PERGAMON GENERAL PSYCHOLOGY SERIES

Editors: Arnold P. Goldstein, *Syracuse University*
Leonard Krasner, *SUNY, Stony Brook*

PSYCHOTHERAPEUTIC ATTRACTION
PGPS-14

Psychotherapeutic Attraction

by

Arnold P. Goldstein
Syracuse University

PERGAMON PRESS

New York • *Toronto* • *Oxford* • *Sydney* • *Braunschweig*

Pergamon Press Inc.
Maxwell House
Fairview Park
Elmsford, N. Y. 10523

Pergamon of Canada Ltd.
207 Queen's Quay West
Toronto 117, Ontario

Pergamon Press Ltd.
Headington Hill Hall, Oxford

Pergamon Press (Aust.) Pty. Ltd.
19A Boundary Street
Rushcutters Bay, N.S.W.

Vieweg & Sohn GmbH.
Burgplatz 1,
Braunschweig

Library of Congress Catalog No. 79-119598
PRINTED IN THE UNITED STATES OF AMERICA

08 016398 ✕

To my collaborators,
the Syracuse University
Psychotherapy Research Group:

Ann Beal
Tom Cheney
Linda Davidoff
Robert Deysach
Richard Gable
Suzanne Gassner
Gilda Gold
Roger Greenberg
Martin Gutride
Peter Hemingway
Joseph Himmelsbach
Toni Hollander
Jay Land
Bernard Liberman
Rosanne Orenstein
Martha Perry
Robert Sabalis
William Walsh

Contents

Acknowledgments

As this book's dedication underscores, the research program described herein was truly a collaborative effort. Hundreds of meetings over the past six years, formal and informal, group and individual, took place between the writer and the students to whom this book is gratefully dedicated. Their stimulation, involvement, and sheer hard work are deeply appreciated.

We have been most fortunate over these years in obtaining the active and interested cooperation of a wide array of institutions to serve as settings for tests of our experimental notions. Thus our gratitude is extended to the administrations and staffs of the Psychiatric Clinic of St. Joseph's Hospital, the Soule Clinic of Crouse-Irving Memorial Hospital, Jamesville Penitentiary, Elmcrest Children's Center, Canastota High School, and the Veterans Administration Hospital—all in or near Syracuse, New York—and the Eagleville Hospital, Eagleville, Pennsylvania; Utica State Hospital, Utica, New York; Worcester State Hospital, Worcester, Massachusetts; Veterans Administration Hospital, Canandaigua, New York; and the Veterans Administration Center, Sioux Falls, South Dakota. We sincerely hope that in most of these relationships we have meaningfully reciprocated for the data made available to us by contributing in some significant way to the functioning of each institution.

Kenneth Heller, Irwin Silverman, and Leonard Krasner have read this book and generously offered many helpful comments and clarifications. Their efforts are very much appreciated. For typing almost countless forms and manuscript drafts, and for "running interference" for me on those days when I needed it most, Mrs. Barbara Murphy and Mrs. Corrine Intaglietta have my warmest thanks.

My wife, Lenore, and my daughters, Cindy and Susan, have been a reservoir of encouragement, both directly and indirectly. They well deserve my deepest appreciation.

Most of the research reported in this book was supported by PHS Research Grants Nos. MH 10720 and MH 16426 from the National Institute of Mental Health.

Chapter I

Introduction

Viewed from a broad perspective, perhaps one of the most significant conceptual developments in contemporary psychotherapy in recent years is the degree to which effective change ingredients have begun to be identified. The therapeutic in psychotherapy is increasingly discernible. The field has moved toward this position by simultaneously giving expression to two opposing research strategies. One has been the search for effective *differences* between psychotherapeutic approaches. Here we find represented an emphasis on psychotherapies and not psychotherapy, a growing attempt to match treatments to patients, to make diagnosis more relevant to therapy, and a rejection of both the patient uniformity myth and the companion notion that a single therapeutic approach is uniformly applicable to all patients seeking psychological assistance. The increasing focus on patient-specific target-symptoms and multifactorial change measures as outcome criteria, and the decreasing emphasis upon global outcome measures are further reflections of this trend. As has been almost singularly true for such other change procedures as education and general medical practice, psychotherapists are increasingly recognizing that no single set of change procedures (in this case, verbal, insight-oriented psychotherapy) is equally appropriate for all patients presenting a given disorder. In the last few years, this movement toward an array of psychotherapies has been augmented by the rapid development of the behavior therapies and the growing community mental health movement—and the difficulties experienced therein in dealing effectively with types of individuals whom we have not previously sought to treat on so wide a scale.

Concomitant with the focus upon differences across therapies has been the perhaps even more salient development of interest in *commonalities*, both across psychotherapeutic approaches as well as non-psychotherapeutic change procedures. In our view, psychotherapy as generally practiced has long included major, efficiency-reducing trappings, that is, procedures and conceptualizations embedded in clinical lore which are largely or totally irrelevant to patient change. This belief is bolstered by the remarkable similarity in reported improvement rates across therapeutic approaches—approaches differing widely in purported techniques. To the extent that such trappings can be identified and their influence diminished, we are that much freer in our efforts toward maximizing the therapeutic impact of those ingredients which are indeed active. The number of such effective therapeutic ingredients is, we suspect, both finite and relatively few. In a recent and particularly thorough review of the psychotherapy research literature, Strupp and Bergin (68) similarly suggest that all major approaches to psychotherapy utilize a small number of specifiable mechanisms of psychological influence—imitation, identification, persuasion, empathy, warmth, interpretation, counterconditioning, extinction, discrimination learning, reward, and punishment. We strongly concur with their sentiment that ". . . to determine the relative contributions of each process and the extent to which it can be optimally employed is a major research task of the future."

In spite of considerable historical sentiment to the contrary, there is today a growing awareness that variables fostering personality or behavioral change are not unique to psychotherapy. Many of the active ingredients noted above characterize a number of other change processes. Frank (19) has most fully articulated this viewpoint and, in so doing, drew attention to those commonalities central to healing in primitive societies, religious revivalism, miracle cures, Communist thought reform, placebo effects in medical practice, and, as we have noted, contemporary psychotherapy. These shared characteristics include initial subjective distress experienced by the sufferer, the arousal of favorable expectation for change through dependence upon a socially sanctioned healer, a circumscribed ritualistic relationship with the healer, a socially shared series of assumptions about illness and the healing process that cannot be disproved by the sufferer's failure to respond, a detailed review of the patient's past life, the mobilization of guilt, the heightening of self-esteem, and social reinforcement of these changes.

The growing impact in the United States today of the community mental health movement adds further thrust to Frank's position regarding potent change ingredients across helping relationships. While "hard" evidence of successful outcomes is not yet available, it appears increasingly likely that a wide array of paratherapy procedures administered by diverse paraprofessionals is yielding encouraging results. The literature now includes clinical reports of successful "treatment" by nurses (5, 15), psychiatric aides (4, 11), patient's parents (2, 27, 65, 72), college undergraduates (51, 61), psychological technicians (12, 50), convicts (8), housewives (42, 54), auxiliary counselors (14, 29), human service aides (41), and foster grandparents (37).

Thus while not ignoring the continuing need to search for the potentially unique contribution derivable from diverse psychotherapies, the companion search for commonalities must be pursued. Strupp and Bergin (68) have distilled for us a particularly potent list of technique commonalities. Although they make no claim to all-inclusiveness, it seems most likely that a very significant proportion of the variance in therapeutic outcome may be accounted for by the variables they indicate. Frank (19) helps us further in this search by shifting our glance elsewhere—toward a host of procedures not formally designated as psychotherapy, but having a very great deal in common with it. From the community mental health movement we discern yet other dyadic and group interactions not formally labeled as psychotherapy, but which nevertheless often seem to eventuate in the very changes psychotherapists seek for their patients. We intend, in the chapters that follow, to focus upon one such commonality, a dimension of psychological change processes of *all* kinds, a dimension we view as of the first rank in change potency—the psychotherapeutic relationship.

The Psychotherapeutic Relationship

The central role accorded relationship variables for therapeutic outcome is characteristic of almost all historical and contemporary theories of psychotherapy. Both classical and more recently developed psychoanalytic approaches place a major emphasis upon transference and countertransference dimensions. Of particular relevance is the psychoanalytic "law of Talion" in which transference and countertransference are held to covary. Snyder's (64) eclectic orientation places similar relationship emphasis upon the reciprocity of therapist and patient affect. The importance of reciprocity of positive interpersonal attitudes is also evident in the Rogerian (55) focus upon "unconditional positive regard," Truax and Carkhuff's (70) stress upon empathy, warmth, and genuineness, Grinker's (26) transactional model of psychotherapy, Jackson's (36) interactional approach, Bach's (6) emphasis upon inspection of interpersonal traffic, and in the more recently developed existential approaches (10, 43) to psychotherapy. Furthermore, Murray (47), Shoben (62), Truax (69), and Wilson *et al.* (75) all suggest that the therapist-patient relationship may be of similar significance in determining the outcome of the various behavior therapies. Bordin (9) has commented that:

> The key to the influence of psychotherapy on the patient is in his relationship with the therapist. Wherever psychotherapy is accepted as a significant enterprise, this statement is so widely sub-

scribed to as to become trite. Virtually all efforts to theorize about psychotherapy are intended to describe and explain what attributes of the interactions between the therapist and the patient will account for whatever behavior change results. (9, p. 235)

Psychotherapeutic *theory*, therefore, is overwhelmingly in accord—the therapist-patient relationship is widely viewed as a major, active therapeutic ingredient.

This broad conclusion has been a frequent focus of psychotherapy research. A very large number of investigations have examined the association between quality of the therapist-patient relationship and therapeutic outcome. The vast majority of these studies have yielded positive, significant results. A significant correlation between relationship and outcome has also emerged in such formally nonpsychotherapeutic contexts as stuttering therapy (13), drug administration (44), general medical practice (58), and in the teacher-pupil relationship (74). However, it is important to note the almost complete absence, in this large array of therapy and nontherapy studies, of attempts to experimentally manipulate the therapist-patient relationship in such a manner that causality can be specified. One *cannot* conclude from this research that the quality of the relationship *influences* therapeutic outcome; one can only conclude that the two are associated. Gardner (20), in a careful review of much of this literature, comments:

> The evidence that the quality of the therapeutic relationship is a correlate of therapeutic change lies not in the conclusive results of any one study but rather in the repeated findings of a series of studies, most of which contain one or more serious defects. Methodology varies greatly, and absence of precise definitions often makes it difficult to discern whether the 'good relationship' of one study contains the same elements as that of another study. In a sense, the diversity of procedure strengthens the force of the conclusion. (20, p. 431)

We are in accord with Gardner's conclusion; the diversity of procedure does strengthen the probability that relationship and outcome are associated. But this same procedural diversity weakens our ability to optimize the impact of relationship on outcome. To this point in this section we have developed a picture of broad theoretical and research agreement—both theoreticians and researchers are in accord regarding the likely potency of relationship ingredients. However, when one looks behind this broad level of agreement, one finds immense definitional diversity. What is "relationship?" The theoretical definitions are numerous—transference-countertransference (46), reciprocal affect (64), interaction (36), transaction (26), commitment, warmth, and understanding (52), empathy, warmth, and genuineness (71), inter-personal trust (45), freedom in self-disclosure (38), reciprocal thera-pist-patient needs (49), generalized reinforcement (39), mutuality of goals (1), and symmetrical and complementary communication (28).

The definitional confusion increases even further when one turns to research definitions of "relationship." Here, the number of different op-erationalizations of "relationship" is approximately equal to the number of investigators. A nonexhaustive list would include Libo's (40) Pic-ture Impressions Test, a projective test consisting of four cards depict-ing therapy-like situations, administered like the TAT; Snyder's (64) Therapist and Client Affect Scales, on which therapist and patient rate their evolving feelings toward each other; Ashby *et al.'s* (3) Therapist and Client Personal Reaction Questionnaires, on which both partici-pants rate aspects of their interview interactions; Fiedler's (17) Q-sorts of the Ideal Therapeutic Relationship; Schrier's (60) Special Rating Scale for Rapport; Truax and Carkhuff's (71) scales for empathy and warmth used in rating the content of therapy sessions; Rawn's (52) Transference Scale; Barrett-Lennard's (7) Relationship Inventory; and a host of additional, psychometrically diverse scales, rating forms, content analysis approaches, and other devices.

If "relationship" is indeed as therapeutically potent as both theory and research suggest, and if it thus follows that maximizing our use of "relationship" augments our therapeutic efficiency, order must be brought to this definitional chaos. In the section that follows we begin to offer an initial attempt at such orderliness by providing yet another definition of relationship—a definition that we feel the remaining chap-ters of this book suggest is a viable one. Such a definition should be meaningfully tied to theory, research findings, and measurement de-vices. Most important, it must be a pregnant definition, one which augments our ability to derive testable and progress-enhancing hy-potheses.

Interpersonal Attraction

Researchers committed to the advancement of psychotherapy, until the mid-1950's, turned primarily to their clinical experience or theories of psychotherapy and psychopathology when seeking to define and de-rive hypotheses about psychotherapeutic variables. In the mid-1950's, research on learning processes began to enter the psychotherapy re-search arena in force. The growing influence of such research upon the study of psychotherapy is attested to by the current viability of the be-havior therapy movement. It has long been our view that a major contribution of the growth of behavior therapy resides in the manner in which it represents a stride toward placing the study of psychotherapy where it most fundamentally belongs—*within* the mainstream of general psychology. For too long has the fiction been maintained that general psychological principles are one thing, psychotherapy quite another. The present book seeks to further consummate the marriage of general psychology and psychotherapy. All of the investigations we will report derive from social-psychological research. Consistent with our desire to more adequately define "relationship," the specific research literature to which we have turned consists of investigations of interpersonal attraction. Interpersonal attraction is a variable with a long and fruitful research history. As such, many of its antecedents, concomitants, and consequences are reliably known—at least in the social-psychological laboratory. If there is indeed a unity to psychological change processes, be they called psychotherapy or something else, procedures which augment interpersonal attraction in the social-psychological laboratory may well be relevant to increasing such attraction as it operates between patient and therapist in clinical settings. Thus it is a series of extrapolatory studies upon which we are embarking here—from the social-psychological laboratory to settings more relevant to clinical concerns. We have developed our *a priori* rationale for this extrapolatory research strategy in considerable detail elsewhere (23, 24, 25) and will not elaborate it greatly here. Of importance, however, is the *a priori* nature of this rationale. It is *evidence* and not favored strategies which must determine the paths our research efforts follow. Our earlier writings presented our favored strategy. The present volume seeks to provide relevant evidence.

YAVIS and NON-YAVIS Patients

We have specified the psychotherapeutic relationship as the intended focus of this book, and indicated that relationship will be operationalized in our research in terms of the social-psychological variable, interpersonal attraction. At this point we wish to delimit the type of therapist-patient dyad toward which our research is primarily oriented. In a recent and penetrating analysis of the sociology of contemporary psychotherapy in the United States, Schofield (59) called our attention to the YAVIS patient—young, attractive, verbal, intelligent, and successful. Mr. YAVIS is apparently the type of patient with whom we all like to work. He tends to be introspective and psychologically-minded, or at minimum is "trainable" by the therapist in such behaviors. He comes to our office typically with volition. He brings with him a participation expectation, an expectation subsequently manifested behaviorally in high rates of in-therapy verbalization and self-exploration. More generally, such patients display a full array of the "good patient" behaviors which clinical lore has taught us is likely to lead to a favorable therapeutic outcome. Perhaps most crucial from our research perspective is the fact that Mr. YAVIS and his therapist characteristically form a favorable psychotherapeutic relationship.

While we are far from indifferent to the relationship implications of our research for YAVIS patients, our investigations have been increasingly oriented toward quite a different type of patient. We might call him Mr. NON-YAVIS: middle-aged or elderly, physically ordinary or unattractive, verbally reticent, intellectually unexceptional or dull, and typically from a lower socioeconomic level. Mr. NON-YAVIS comes to our office, often not with full volition, with a guidance expectation. He is neither introspective nor psychologically-minded. He anticipates being directively guided toward problem resolution. His expectations and behaviors are at wide variance with the typical psychotherapist's preference for YAVIS patients. How else might we identify Mr. NON-YAVIS? Surveys at three large outpatient clinics serving individuals of lower socioeconomic status report dropout rates of over 50 percent after the initial interview (35, 48, 56). These dropouts are Mr. NON-YAVIS. We meet him again in the well-known Hollingshead and Redlich (34) study:

> Class V patients accept professional procedures which have no meaning to them and which often arouse their anxiety. . . . Practically all Class V neurotics drop out of treatment. The few who remain beyond the intake period are unable to understand that their troubles are not physical illnesses. . . . The most frequent source of difficulty between the lower status patient in psychotherapy and the therapist is the patient's tacit or overt demand for an authoritarian attitude on the part of the psychiatrist and the psychiatrist's unwillingness to assume this role because it runs counter to certain therapeutic principles. (34, p. 340)

And we meet Mr. NON-YAVIS again in the research of Gliedman *et al.* (22), Heine and Trosman (30), Hoehn-Saric *et al.* (33), and Overall and Aronson (48). All of these investigations demonstrate that incongruent therapist and patient expectations regarding the nature of psychotherapy lead to rapid termination. More important for purposes of our research, however, are the relationship implications of these findings. These investigations clearly indicate that not all the dyadic difficulty lies with Mr. NON-YAVIS, but also in the therapist's negative reaction to such patients. As Wallach (73) has demonstrated, therapists prefer less disturbed patients, patients willing to talk of their feelings, or, more generally, Mr. YAVIS. Furthermore, Heller *et al.* (31), Russell (57), Snyder (64), and Winder *et al.* (76) have all reported results indicating reciprocity in therapist and patient feelings toward each other. Thus the rapid termination so characteristic of NON-YAVIS patients follows not only from their own processing of early therapy events, but also from the therapist's perceptions and be- haviors. The therapist may hide behind the process of labeling such patients "resistant" or "unsuitable," but in reality the therapist is ac- knowledging both our field's poverty of therapeutic skills when deal- ing with such patients as well as perhaps more personalized feelings of both inadequacy and dislike. A few creative therapists, a very few, have suggested new therapeutic maneuvers for aiding such patients (16, 21, 63, 66), but the field in general has made extremely little progress in this direction.

If relationship is indeed a crucial therapeutic ingredient, and the hallmark of psychotherapy with NON-YAVIS patients is a poor quality relationship, steps must be taken to develop procedures for augment- ing the favorableness of such relationships. Development of proce- dures for such relationship enhancement is the primary objective of our research program. Having taken this stance and, in a sense, staked out our primary area of clinical focus, we wish to indicate our aware- ness that the terms YAVIS and NON-YAVIS represent in reality end points on a continuum and not a dichotomy. Strupp (67) has ob- served:

> Every neurotic patient is unconsciously committed to maintain the status quo, and psychotherapy, particularly if aimed at confront- ing the patient with his inner conflicts, proceeds against the ob- stacle of powerful unconscious resistances. Therefore, unless there is a strong conscious desire to be helped and to collaborate with the therapist, the odds against a favorable outcome may be insuperable. (67, p. 6)

The major implication of Strupp's position for our purposes is that the task of relationship enhancement is potentially worthwhile not only in therapies involving patients at the NON-YAVIS extreme of our YAVIS-NON-YAVIS continuum, but also well along almost all of this continuum.

Experimental Design Strategy

Having expressed both our relationship-oriented clinical motivations and our social-psychologically-oriented extrapolatory research philosophy, but one introductory task remains. We wish in this section to specify concretely our orientation to the design and execution of the studies that follow. Reflecting both the complexity of the therapist-patient interaction and the manner in which important psychotherapeutic variables act upon one another, almost all of our investigations have made use of some type of factorial design. Conducting psychotherapy research often demands compromise and experimental design flexibility. One cannot conduct a large research program involving a variety of institutional settings unless one is willing to accommodate at least some aspects of one's experimental designs to the requirements of the settings in which one works. In part for this reason, the reader will note we have utilized a variety of experimental approaches. That is, while all of our studies derive from research on interpersonal attraction and most make use of a factorial design, some are analogue studies while others were conducted in actual clinical contexts. Setting demands notwithstanding, our primary rationale for this experimental design strategy rests upon our earlier formulation of the analogical bridge (24). More concretely, since we view the study of psychotherapy as falling within the mainstream of the more general psychology of behavior change, behavior change studies of all types that involve interpersonal attraction are viewed by us as relevant to our research program's goals. This bridging formulation envisions a dimension along which studies of behavior change may be ordered. Studies toward the laboratory end of this dimension or bridge essentially represent, for our purposes, social-psychological studies of interpersonal attraction. Toward the clinic pole we come more directly to investigations focusing upon the therapist-patient relationship.

As one moves from laboratory to clinic on such a dimension, one's subjects change from nonpatients to patients; the research setting becomes more clinically relevant; and the processes investigated become more readily identified as psychotherapeutic processes. Ford and Urban (18) have proposed a similar notion. Principles of behavior change, they note, are first distilled in a series of experimental studies. Clinical research then grows from such experimentation, i.e., research which focuses on the interaction of experimental and individual difference variables. Clinical trials optimally follow, trials in which the findings of clinical research are examined using real patients undergoing psychotherapy. Hilgard and Bower (32) have also developed a bridging schema, in this case with an educational focus in which findings from learning research conducted in the experimental laboratory are examined in contexts ever more relevant to classroom learning. In response to this research strategy, as well as in response to the practical demands noted above, our studies represent several points on our analogical bridge. Whenever possible, we entered an area of potential relationship enhancement by proceeding stepwise and conducting a study using YAVIS-like patients first. In most instances, we then were able to move in subsequent studies toward the types of patient-therapist pairs for whom establishing a favorable relationship is characteristically difficult. Thus our early studies in most series were conducted as psychotherapy analogues using university student subjects or at a university counseling center using student patients. The settings of our later studies were a penitentiary, two state mental hospitals, a private hospital for alcoholic patients, two community psychiatric clinics, and three Veterans Administration hospitals.

The temporal focus in all our investigations was the candidacy and initial stages of psychotherapy. We sought to augment the favorableness of the therapist-patient relationship by instituting procedures during the immediate pretherapy or post initial interview phases of the patient's treatment career. Our goal has been to develop techniques for "hooking" patients, that is, for maximizing the favorableness of the initial relationship so that, at minimum, the patient returns for further sessions and, more maximally, is open to the therapist's influence attempts. Historically, early studies of psychotherapeutic outcome were singularly global in nature. The primary questions addressed to the data of these investigations were, "Does therapy work?," "Is therapy better than no therapy?," or "Is therapy A superior to therapy B?" Answers to such rudimentary questions were not forthcoming, however, for the early psychotherapy research enterprise faltered as it unsuccessfully attempted to come to grips with the major inadequacies of the global measures of outcome then available. Investigators largely responded by turning away from concern with, "Does it work?" and, instead, began to focus on what came to be called process research. The impact of psychotherapy upon the lives of patients, its very reason for existence, was no longer the concern of most psychotherapy researchers. Instead, the investigation of psychotherapy became the study of a "rich, interpersonal laboratory" in which many interesting, researchable questions were examined—as the patient stood ignored on the sidelines.

Today, psychotherapy outcome research has entered a third phase. Just as the unsatisfying nature of global outcome studies gave birth to process research, the patient-irrelevant quality of most process research has given rise to a growing number of studies examining outcome-related process variables. These are investigations of psychotherapeutic process variables which research to date has suggested as having a high probability of association with therapeutic outcome. One such variable is the therapist-patient relationship. Thus we propose no *direct* association between an enhanced initial therapeutic relationship and the eventual therapy outcome. However, we do view such a relationship as serving as a potentiator of events whose consequences can themselves lead to a more fruitful therapeutic outcome. Therefore it seems likely that an enhanced initial therapeutic relationship can lead to heightened self-disclosure, decreased resistiveness, and other favorable steps toward outcome. In a number of our studies we have focused directly upon just such relationship consequents.

Most of the procedures examined in our studies for their relationship-enhancing effects are highly manipulative in nature. While consistent with a laboratory research tradition, the *stated* values of most members of the psychotherapeutic community are such that strong exception is often taken to manipulative strategies. We feel the latter to be a head-in-the-sand position, since there now exists a great deal of evidence that *all* psychotherapies are in fact manipulative (e.g., 24, 39, 70). Nevertheless, our experimental manipulations will be decried by some, and so it is appropriate that our rationale for the ethics of such manipulation be stated more fully. We have done so elsewhere (25) and offer here a statement which represents the core of our rationale:

> Manipulative approaches may be attacked on the grounds that they dehumanize, treat the patient as a machine or object, or, more generally, that they reflect a nonhumanitarian orientation to sick or unhappy people. Our position, quite the contrary, is that *current* psychotherapeutic approaches are deficient on a humanitarianism continuum largely because they do not incorporate or reflect research findings regarding the most effective means of altering an individual's behavior—the very reason for the existence of psychotherapy. To know that solid research dealing with attitude change, learning, group dynamics, and a score of other domains offering other manipulative means of altering an individual's behavior exists, and to deny in an *a priori* manner the potential relevance of such research to the psychotherapy patient is to perform a disservice to both the advance of psychotherapy and to one's psychotherapy patients. Obviously there will be limits that society will impose upon its psychological practitioners. But to imply that these limits can be imposed without evidence, without research on behavior control, is to deny the experimental foundation on which science rests. We have an obligation to society and to our psychotherapy patients, and this obligation demands that we publicize and use the best possible scientific findings in our own field. To do less than this, we hold, is a failure to meet our ethical responsibilities. (25, pp. 8–9)

References

1. Adler, A. *The practice and theory of individual psychology*. New York: Harcourt, Brace, 1924.

2. Allen, K. E. & Harris, F. R. Elimination of a child's excessive scratching by training the mother in reinforcement procedures. *Behaviour Research and Therapy*, 1966, 4, 79–84.

3. Ashby, J. D., Ford, D. H., Guerney, B. G., Jr., & Guerney, L. Effects on clients of a reflective and a leading type of psychotherapy. *Psychological Monographs*, 1957, 7, 1–32.

4. Ayllon, T. & Haughton, E. Modification of symptomatic verbal behavior of mental patients. *Behaviour Research and Therapy*, 1964, 2, 87–98.

5. Ayllon, T. & Michael, J. The psychiatric nurse as a behavioral engineer. *Journal for the Experimental Analysis of Behavior*, 1959, 2, 323–334.

6. Bach, G. R. *Intensive group psychotherapy*. New York: Ronald Press, 1954.

7. Barrett-Lennard, G. T. Dimensions of therapist response as causal factors in therapeutic change. *Psychological Monographs*, 1962, 76, Whole No. 562.

8. Benjamin, J. G., Freedman, M. K., & Lynton, E. F. *Pros and cons: New roles for non-professionals in corrections*. Washington, D.C.: Department Health, Education and Welfare, 1966.

9. Bordin, E. S. Inside the therapeutic hour. In E. A. Rubinstein & M. B. Parloff (Eds.), *Research in psychotherapy*. Washington, D.C.: American Psychological Association, 1959. Pp. 235–246.

10. Bugental, J. F. T. *The search for authenticity*. New York: Holt, Rinehart & Winston, 1965.

11. Carkhuff, R. R. & Truax, C. B. Lay mental health counseling. *Journal of Counseling Psychology*, 1965, 29, 426–431.

12. Cattell, R. B. & Shotwell, A. M. Personality profiles of more successful and less successful psychiatric technicians. *American Journal of Mental Deficiency*, 1954, 58, 496–499.

13. Cooper, E. B. Client-clinician relationships and concomitant factors in stuttering therapy. *Journal of Speech and Hearing Research*, 1966, 9, 194–207.

14. Costin, S. B. Training nonprofessionals for a child welfare service. *Children*, 1966, 13, 63–68.

15. Daniels, A. M. Training school nurses to work with groups of adolescents. *Children*, 1966, 13, 210–216.

16. Eissler, K. R. Some problems of delinquency. In K. R. Eissler (Ed.),

Searchlights on delinquency. New York: International University Press, 1949. Pp. 3–25.

17. Fiedler, F. E. The concept of an ideal therapeutic relationship. *Journal of Consulting Psychology,* 1950, 14, 39–45.

18. Ford, D. H. & Urban, H. *Systems of psychotherapy.* New York: Wiley, 1963.

19. Frank, J. D. *Persuasion and healing.* Baltimore: Johns Hopkins Press, 1961.

20. Gardner, G. G. The psychotherapeutic relationship. *Psychological Bulletin,* 1964, 61, 426–437.

21. Gendlin, E. T. Initiating psychotherapy with "unmotivated" patients. *Psychiatric Quarterly,* 1961, 35, 134–139.

22. Gliedman, L. H., Stone, A. R., Frank, J. D., Nash, E. H., Jr., & Imber, S. D. Incentives for treatment related to remaining or improving in psychotherapy. *American Journal of Psychotherapy,* 1957, 11, 589–598.

23. Goldstein, A. P. Psychotherapy research by extrapolation from social psychology. *Journal of Counseling Psychology,* 1966, 13, 38–45.

24. Goldstein, A. P. & Dean, S. J. *The investigation of psychotherapy.* New York: Wiley, 1966.

25. Goldstein, A. P., Heller, K., & Sechrest, L. B. *Psychotherapy and the psychology of behavior change.* New York: Wiley, 1966.

26. Grinker, R. R. A transactional model for psychotherapy. In M. I. Stein (Ed.), *Contemporary psychotherapies.* New York: Free Press, 1961. Pp. 190–213.

27. Guerney, B. G., Jr. Filial therapy: Description and rationale. *Journal of Consulting Psychology,* 1964, 28, 304–310.

28. Haley, J. *Strategies of psychotherapy.* New York: Grune & Stratton, 1963.

29. Harvey, L. V. The use of non-professional auxiliary counselors in staffing a counseling service. *Journal of Counseling Psychology,* 1964, 11, 348–351.

30. Heine, R. W. & Trosman, H. Initial expectations of the doctor-patient interaction as a factor in continuance in psychotherapy. *Psychiatry,* 1960, 23, 275–278.

31. Heller, K., Myers, R. A., & Kline, L. Interviewer behavior as a function of standardized client roles. *Journal of Consulting Psychology,* 1963, 27, 117–122.

32. Hilgard, E. R. & Bower, G. H. *Theories of learning.* New York: Appleton, Century, Crofts, 1966.

33. Hoehn-Saric, R., Frank, J. D., Imber, S. D., Nash, E. H., Stone, A. R., & Battle, C. C. Systematic preparation of patients for psychotherapy. I. Effects on therapy behavior and outcome. *Journal of Psychiatric Research,* 1964, 2, 267–281.

34. Hollingshead, A. B. & Redlich, F. S. *Social class and mental illness*. New York: Wiley, 1958.

35. Imber, S. D., Nash, E. H., Jr., & Stone, A. R. Social class and duration of psychotherapy. *Journal of Clinical Psychology*, 1955, **11**, 281–285.

36. Jackson, D. D. Interactional psychotherapy. In M. I. Stein (Ed.), *Contemporary psychotherapies*. New York: Free Press, 1961. Pp. 256–271.

37. Johnston, R. Foster grandparents for emotionally disturbed children. *Children*, 1967, **14**, 46–52.

38. Jourard, S. M. & Lasalow, P. Some factors in self-disclosure. *Journal of Abnormal and Social Psychology*, 1958, **56**, 91–98.

39. Krasner, L. The therapist as a social reinforcement machine. In H. H. Strupp & L. Luborsky (Eds.), *Research in psychotherapy*. Washington, D.C.: American Psychological Association, 1962. Pp. 61–94.

40. Libo, L. The projective expression of patient-therapist attraction. *Journal of Clinical Psychology*, 1957, **13**, 33–36.

41. MacLennon, B. W. New careers as human service aides. *Children*, 1966, **13**, 190–194.

42. Magoon, T. M., Golann, S. E., & Freeman, R. W. *Mental health counselors at work*. New York: Pergamon Press, 1969.

43. May, R. *Existence*. New York: Basic Books, 1958.

44. McNair, D. M., Kahn, R. J., Droppleman, L. F., & Fisher, S. Compatibility, acquiescence and drug-effects. Presented at International Congress of Psychology, Washington, D.C., 1966.

45. Mellinger, G. D. Interpersonal trust as a factor in communication. *Journal of Abnormal and Social Psychology*, 1956, **52**, 304–309.

46. Munroe, R. L. *Schools of psychoanalytic thought*. New York: Dryden Press, 1955.

47. Murray, E. J. Learning theory and psychotherapy: Biotropic versus sociotropic approaches. *Journal of Counseling Psychology*, 1963, **10**, 250–255.

48. Overall, B. & Aronson, H. Expectations of psychotherapy in patients of lower socioeconomic class. *American Journal of Orthopsychiatry*, 1963, **33**, 421–430.

49. Patterson, C. H. The place of values in counseling and psychotherapy. *Journal of Counseling Psychology*, 1958, **5**, 216–223.

50. Poser, E. G. The effect of therapists' training on group therapeutic outcome. *Journal of Consulting Psychology*, 1966, **30**, 283–289.

51. Poser, E. G. Training behavior therapists. *Behaviour Research and Therapy*, 1967, **5**, 37–42.

52. Raush, H. L. & Bordin, E. S. Warmth in personality development and in psychotherapy. *Psychiatry*, 1957, **20**, 351–363.

53. Rawn, M. L. An experimental study of transference and resistance phenomena in psychoanalytically oriented psychotherapy. *Journal of Clinical Psychology*, 1958, **14**, 418–425.

54. Rioch, M. J., Elkes, C., Flint, A. A., Usdansky, B. S., Newman, R. G., & Silber, E. National Institute of Mental Health pilot study in training mental health counselors. *American Journal of Orthopsychiatry*, 1963, **33**, 678–689.

✗ 55. Rogers, C. R. The characteristics of a helping relationship. In M. I. Stein (Ed.), *Contemporary psychotherapies*. New York: Free Press, 1961. Pp. 95–112.

56. Rosenthal, D. & Frank, J. D. The fate of psychiatric clinic outpatients assigned to psychotherapy. *Journal of Nervous and Mental Diseases*, 1958, **127**, 330–334.

57. Russell, P. D. Counselor anxiety in relation to clinical experience and hostile or friendly clients. Unpublished doctoral dissertation, Pennsylvania State University, 1961.

58. Sapolsky, A. Relationship between patient-doctor compatibility, mutual perception and outcome of treatment. *Journal of Abnormal Psychology*, 1965, **70**, 70–76.

59. Schofield, W. *Psychotherapy, the purchase of friendship.* Englewood Cliffs, N.J.: Prentice-Hall, 1964.

60. Schrier, H. The significance of identification in therapy. *American Journal of Orthopsychiatry*, 1953, **33**, 585–604.

61. Schwitzgebel, R. & Kolb, D. A. Inducing behavior change in adolescent delinquents. *Behaviour Research and Therapy*, 1964, **1**, 297–304.

62. Shoben, E. J., Jr. The therapeutic object: Men or machines? *Journal of Counseling Psychology*, 1963, **10**, 264–268.

63. Slack, C. W. Experimenter–subject psychotherapy. *Mental Hygiene*, 1960, **44**, 238–256.

64. Snyder, W. U. *The psychotherapy relationship.* New York: Macmillan, 1961.

65. Straughan, J. H. Treatment with child and mother in playroom. *Behaviour Research and Therapy*, 1964, **2**, 37–42.

66. Strean, H. S. Difficulties met in the treatment of adolescents. *Psychoanalysis and the Psychoanalytic Review*, 1961, **48**, 69–80.

67. Strupp, H. H. Patient-doctor relationships. In A. J. Bachrach (Ed.), *Experimental foundations of clinical psychology*. New York: Basic Books, 1962. Pp. 576–615.

68. Strupp, H. H. & Bergin, A. E. Some empirical and conceptual bases for coordinated research in psychotherapy. *International Journal of Psychiatry*, 1969, **7**, 18–90.

69. Truax, C. B. Reinforcement and non-reinforcement in Rogerian psychotherapy. Unpublished manuscript, University of Kentucky, 1960.

70. Truax, C. B. Some implications of behavior therapy for psychotherapy. *Journal of Counseling Psychology*, 1966, **13**, 160–170.

✗ 71. Truax, C. B. & Carkhuff, R. R. *Toward effective counseling and psychotherapy*. Chicago: Aldine, 1967.

72. Wahler, R. G., Winkel, G. H., Paterson, R. F., & Morrison, D. C. Mothers as behavior therapists for their own children. *Behaviour Research and Therapy*, 1965, **3**, 113–124.

73. Wallach, M. S. Therapists' patient preferences and their relationship to two patient variables. *Journal of Clinical Psychology*, 1962, **18**, 497–501.

74. Wilderson, F. B. A concept of the "ideal" therapeutic relationship in classes for emotionally disturbed children. *Journal of Special Education*, 1967, **1**, 91–97.

75. Wilson, G. T., Hannon, A. E., & Evans, W. I. M. Behavior therapy and the therapist-patient relationship. *Journal of Consulting and Clinical Psychology*, 1968, **32**, 103–109.

76. Winder, C. L., Ahmad, F. Z., Bandura, A., & Rea, L. C. Dependency of patients, psychotherapists' responses, and aspects of psychotherapy. *Journal of Consulting Psychology*, 1962, **26**, 129–134.

Chapter II

Direct Structuring

Patients come to psychotherapy from numerous and diverse referral sources, and in the process of doing so are provided with equally diverse referral messages. One characteristic of such referral messages will be examined in the present chapter for its relevance to attraction enhancement. The studies presented below investigate the effects on patient attraction and influenceability of pretherapy messages whose content directly proposes to the patient that he "will like" his psychotherapist.

Direct Structuring—Laboratory Subjects

A number of social-psychological laboratory and field investigations have focused upon the effects on attraction and influenceability of direct attraction-structuring messages. The first of these, a study that our own initial investigation largely parallels, was conducted by Back (7). Back's design involved seven experimental conditions, i.e., strong and weak structured attraction based upon (a) personal attraction, (b) task importance, or (c) group prestige, and a "Negative Treatment" Condition in which all three bases for attraction were minimized. He randomly constituted his subjects into pairs, and assigned 10 such pairs to each experimental condition. His overall design called for induction of strong or weak within-pair attraction (based on one of the three methods noted above) and measurement of the consequent within-pair level of influenceability. Back's basic hypothesis predicted that heightened attraction would lead to heightened influenceability. When the college student subjects initially signed up for this study, they were asked a number of questions which purportedly were to be used for pairing purposes. Each subject was structured for strong or weak attraction prior to meeting his partner. For example, as part of the structuring for weak attraction based upon personal liking, both subjects in the pair were individually told:

> You remember the questions you answered when you signed up in class? We tried to find a partner with whom you could work best. Of course, we couldn't find anybody who would fit the description exactly, but we found a fellow who corresponds to the

main points, and you probably will like him. You should get along all right.

In contrast, members of strong attraction pairs in this condition (Personal Liking) were told:

> You remember the questions you answered in class about the people you would like to work with? Of course, we usually cannot match people the way they want but, for you, we have found almost exactly the person you described. As a matter of fact, the matching was as close as we had expected to happen once or twice in the study, if at all. You'll like him a lot. What's even more, he described a person very much like you. It's quite a lucky coincidence to find two people who are so congenial, and you should get along extremely well.

In an analogous manner, in the strong and weak attraction conditions based upon task importance, the structured importance to the subjects of task results was varied. In the group prestige conditions, structured attraction was induced in terms of variations in the purported value of belonging to the specific pair. Subjects assigned to the Negative Treatment (Minimal Attraction) Condition were told:

> I am sorry, but the idea of putting people together who are congenial didn't work. Especially in your case we had some trouble because of scheduling. So the fellow you are going to work with may irritate you a little, but I hope it will work out all right. The trouble is that the whole thing is quite frustrating and the conversation somewhat strained, so we would have preferred to have you with a person you liked. But, anyway, do the best you can.

Following attraction structuring but still prior to meeting the partner, each subject was given a set of three pictures about which he was to write a story. Although each subject was led to believe that he and his partner had responded to the same set of pictures, there were in fact slight differences between the sets of pictures given to the members of each pair. After completion of their initial story writing, subjects met their partners for the first time. This meeting was described as an opportunity to discuss one's stories with one's partner and, if appropriate, to improve them. Following this discussion, and again working apart, each subject rewrote his stories as he wished. The study's criterion, interpersonal influence, was reliably measured in terms of changes from the preliminary to the final stories that were in the direction of the subject's partner's stories. Back's results indicated significantly more (a) effort to reach within-pair agreement, (b) influence attempts, and (c) successful influence in all three strong attraction conditions as compared to both the weak attraction and negative treatment conditions. Furthermore, sociometric measurement provided independent evidence of the success of the attraction inductions. Thus in this initial laboratory attempt—involving nonpatients and nonclinical spheres of influence—interpersonal attraction was enhanced by direct structuring and led to heightened levels of interpersonal influence.

Using very different criteria of influence, Sapolsky (49) has reported concurring findings. Prior to meeting the experimenter, his subjects were structured for either high or low attraction (to the experimenter) via procedures parallel to those used by Back in his "Personal Liking" conditions. All subjects then met individually with the experimenter and participated in a standardized verbal conditioning task. The task involved presenting the subject with a series of verbs in combination with one of six personal pronouns; the subject then had to construct sentences with each of these two word sets. For *all* subjects, after 20 base rate trials, "E provided reinforcement by saying 'mmm-hmm' in a flat, unemotional tone at the end of any sentence that began with the 'I' or 'We' pronouns." Following the conditioning trials, as a check on the effectiveness of the attraction induction, a self-anchored sociometric scale was administered. This check demonstrated the predicted significant difference between the two groups of subjects in their attraction to the experimenter. There was a similarly significant between-groups difference in response to the conditioning trials. On subsequent test trials, subjects in the high attraction condition used the reinforced pronouns with significantly greater frequency than did subjects structured for low attraction.

Thus these two laboratory attempts to directly augment dyadic attraction were successful. Furthermore, in both of these studies, as well as in a number of others (9, 17, 19, 21, 40, 45), we find robust evidence for a major effect of interpersonal attraction upon interpersonal influence. It was these specific findings which provided the extrapolatory foundation for our initial investigation of the effects of direct structuring on attraction and influence in a psychotherapeutic context.

Direct Structuring—YAVIS Patients

This initial investigation was conducted at our University Counseling Center. The six participating psychotherapists were all advanced graduate students in clinical psychology. Eighty-two patients were involved, all of them college undergraduates presenting problems of an essentially psychoneurotic nature. Our primary hypothesis, following Back and Sapolsky, was that patients structured to expect high attraction toward their therapist would be more receptive to his influence attempts than would patients in whom low attraction to the therapist was induced. A secondary hypothesis, responsive to our earlier discussion of the effect of therapist preferences on the therapeutic relationship, predicted a reciprocal effect such that patients highly attracted to their therapists would themselves be rated as more attractive by their therapists than would patients experiencing low attraction to their therapist. This prediction is consistent with both Jones and Thibaut's (25) formulations regarding reciprocally contingent dyadic relationships, as well as the psychoanalytic "law of Talion." Exploratory questions were also addressed to the data of this study regarding the relationship between patient attraction and influenceability to his confidence in the treatment Center and his expectation of change from psychotherapy.

As a purportedly routine aspect of the Center's therapy procedures, all patients began their participation in the investigation by completing the following test battery.

1. *Picture Impressions Test* (*PIT*). This is a projective device consisting of four plates depicting therapy-like situations. The test is administered in a manner very similar to standard TAT administration procedures. Libo (34, 35), the developer of the PIT, has provided a degree of predictive validity evidence for this measure in a psychotherapy study using the PIT as an operational definition of patient attraction to psychotherapists in general.

2. *Patient Prognostic Expectancy.*[1] Two versions of a symptom intensity inventory were administered to obtain a prognostic expectancy estimate from each patient. The inventory consists of 50 problems and symptoms commonly presented by psychoneurotic patients. In the Present Self form of this inventory, the patient responds in terms of the current status of his complaints, indicating which problems he ascribes to himself and their perceived intensity. In the Expected Self version, consisting of the same 50 items, the instructional set requires the patient to respond in terms of his anticipated problem status and problem intensity following his psychotherapy. The Expected Self-Present Self total difference score is taken to reflect the patient's prognostic expectancy. Construct validity evidence relevant to these inventories, as well as to that described below, are provided in Goldstein (20).

3. *Friend's Problem Inventory* (FPI).[2] This instrument seeks to mea-

---

[1] See Appendix I, pp. 172-188.
[2] *Ibid.*, pp. 189-191.

sure the patient's generalized confidence in the treatment clinic (Center). It consists of the same 50 items which comprise the Present Self and Expected Self Inventories. In this instance, however, each problem statement is followed by five, randomly ordered, alternative sources of help for the problem: friend, parent, no one, this clinic, clergyman. The patient is requested to respond to each problem statement by ranking the five alternative sources of help in the order he would recommend them to a friend if the latter had the given complaint. The lower the mean rank assigned by the patient to "this clinic," the greater is his assumed confidence in its treatment personnel.

4. *Patient-Therapist Matching Scale.*[3] Like Back's preliminary questions to his subjects, this scale was not used for assessment purposes in this investigation. Its sole use was to enhance the credibility of experimental Conditions A and B (see below). This scale consists of 24 statements describing ways in which a psychotherapist may behave or respond to his patients during a therapy interview. Scale instructions are such that the patient is requested to rate each statement in terms of how strongly he wishes *his* (prospective) therapist to behave in the manner described by each statement.

Subsequent to the testing session, all patients were randomly assigned to both a psychotherapist and to one of the study's five experimental conditions. The sole restriction on randomization was that each therapist was assigned an equal number of patients per condition. The four attraction to therapist manipulations and the control group defining the five experimental conditions were as follows:

Condition A. High Attraction-Personal Liking. The verbatim structuring statement that follows, as well as those employed in Conditions B, C, and D, parallel very closely those used for analogous purposes by Back. Patients assigned to Condition A were told (by the tester):

> We have carefully examined the tests you took in order to assign you to a therapist whom you would like to work with most. We usually can't match a patient and therapist the way they want most, but for you we have almost exactly the kind of therapist you described. (Tester then shows patient how well his Matching Scale matches one purportedly representing a composite of the judgments of many patients already seen by the therapist to whom he is to be assigned). As a matter of fact, the matching of the kind of person you wanted to work with and the kind of person Mr. _____ is, is so close that it hardly ever happens. What's even more, he has often described the kind of patient he likes to

[3] *Ibid.,* p. 192.

work with most as someone just like you in many respects. You two should get along extremely well.

Condition B. Low Attraction-Personal Liking. The beginning of the structuring of patients in this Condition was the same as that employed in Condition A. The structuring tag line, however, was: "Frankly, we don't have anyone on our staff who fits your description closely, but Mr. _____ is like your description in some ways. You and he will probably get along all right."

Condition C. High Attraction-Therapy Outcome. Whereas the intended basis for the Condition A and B attraction manipulations was the degree to which the patient would "like" the therapist and his in-therapy behaviors, Conditions C and D centered upon the supposed likelihood that the therapist would or would not be able to help the patient resolve his specific presenting problems. Thus in lieu of the Matching Scale (which was not administered to Condition C and D patients) the Present Self Inventory was used to enhance the credibility of the attraction induction procedures for these patients. In conjunction with the structuring statement made to Condition C patients, the tester displayed several copies of the Present Self Inventory and stated that each was a composite for each of the Center's therapists, a composite indicating which patient problems each therapist had proven most skilled at handling in the past. Condition C patients were told:

> We have carefully examined the tests you took in order to assign you to a therapist who would be most likely to help you solve the problems which brought you here. We usually can't match a patient with a therapist who is clearly the very best therapist for that person, but for you we've been able to do almost exactly that. Mr. _____ has worked with many patients whose problems are just like yours, and apparently has been very successful with them. Your therapy with him will likely work out very well.

Condition D. Low Attraction-Therapy Outcome. Patients assigned to this Condition were treated as described for Condition C, with the major difference being the last part of the structuring: "It is never really possible to match a patient with a therapist who is clearly the very best therapist for that person. In your case we've assigned you to Mr. _____, who like most therapists, has generally been helpful to the patients he has worked with. Your treatment with him will probably work out all right."

Condition E. Control Group-No Attraction Structuring. Patients assigned to this Condition completed the intake test battery, but underwent no posttesting attraction induction. Note that, largely in response to ethical considerations, we depart with this condition from our effort to utilize procedures parallel to those employed by Back. It is also worth noting in this regard that Back's most robust findings involved comparisons against his Negative Treatment (Minimal Attraction) Condition, i.e., the condition we have intentionally omitted from the present investigation. After a wait period of from three to seven days, each patient was seen for his initial psychotherapy session by the therapist to whom he had been assigned. No requests were made of the participating therapists regarding the nature of these sessions. It was assumed they would be conducted in a manner according with that usual for nonresearch patients.[4] All sessions were tape-recorded and, at the close of each session, the therapist completed a Therapist's Personal Reaction Questionnaire (TPRQ).[5] This instrument was developed by Ashby et al. (2), who report evidence indicating the usefulness of this device as a measure of the therapist's attraction to the patient and the developing therapy relationship. A parallel measure, the Client's Personal Reaction Questionnaire (CPRQ)[6] was completed by each patient after the initial therapy session. Also developed by Ashby et al. (2), the CPRQ has associated with it considerable evidence regarding construct and predictive validity as a measure of patient attraction to the therapist and therapy.

Patient influenceability, hypothesized here as a major consequent of attraction to the therapist, was operationalized in two ways—both of which are in-therapy behaviors. First, patients structured for high attraction (Conditions A and C) should talk more in psychotherapy than those structured for low attraction (Conditions B and D) or unstructured (Condition E). This criterion was operationalized in terms of Mahl's (36) Patient Silence Quotient as determined from a timing analysis[7] of the initial interview recordings. A content analysis[8] of these same tapes formed the second set of openness to influence criteria, also predicted to be more favorable for Condition A and C versus B, D, and E patients. The content analysis system developed by Ashby et al. (2) was used for this purpose, particularly the categories of openness, guardedness, overt resistance, and covert resistance.[9]

A series of one-way analyses of variance was conducted on the

---

[4] While participating therapists all knew a study was in progress, all were completely blind as to the nature and hypotheses of this investigation.
[5] See Appendix I, pp. 193-194.
[6] Ibid., pp. 195-196.
[7] Interjudge reliability = .997 (Pearson r).
[8] Interjudge reliability = .885 (Pearson r).
[9] A full description of these content categories is provided in Appendix II, pp. 227-233.

study's data. The overall F for attraction induction was not significant. Thus unlike Back's and Sapolsky's results, the absence of between-condition differences on the CPRQ indicated the failure of our
structuring to influence patient attraction to the therapist. Consistent
with this failure of induction, the analyses of variance for the TPRQ,
Patient Silence Quotient, and the content analysis scores for influenceability similarly yielded nonsignificant results. We can offer at best
only a partial speculation for this series of findings. Back's results were
most robust on his comparisons of strong induced attraction versus the
negative treatment condition. His strong versus weak attraction comparisons were clear in trend, somewhat more equivocal in definiteness.
Perhaps the conditions of our study, excluding for ethical reasons a
negative treatment condition, represent primarily a truncated segment
of the range of attraction inductions represented in Back's study. That
is, while he had represented strong positive attraction, weak positive
attraction, and negative attraction, we have represented only the first
two of these. Had the full range of inductions been possible in our
study, perhaps the likelihood of a positive effect would have increased.

There are other findings from the present investigation to be noted.
The correlation between CPRQ and TPRQ scores was .344 ($p < .05$).
While statistically significant, the magnitude of this correlation indicates only minimal variance accounted for. However, as subsequent
chapters will indicate, this same finding at about the same order of
association was obtained in several studies. Thus while the percentage
of variance accounted for is not large, the finding appears to be quite
reliable.

To this point we have focused upon induced attraction, that is, the
level of patient attraction to the therapist resulting from experimental
structuring. A second type of attraction is relevant however. We refer
here to what might be termed "resultant" attraction, that is, patient
attraction to the therapist (independent of experimental procedures)
that follows from the sum of his previous therapy-relevant experiences—
his past experience with other therapists or physicians, impressions
gleaned about therapy and therapists from the mass media and other
individuals, his referral to the Center—as well as his initial interactions
with his therapist. If the patient's CPRQ score is construed as reflecting
such resultant attraction (since there is no evidence in this study indicating it represents induced attraction), we may examine the degree of
association between patient attraction and the criteria of influenceability. Table 2.1 presents this and related information.

Table 2.1 indicates that both patient pretherapy (PIT pre) and
postsession (CPRQ) attraction to the therapist varies inversely with

Table 2.1

Correlation of Attraction and Influence Scores[a]

Attraction Score	Silence Quotient	Openness	Guardedness	Overt Resistance	Covert Resistance
PIT (pre)	− .203	− .058	.150	− .311*	− .461**
CPRQ	− .471**	.275	.176	− .312*	− .468**
TPRQ	− .425*	.286	− .044	− .220	− .314*

[a] Biserial correlations
* $p < .05$, ** $p < .01$

the two interview levels of resistiveness. The timing analysis of these interviews also reveals a significant association of postattraction with the amount of patient talk. A generally similar set of relationships emerges with regard to therapist attraction to the patient. Both high levels of patient talk and low levels of covert resistance covary with high levels of therapist attraction. The correlational nature of these findings must be underscored. We have not demonstrated an effect here of attraction on influence, only a covariation. From such findings we derive encouragement for further exploration of this broad domain of attraction and influence; and a measure of discouragement regarding the potential usefulness in a clinical context of direct structuring as we have operationalized it.

Table 2.2

Correlates of Patient Expectancy and Confidence

	Expectancy	Confidence
PIT (pre)	.026	− .058
CPRQ	.277	.073
Silence Quotient	− .186	− .534**
Openness	.416*	.387*
Guardedness	− .328*	.094
Overt Resistance	.124	− .010
Covert Resistance	− .202	− .367*

* $p < .05$, ** $p < .01$

Finally, for hypothesis generating or exploratory purposes, it will be recalled that measures of Patient Prognostic Expectancy and confidence in the treatment Center were obtained from all patients. The relationship of these scores to our other study measures are presented in Table 2.2.

Table 2.2 indicates that high levels of patient expectation of gain from psychotherapy are associated with high levels of openness and low levels of guardedness in initial interview behavior. Furthermore, the greater the patient's confidence in the treatment Center, the more he talks, the more open his verbalizations, and the less covertly resistive he is.

Thus this study's attraction manipulations failed in their intended effects. Yet when viewed naturalistically, attraction appears to covary with a host of seemingly significant psychotherapeutic dimensions. While there is nothing implying directionality which may be concluded from these data, the covariational evidence stands as suggestive for further study of direct structuring for attraction enhancement.

Direct Structuring—NON-YAVIS Patients

Davidoff (13), the principal investigator for this investigation, sought to examine the combined effects of direct patient structuring for attraction and the ambiguity of information provided patients regarding the interview in which they were to participate. Her dependent measures focused upon patient performance during the interview and his attraction toward the interviewer. A two by three factorial design was utilized, involving two levels of direct structuring of attraction (positive and unstructured) and three levels of ambiguity (high, medium, and no information provided). The nature of the study's procedures was such that this investigation may appropriately be considered an operant conditioning analogue of significant dimensions of verbal, insight-oriented psychotherapy.

In brief overview of the study's procedures, each patient participated in an individual, one and one-half hour session. The session began with a brief testing period, followed by structuring to the patient about his likely compatibility with the interviewer he was soon to meet (High Attraction Condition) or an explanation of his participation on a research basis (attention control). A 50-minute interview followed. In the first 10 minutes a base level for self-referring statements was determined. In the following 40 minutes, all self-referring statements were reinforced. The interview was interrupted after 30 minutes for a break during which another E delivered one of three messages varying in ambiguity about the contingencies involved in the interview. The interview was then completed and postinterview testing for awareness and attraction to the interviewer was conducted.

The participating patients were selected from the population of a Veterans Administration psychiatric hospital by the ward psychologists who used a series of rudimentary screening criteria, all of which sought to establish that the patient could understand and enact the study's procedures. One hundred and eighteen patients were so selected. Of these, 28 refused to participate in the investigation. The remaining 90 patients thus constituted the study's sample.

The failure of the attraction inductions by direct structuring in our earlier study combined with ethical considerations to lead to the decision not to seek to structure low or negative attraction in this investigation. Thus all participating patients, after completing the Patient-Therapist Matching Scale, were either provided high attraction structuring (based on "personal liking") identical with that used in our earlier study, or received what we viewed as "attention control" structuring, that is, material independent of the issue of attraction, but providing the patient with attention from the structurer equivalent to that received by patients structured for high attraction. Both attraction and attention structuring were provided by an E other than the study's interviewer. The attention control structuring was:

> Your ideas about the kind of interviewer you'd like to have are going to be used in another research project we are doing on what qualities people like in their interviewers. As you know, the university is involved in training interviewers, and this will help them understand the kinds of abilities and qualities that are important to patients in training good interviewers.

This study's second independent variable was ambiguity, operationalized in terms of levels of information provided the patient regarding the nature and purposes of the interview. Our interest in ambiguity grew from Ausubel's research on "advanced organizers," defined as "an individual's organization, stability, and clarity of knowledge in a particular subject matter field." Such prior structuring of information or advanced organizers were, Ausubel held, a major positive influence on the learning and retention of new material. He and his co-workers (3, 4, 5, 6), in a series of verbal learning studies, successfully demonstrated that the provision of advanced organizers clearly improved discrimination among concepts already learned, and enhanced performance where established ideas were less clear or stable. Concern with the provision of prior information as to organizing rules and relationships, and hence ambiguity reduction, is also of major concern to contemporary psychotherapy. In contrast to classical psychoanalytic traditions encouraging ambiguity of in-therapy goal-attainment procedures, several current psychotherapeutic innovations strongly urge supplying the patient with therapy-relevant advanced organizers. We refer here to the use of such techniques as Rotter's (48) successive structuring, Truax's (55) vicarious therapy pretraining, Hoehn-Saric et al.'s (24) role induction interview, and our own earlier formulations (20) regarding the structuring of realistic pretherapy patient expectations. Both Bordin (8) and Carkhuff (11) have suggested that such ambiguity reduction may be particularly beneficial in psychotherapies involving schizophrenic patients. This suggestion is consistent with evidence presented by Buss (10) and Mahrer (37) regarding cognitive functioning in schizophrenics. Such evidence emphasizes the fundamental difficulty experienced by such patients in selecting from, attending to, and regulating the stimuli that impinge upon them. Particular difficulty appears to occur in situations requiring a long attention span, sophisticated observation, or complex discriminations. Ambiguous tasks often demand these very skills. Thus in addition to her prediction of higher performance and attraction under attraction structuring as compared to the attention control conditions, Davidoff hypothesized that the more information provided patients regarding the nature of their interview the greater would be their postinterview attraction.

This investigation's final prediction was of an attraction-structuring by information-structuring interaction such that patients operating under conditions of high structured attraction and most prior information were hypothesized to perform at a higher level than patients in any of the study's five other conditions. This prediction stemmed directly from the growing evidence on the necessary role played by subject awareness of reinforcement contingencies for successful conditioning in verbal conditioning studies (15, 30, 33, 44, 53, 54). These studies have demonstrated that performance gains tend to be limited to those subjects who are able to verbalize a correct or correlated contingency between the reinforcement and their own response. However, not all subjects who can so verbalize do indeed increase in performance. Spielberger et al. (54) and Dulany (14) have demonstrated that such awareness enhances performance only when the subject feels positively toward the experimenter. By extrapolation, Davidoff thus predicted that aware patients (those provided much information about the contingencies in the interview) would perform at the highest level under the condition of high attraction structuring.

Following the delivery of the preinterview attraction or attention control structuring, the patient was introduced to the interviewer by

$E.$[10] The interview was opened with the following statement by the interviewer to *all* participating patients:

> I'm going to be asking you some questions, but I won't be saying much myself. I'll mostly be listening. I cannot answer any questions until the interview is over. I'm going to ask you to talk for 10 minutes on each question. There will be five questions; the interview will last about 50 minutes. It sounds very hard to talk 10 minutes, but I think you can do it if you try. And I will help you out if you get stuck. So that I don't have to take notes, I'm going to tape-record the interview. Your name is not on it, so no one will know what you tell me.

Each of the five 10-minute periods which then followed began with one of the following interviewer questions. These questions were rotated across patients in a completely counterbalanced order.

1. Tell me about the hospital here. You could tell me about your experiences with the people you know, that is, doctors, nurses, aides, or other patients and the things you do.

2. Tell me about your parents, brothers, sisters, and relatives. You could tell me about some of your experiences with your mother and father, brothers, sisters, and relatives.

3. Tell me about the armed services, having a job, being in school. You could tell me about some of your experiences with the armed services, jobs, school.

4. Tell me about your hobbies and interests. You could tell me about some of your experiences with hobbies and interests.

5. Do you have a wife and children? (If yes) Tell me about your wife and children, friends, clubs, and church. You could tell me about some of your experiences with your wife and children, friends, clubs, and church. (If no) Tell me about your friends, clubs, and church. You could tell me about some of your experiences with your friends, clubs, and church.

Prompting by the interviewer was used following obvious confusion, lack of direction, or pauses of over 15 seconds. The number of prompts per 10-minute period was later tabulated. During the answering of the first question asked (base rate period), the interviewer provided the patient no reinforcements. During the answering of the next two questions, the interviewer reinforced all self-referring statements by showing interest and approval, by such comments as, "That's interesting," "mm-hmm," "yes," "I see," and by smiling and providing eye contact.

[10] The interviewer had no knowledge of each patient's preinterview structuring.

Following the third question, the interviewer excused herself for a brief break and left the interview room. At this time, the original E consulted a previously concealed slip of paper to inform herself to which ambiguity condition the given patient had been assigned. She then entered the room and delivered one of the following communications:

High Information Condition

There was something I forgot to tell you. Mrs. Davidoff wanted you to know that in asking these questions she's especially interested in hearing about you. Even though she says, 'Tell me about some experience or another,' she's really much more interested in your talking about yourself. In other words, the purpose of asking all these questions is for her to learn about you—your feelings, your reactions, your opinions, your likes and dislikes. She'll let you know that you're talking about things she wants to hear by saying, 'mm-hmm' or, 'That's interesting,' or something like that.

Medium Information Condition

There was something I forgot to tell you. Mrs. Davidoff wanted you to know that in asking these questions she's especially interested in hearing about certain kinds of things. I know Mrs. Davidoff will let you know when you're talking about the things she wants to hear about by saying, 'mm-hmm' or, 'That's interesting,' or something like that. If you watch and listen carefully, you can probably figure out what she's really interested in having you tell about.

No Information Condition

How are you? How are things going? (A one-minute discussion in response to these questions then followed and, if necessary, conversation regarding the weather.)

The E left the room; the interviewer returned, put the tape recorder back on, and conducted the remaining two segments of the interview. The awareness and attraction (CPRQ) questionnaires were then administered, the former by the interviewer, the latter by E.

Performance was operationalized in this investigation by four different measures. Period 1 was considered representative of the patient's naturally occurring output of self-reference.[11] Subtracting this base rate output from the average output of periods 2 and 3 ($\frac{2+3}{2} -1$) yielded our first measure of performance (conditioning). The second performance measure sought to reflect the interactive effects of both

---

[11] For criteria for self-referring statements, see Appendix II, pp. 240-241.

conditioning and the ambiguity manipulation. Here, self-references during periods 2 and 3 were considered the base rate; self-references during 4 and 5 a function of conditioning plus ambiguity structuring. Our measure here was $\frac{4+5}{2} - \frac{2+3}{2}$. Before actual usage, both of these conditioning indices of performance were weighted by dividing for each patient his self-references per period by his total self-references across periods. This procedure enabled us to compare patients with vastly different outputs of self-referring statements. Our third performance measure, productivity, was simply the sum of self-references given by the patient during periods 2, 3, 4, and 5. Finally, the number of prompts needed by the patient to complete each 10-minute interview segment was our last measure of performance. In sum, the performance measures utilized in this investigation were two indices of *conditioning: productivity*, as measured by total number of self-references, and number of *prompts* needed.

A further study measure which should be noted was a patient rating scale completed on each patient by the ward psychologist. Designed primarily for use in exploratory analyses, this scale yielded ratings on functional intelligence, span of attention, prognosis, approval and companionship seeking from the staff and from other patients. Finally, and also for purposes of exploratory analyses, one week after participation in the interview session, each patient was given the Defensiveness and Hostility Scales from Sarason's Autobiographical Survey (51), the Control Scale from the MMPI (57), and Rotter's (48) Internal-External Locus of Control Scale. The MMPI Control Scale purports to assess the degree to which a patient describes himself in overly conventional, rigid, and moralistic terms. The Internal-External measure assesses the degree to which an individual believes the outcomes of his behavior are due to chance, luck, or fate versus his own actions and intentions.

Results

Before examining the study's hypotheses, a check was performed on randomization of assignment to experimental condition. No significant between-cell differences were obtained on any of the demographic or psychometric dimensions examined.[12] Similarly, no significant differ-

---

[12] Education, years hospitalized, number of hospitalizations, vocational category, diagnosis, marital status, race, defensiveness, hostility, internal-external, control and the five ratings obtained from the ward psychologists (functional intelligence, prognosis, attention span, approval seeking from staff, approval seeking from other patients).

ences were obtained on these dimensions between the overall study sample and the 28 patients selected for the study who declined to participate.

The interviewer and an independent judge listened to all interview tapes and tallied the number of self-referring patient statements per segment.[13] There were no significant between-condition differences on number of self-referring statements or on number of prompts needed during the first (base rate) segment of the interview. As our final, prehypothesis-testing check, a series of one-way analyses of variance revealed no significant differences on attraction or on any of the performance measures for the different orders of interview questions used.

It was hypothesized that patients provided direct structuring for positive attraction would be more attracted than those receiving attention, but no attraction structuring. An analysis of variance on the CPRQ data failed to support this prediction (p between .10 and .25). As in our first study of direct structuring, therefore, the relevant laboratory structuring procedures extrapolated here to a clinical context appear to be insufficiently powerful regarding their predicted effect on patient attraction.

Our second hypothesis predicted that patients provided high information (low ambiguity) about their forthcoming interview would be more attracted to the interviewer than those provided medium information, and these latter patients would, in turn, be more attracted than patients provided no information. The analysis of variance across these conditions for attraction revealed a significant main effect ($F = 4.03$, $df = 2, 84$, $p < .05$). Scheffe tests on these data, however, revealed that the cell differences were not in the direction predicted. Patients provided no information were significantly more attracted to the interviewer than were medium information patients or were medium and high information patients combined. It may well be the case, therefore, that ambiguity regarding the nature of an anticipated interview, at least under the conditions of the present investigation, augments and does not decrease attraction. An alternative explanation for this finding lies with the exact nature of the information inductions. The medium information induction may have been interpreted negatively by the patient, as a taunt, transforming what until then was a straightforward interview into a mystery to be deciphered. Perhaps this challenging quality of the induction, rather than the amount of information provided per se, led to the lowered patient attraction scores. Contrary to

---

[13] Interjudge reliability $= .99$ (Pearson r).

prediction, high information patients were not more attracted than no information patients. This finding may have grown from the possibly superfluous nature of the high information communication for many of the patients. The high information communication was formulated through pilot efforts to be understood by the least common denominator in the patient sample. Self-referring statements were a natural response to the situation and the interview questions themselves (independent of information structuring), and both preinterview structuring and the interviewer's prompting behavior were further reducing of ambiguity. Perhaps the combination of these considerations led the ambiguity status of no information patients to be not as discrepant as we had orginally hoped from the ambiguity status of our high information patients.

Our final hypothesis predicted highest performance in patients structured for attraction and provided high information. Analyses of variance involving the study's four measures of performance failed to support this prediction. Thus both attraction and information structuring, as operationalized in this investigation, failed to influence either attraction or performance in the manner predicted. A clearly appropriate response to such negative findings concerns post hoc examination of the interactive effects played by subject variables. Thus, for strictly exploratory purposes, and leading to only suggestive conclusions, a series of post hoc analyses on these data were performed. To identify which subject variables were most worth pursuing, our initial post hoc analysis was correlational. We will focus in the discussion that follows primarily on those correlations that contribute to understanding the results of the study's hypotheses. It should be noted, however, that of the 179 correlations run, 53 were significant at or beyond the .05 confidence level. Thus the findings to be discussed below are unlikely to be attributable to chance.

The Internal-External Control Scale (high scores indicate Externality) correlated significantly with CPRQ attraction ($-.28$), with the postinformation structuring measure of performance ($-.32$), and with number of prompts needed ($.31$). Thus, the greater the patient's external orientation, the less he liked the interviewer, the fewer self-references he gave following information induction, and the more prompts he needed. In response, then, to the possible significance of this patient characteristic, patients were split at the median on internal-external control and an analysis of variance was performed on this split against the study's conditions on the attraction and performance dependent variables. These analyses revealed no effect for internal-external control on performance. However, a significant effect on attraction was obtained ($F = 5.52$, $df = 1$, 35, $p < .05$). Highly external patients who received direct structuring for attraction were significantly more attracted to the interviewer than were high externals provided attention structuring. As noted earlier, Rotter (48) has described the externally controlled individual as a person who views his destiny as falling in hands other than his own. Fate, luck, chance, and the wishes of others, and not one's own efforts, determine one's personal circumstances. This disposition is fully consistent with the greater responsiveness of such patients to attraction structuring rather than attention structuring.

The ward psychologists' ratings[14] of patient prognosis were significantly associated with interviewer liking (TPRQ) for the patient (.23), with both pre- and postinformation induction conditioning (.24, .30), and with number of prompts needed (— .37). Thus patient prognosis as rated by the ward psychologist is associated with attractiveness, conditionability, and the disinclination to need help. The ward psychologists' prognostic ratings were blocked into high and moderate versus low and an analysis of variance was performed on this split against the study's conditions on the attraction and performance dependent variables. Significant main effects were obtained such that high and moderate prognosis patients, in contrast to those rated low, were more attractive to the interviewer ($F = 7.40$, $df = 1$, 31, $p < .05$), verbalized a greater number of self-referring statements both before and after the information induction ($F = 8.04$, $df = 1$, 35, $p < .05$; $F = 4.20$, $df = 1$, 35, $p < .05$), and needed fewer prompts ($F = 4.78$, $df = 1$, 35, $p < .05$).

While ward psychologist ratings of functional intelligence failed to look promising in our correlational analysis, our pursuit here of subject variables seeks to be particularly responsive to the implications of those patient characteristics subsumed under the term NON-YAVIS. Externality and prognosis are two such characteristics, apparent functioning intelligence is a third. Thus the following analysis was conducted. Average or high intelligence ratings versus low ratings were compared across conditions and dependent variables. Results indicated that patients rated high or average on intelligence, as compared to those rated low, were more attracted to the interviewer ($F = 4.51$, $df = 2$, 35, $p < .01$), gave more self-references in periods 2 and 3 ($F = 4.50$, $df = 2$, 35, $p < .05$) and periods 4 and 5 ($F = 4.93$, $df = 2$, 35, $p < .05$), needed fewer prompts ($F = 4.62$, $df = 2$, 35, $p < .05$), and were better liked by the interviewer ($F = 3.38$, $df = 2$, 35, $p < .05$).

[14] See Appendix I, pp. 212-213.

Thus, while the major predictions of this investigation failed to receive support, a series of post hoc analyses focusing on subject variables of likely relevance to attraction and performance provides us with a consistent and provocative series of leads for further investigation. Externally-oriented patients are less attracted to the interviewer than are internals. Yet, when structured for attraction, such patients are significantly more attracted than are unstructured externals. Patients rated as high or moderate in prognosis and intelligence are more attracted to the interviewer and perform better in therapy-relevant ways than do their low rated counterparts. We have here further confirmation of the internality, favorable prognosis, and high intelligence components of the YAVIS syndrome. At least with regard to the responsiveness of externally-oriented patients to direct structuring, we also have some tentative evidence that one aspect of being a NON-YAVIS patient, namely low attraction to the interviewer, is not immutable.

Finally, in a manner consistent with the correlational findings of our earlier study of direct structuring, as well as the findings dealing with the reciprocity of therapist and patient attraction to be discussed in later chapters, we examined the relationship of CPRQ and TPRQ scores. Patient attraction to the interviewer correlated .44 ($p < .01$) with interviewer attraction to the patient, and .41 ($p < .01$) with experimenter attraction to the patient. In addition, still viewing CPRQ scores independent of experimental manipulations, such scores were split at the median and one-way analyses of variance performed against both interviewer and experimenter attraction. Both analyses yielded significant results (respectively: $F = 5.62$, $df = 1, 88$, $p < .01$; $F = 7.80$, $df = 1, 88$, $p < .01$) thus indicating that patients who are more attracted to the interviewer are, in turn, more attractive to both the interviewer and the experimenter.

Direct Structuring and Desensitization

Throughout this book our implicit, and often explicit, focus will be upon techniques of relationship enhancement instituted in order to maximize the likelihood of successful outcome in *verbal, insight-oriented psychotherapy*. Thus disclosure and guardedness will be the type of relationship consequent of interest to us. However, we are very much in accord with Kiesler (27), Heller (22), and others who have pointed to the need for psychotherapies and not psychotherapy, for a heterogeneous array of treatment approaches responsive to the diversity of psychopathologies with which we must deal. The recent and rapid development of the behavior therapies is clearly responsive to this sentiment, and augers well for our growing ability to more effectively match patients and treatments. In contemplating such an array of insight-oriented, behavioral, and other psychotherapies, we have proposed earlier that both commonalities and differences across therapies must be investigated if we are to more fully discern the therapeutic in psychotherapy. One such active ingredient, viewed by us as likely shared in common by all existing therapies, is the therapist-patient relationship. The remainder of this chapter represents a beginning focus upon direct structuring for purposes of relationship enhancement in the context of desensitization therapy.

Wolpe and Lazarus (60) have commented in this regard:

> In the conventional literature on psychotherapy much has been made of the patient-therapist relationship. A widely prevalent belief is that the quality of the therapeutic relationship is more basic to therapeutic outcome than the therapist's specific methods and techniques, and this is probably true of the conventional therapies. . . . But the active implementation of conditioning procedures add to the generalized benefits which accrue when people establish close rapport. The practice of behavior therapy may thus be viewed as a 'double-barrelled' means of alleviating neurotic distress. As in most systems of psychotherapy, the patient enjoys the nonjudgmental acceptance of a person whom he perceives as possessing the necessary skills and desire to be of service, but in behavior therapy he receives, in addition, the benefits of special conditioning procedures which may have independent validity. (60, pp. 9-10)

These same authors, in another context (28), have gone on to note that:

> . . . relationship variables are often extremely important in behavior therapy. Factors such as warmth, empathy, and authenticity are considered necessary but often insufficient. (28, p. 262)

Andrews (1), Gelder et al. (18), Meyer and Gelder (39), Murray and Jacobson (41), Patterson (42), Wilson et al. (58), and Wolpin and Raines (61) are others who, viewing behavior therapy from rather different perspectives, have pointed to the likely significant role played by relationship forces in the therapeutic learning process. Yet evidence speaking directly to this issue is both sparse and equivocal. Both Wolpe (59) and Lazarus (32) have had other therapists substitute for themselves part way through the desensitization of monophobic patients, and report no deleterious effects following from such a procedure. Such an interchange of therapists may indeed have diminished those positive benefits associated with the specific therapist-patient dyad, but may have augmented the total of status, attentional, and other placebo-like relationship benefits accruing to the patient. Melamed and Lang (38) compared the therapeutic effectiveness of a live behavior therapist with that of a programmed apparatus known as DAD (Device for Automated Desensitization). DAD and the therapist appeared to be equally effective fear reducers. It should be noted, however, that DAD patients met with a therapist prior to the desensitization sessions for a series of sessions involving hierarchy building and relaxation instruction. However, in an investigation in which human interaction with the patient was much more fully minimized, Krapfl and Nowas (29) found, as had Melamed and Lang, no difference in outcome between the automated and therapist-administered treatment conditions and, in addition, both of these treatments proved superior in fear reduction to untreated or pseudo-desensitized controls. Paul (43) similarly found specific therapeutic effects for desensitization and, to a less powerful extent, for relationship ingredients. He compared the relative effectiveness of desensitization, insight therapy, attention-placebo, and no treatment. Significantly greatest patient anxiety reduction occurred with desensitization. In addition, both insight therapy and attention-placebo patients improved significantly more than patients receiving no treatment. Yet, in a similarly well-controlled investigation comparing treatments not dissimilar from Paul's, Lang et al. (31) replicated the significant effect for desensitization, but found no difference between untreated controls and patients receiving attention and related relationship ingredients.

To confuse the picture even further, Ritter (46) compared the effects of (a) "contact desensitization," (b) desensitization involving all the components of (a) except the physical contact with the therapist, and (c) no treatment in reducing fear and avoidance of heights in agoraphobic patients. Patients receiving contact desensitization demonstrated significantly greater fear reduction than the other two conditions—which did not differ from one another.

In summary of these studies, we find a rather consistent demonstration of a positive therapeutic effect for desensitization, but somewhat equivocal evidence regarding the role played by relationship factors in augmenting this desensitization effect. We will present two investigations in the remainder of this chapter. The first, which we will consider rather briefly, had as its primary goal the investigation of aspects of the desensitization process other than the role played by the therapist-patient relationship. It will, however, provide us with important correlational data bearing upon quality of relationship and outcome of desensitization therapy. The second investigation will focus more directly upon the major questions we wish to deal with here—the effec-

tiveness of direct structuring for attraction enhancement, and the outcome consequences of such structuring in the context of desensitization
therapy.

Group Desensitization:
I. The Role of Group Interaction and
a Progressive Anxiety Hierarchy

Cohen (12), the principal investigator for this study,[15] was interested in examining two aspects of the desensitization process for their
effects upon anxiety reduction. Working in the context of group desensitization for test anxiety, the first variable investigated was the opportunity provided or denied group members for group interaction during
desensitization sessions. Cohen posited that such interaction among
members of a group undergoing desensitization would serve to further
augment the effects of the desensitization proper on anxiety reduction.
Such augmentation, he held, might follow from the added opportunity
thus provided to learn behavioral discriminations, from the motivational
properties associated with hearing of other patient's progress, and/or
from the desensitization component per se possibly inherent in such
group interactions. Cohen also sought to question the typical desensitization procedure of beginning with slightly anxiety-arousing situations
and gradually introducing items eliciting greater anxiety. While it may,
he held, take more trials to respond without anxiety to top-
of-the-hierarchy items when they are presented with no desensitization
of less intense items, the total number of trials necessary to achieve
overall inhibition of anxiety may be fewer. Five experimental groups
were randomly constituted from a pool of college student subjects reporting markedly high test-taking anxiety. Utilizing a 2 x 2 design,
these groups involved two levels of opportunity for group interaction
(presence versus absence) and two levels of hierarchy presentation
(all items beginning with least anxiety-provoking versus use of only
the four most anxiety-provoking items). Subjects assigned to a fifth
study group, no contact controls, took the study's pre- and postmeasures as part of a class requirement, but participated in no desensitization sessions. Each experimental subject participated in 12 one-hour
group desensitization sessions. Results of this investigation indicated
that subjects in all experimental groups reported significantly greater
reduction in text anxiety [pre-post-desensitization change score on
Sarason (51) Test Anxiety Scale] than did no contact controls. A
significant main effect on self-reported anxiety reduction also emerged

---

[15] Sanford Dean served as primary advisor for this investigation.

such that subjects permitted group interaction during desensitization sessions obtained greater anxiety reduction than did subjects in the no group interaction conditions. No such difference was obtained in the comparison of progressive hierarchy versus top of the hierarchy subjects. It should also be noted that the latter subjects took significantly fewer trials (scene exposures) than progressive hierarchy subjects to reach the same level of anxiety reduction.

With regard to our major concern, attraction, two measures were developed for use in this study. Both measures derived from related scales used by us in our investigations of the therapy relationship in individual psychotherapy. The Attraction to Group Scale,[16] rather similar in content to several contemporary measures of group cohesiveness (16, 52, 56), sought to measure subject attraction to his desensitization group. The Attraction to Treatment Scale[17] sought estimates from the subjects regarding their feelings about the group leader and several specific aspects of the treatment process, e.g., relaxation, visualization, discussion, etc. Both measures were administered after the third desensitization session and at termination. Consistent with Libo's (34) finding that attraction to treatment is predictive of remaining or terminating in individual psychotherapy, subjects in the four experimental conditions who completed treatment reported significantly greater attraction to treatment than did those subjects who dropped out of the study prior to completion of treatment. Furthermore, on the Attraction to Group Scale, dropout subjects were significantly less attracted at termination than they were following their third session. Group interaction subjects strongly tended to report greater attraction to group than noninteraction subjects, though not significantly so. A significant interaction effect favoring the group interaction-top of hierarchy condition over the group interaction-progressive hierarchy emerged in terms of attraction to treatment.

A correlational analysis across all experimental groups revealed highly significant positive associations between subject estimates of anxiety reduction due to treatment and both measures of attraction. Of course, as is true of the numerous similar findings in the individual psychotherapy literature, there is no reason to assume from these data that attraction to group or to treatment *leads to* greater anxiety reduction. Particularly in this context, in which both attraction and anxiety reduction measures are based on self-report, an equally plausible directional inference is that perceived change leads to enhanced attraction.

[16] See Appendix I, p. 198.
[17] *Ibid.*, p. 199.

With similar correlational tentativeness, and in a manner consistent with the findings of our first study of direct structuring, Cohen also found significant positive associations between his attraction measures and both the level of pretreatment subject anxiety and pretreatment subject expectation of anxiety reduction due to treatment.

Group Desensitization:
II. Direct Structuring for
Attraction Enhancement

Both the Cohen study and our own initial attempts at attraction enhancement by direct structuring provide us with consistent correlational evidence of the association of attraction and a variety of outcome or outcome-relevant dependent variables. In neither our initial study nor in our second attempt at direct structuring was there any substantial evidence pointing to the success of such structuring attempts. Davidoff's post hoc analysis on selected patient subsamples altered this conclusion somewhat and tentatively suggested that there might exist certain subclasses of patients for whom attraction enhancement by direct structuring may be an appropriate and useful technique. Kiesler's (27) formulations regarding the "patient uniformity myth" similarly, if more generally, suggest that researchers have conceptualized too grossly in defining patient samples for studies of psychotherapy, and thus that greater investigative progress may be realized to the extent that we can make segmented predictions regarding specific subsamples of patients receiving well-defined treatments. Our next investigation, conducted by Hemingway (23), sought to be responsive to these notions. Direct structuring failed to occur in our first study in which patients were college students undergoing insight-oriented verbal psychotherapy, and occurred only very partially in our second study, involving psychotic patients also undergoing interview interactions. Hemingway's effort shifted our focus away from an interview approach, and examined instead the effects of direct structuring on both attraction and outcome in the context of desensitization therapy.

Subjects for this investigation were university undergraduates reporting marked test-taking anxiety. As in Cohen's investigation, the selection instrument was Sarason's Test Anxiety Scale (51). From an original pool of over 400 students, 88 were selected representing the upper quartile of test-taking anxiety. Twenty-two students were randomly selected from the new pool of 88 to serve as an uninvited control group. They were not informed in any way that they were part of an investigation. The remaining 66 students were sent letters inviting them to participate in a class designed to assist them in reducing their anxiety associated with taking examinations. The 27 students responding affirmatively to this invitation were randomly assigned to the following experimental conditions:

1. *High Attraction, Systematic Desensitization.*—Subject assigned to this condition were led to believe, following matching and structuring procedures almost identical to those used in our first direct structuring study, that they had been exceptionally well-matched with their instructor (group desensitization class instructor) and that they and the instructor would get along very well together. Subsequent to attraction structuring, these subjects participated in eight weekly, one-hour group desensitization sessions.

2. *Moderate Attraction, Systematic Desensitization.*—Matching and structuring procedures utilized for subjects assigned to this condition were very similar to those used for what, at that point, we labeled the Low Attraction Condition in our earlier study. Specifically, following administration and purported scoring of the Student-Instructor Matching Scale,[18] an adaptation of our Patient-Therapist Matching Scale, subjects assigned to this condition were told:

> As I told you before, the tests given to you earlier were designed to match you with an instructor that you would be able to get along with. It makes sense to try to insure your comfort in the class if your success is related to the degree of comfort you experience in class. In the case of this particular group it was possible to make a match. I can assure you that there is no reason to believe that you will not get on well together.

Subsequent to attraction structuring, subjects assigned to this condition participated in eight weekly, hour-long group desensitization sessions.

3. *Contracted Control Group.*—Following administration and "scoring" of the matching scale, subjects assigned to this condition were told that it was impossible to match them with an instructor during the present semester, but that an instructor with whom they could be matched would be available during the following semester, and the class would thus be offered to them at that time. No systematic desensitization was provided these subjects during the period the two treatment groups were in treatment.

In addition to the High and Moderate treatment groups and the

[18] See Appendix I, p. 200.

Contacted and Uninvited control groups, this study contained an additional experimental condition. Following completion of the eight-week period during which treatment groups were undergoing desensitization, subjects in the Contacted and Uninvited control groups were postmeasured and then invited to participate in systematic desensitization. Their pretreatment structuring was identical to that provided earlier to High Attraction subjects, thus constituting this additional condition into essentially a High Attraction, Replication group.

The "instructor" conducting all desensitization "classes" was unaware of the study's hypotheses or attraction manipulations. Each subject met with his group for an initial session during which the attraction inductions were administered. The eight weekly desensitization sessions which followed were all video-taped in order to provide any subjects who might be absent for the given session the opportunity to "make it up." The Attraction to Treatment Scale was administered to all treatment subjects prior to and following the initial session, for purposes of a check on the attraction manipulations. Approximately half of sessions two and three were spent by subjects in the two treatment groups in relaxation training, using taped relaxation instructions for standardization purposes. By the end of the third session, all subjects reported being able to attain a comfortable state of relaxation in a few minutes without the assistance of the taped instructions. Most of the remainder of these two periods were devoted to lecture and discussion of learning theory as applied to anxiety and desensitization. A few moments were devoted to desensitization during these two sessions. Almost all of sessions four through eight were spent in desensitization. The test-anxiety hierarchy items used were drawn from those developed by Cohen (12) and Katahn et al. (26). Subjects were given copies of this list at the first session and asked to arrange the items in ascending order of degree of anxiety elicited. All subjects began the desensitization procedure with the least anxiety-provoking scene and progressed toward the scene which evoked the most anxiety for them.

Dependent variable measures for this investigation consisted of the outcome criteria of pre-post-desensitization change in Test Anxiety Scale score and in grade point average, and such process measures as absenteeism, attrition, sessions made up, and an efficiency measure (work/success) in which work was defined as the number of presentations during a given session and success was defined as the number of hierarchy items successfully deconditioned[19] during the same session.

[19] An item was considered successfully deconditioned when S reported visualizing the given scene for two minutes without evoking an anxiety response, three times in succession.

Results

No significant differences on attraction existed between the three treatment groups [High Attraction, Moderate Attraction, Replication (of High Attraction)] prior to the direct structuring manipulations. Following structuring, subjects in the original High Attraction and Replication groups, while not differing significantly from one another, were both significantly more attracted to treatment than were Moderate Attraction Condition subjects ($t = 2.45$, $df = 16$, $p < .02$; $t = 3.78$, $df = 11$, $p < .005$). Thus, in contrast to our two earlier attempts at attraction enhancement by direct structuring, Hemingway's use of these procedures antecedent to desensitization therapy were successful.

With regard to this study's process measures, the first finding of interest relates to absenteeism. Consistent with Cohen's finding regarding attraction and dropping out of treatment, Hemingway found that subjects structured for moderate attraction missed a significantly greater number of desensitization sessions than both High Attraction and Replication subjects ($X^2 = 5.63$, $df = 1$, $p < .02$; $X^2 = 2.73$, $df = 1$, $p < .05$). An analogous result was obtained with regard to efficiency, defined earlier as the ratio of work to success. Both High Attraction and Replication subjects were significantly more efficient than Moderate Attraction subjects ($F = 13.01$, $df = 1, 8$, $p < .01$; $F = 29.99$, $df = 1, 5$, $p < .01$). The two High Attraction groups also tended to have fewer dropouts and more corrected absences (use of video-tapes) than did the Moderate Attraction group.

With regard to outcome measures, no significant differences were obtained between the five study conditions on grade point average. Change scores on the Test Anxiety Scale, however, revealed significantly greater change by Replication group subjects as compared to Moderate Attraction ($t = 2.12$, $df = 5$, $p < .05$), Contact control ($t = 3.03$, $df = 5$, $p < .02$), and Uninvited control ($t = 2.90$, $df = 6$, $p < .01$) subjects but not in comparison with High Attraction Condition subjects.

The four investigations we have presented, consistent with much that has been reported by others in the psychotherapy research literature, provide a great deal of correlational evidence suggesting that patient attraction covaries with a host of other therapy-relevant variables. Our extrapolatory attempts to enhance patient attraction by use of direct structuring procedures were primarily successful in the context of group desensitization therapy administered to college students, although there was some post hoc evidence for the success of such structuring with a particular subsample of psychotic patients. Further investigation of the treatment and patient contexts in which these procedures may be most fruitfully applied are necessary before more final conclusions can be offered regarding the therapeutic value of direct structuring for attraction enhancement.

References

1. Andrews, J. D. Psychotherapy of phobias. *Psychological Bulletin*, 1966, 66, 455–480.

2. Ashby, J. D., Ford, D. H., Guerney, B. G., Jr., & Guerney, L. Effects on clients of a reflective and a leading type of psychotherapy. *Psychological Monographs*, 1957, 7, 1–32.

3. Ausubel, D. P. *The psychology of meaningful verbal learning*. New York: Grune & Stratton, 1963.

4. Ausubel, D. P. & Blake, E. Pro-active inhibition in the forgetting of meaningful school material. *Journal of Educational Psychology*, 1958, 52, 145–149.

5. Ausubel, D. P. & Fitzgerald, D. The role of discriminability in meaningful verbal learning and retention. *Journal of Educational Psychology*, 1961, 52, 266–274.

6. Ausubel, D. P. & Fitzgerald, D. Organizer, general background, and antecedent learning variables in sequential verbal learning. *Journal of Educational Psychology*, 1962, 53, 243–249.

7. Back, K. W. Influence through social communication. *Journal of Abnormal and Social Psychology*, 1951, 46, 9–23.

8. Bordin, E. Ambiguity as a therapeutic variable. *Journal of Consulting Psychology*, 1955, 19, 9–15.

9. Burdick, H. A. & Burnes, A. J. A test of "strain toward symmetry" theories. *Journal of Abnormal and Social Psychology*, 1958, 57, 367–370.

10. Buss, A. H. *Psychopathology*. New York: Wiley, 1966.

11. Carkhuff, R. Ambiguity: A proposed dimension of the psychotherapeutic process. Wisconsin Psychiatric Institute, 1963, mimeographed.

12. Cohen, R. Group desensitization of test anxiety. Unpublished doctoral dissertation, Syracuse University, 1967.

13. Davidoff, L. L. Schizophrenic patients in psychotherapy: The effects of degree of information and compatibility expectations on behavior in the interview setting: An operant conditioning analogue. Unpublished doctoral dissertation, Syracuse University, 1969.

14. Dulany, D. E. The place of hypotheses and intentions: An analysis of verbal control in verbal conditioning. In C. W. Eriksen (Ed.), *Behavior and awareness*. Durham: Duke University Press, 1962. Pp.102–129.

15. Eriksen, C. W. Figments, fantasies, and follies: A search for the subconscious mind. In C. W. Eriksen (Ed.), *Behavior and awareness*. Durham: Duke University Press, 1962. Pp. 3–26.

16. Festinger, L., Schachter, S., & Back, K. W. *Social pressures in informal groups*. New York: Harper, 1950.

17. French, J. R. P., Jr.& Snyder, R. Leadership and interpersonal power. In D. Cartwright (Ed.), *Studies in social power*. Ann Arbor: Institute for Social Research, 1959. Pp. 118–149.

18. Gelder, M. G., Marks, I. M., & Wolff, H. N. Desensitization and psychotherapy in the treatment of phobic states. *British Journal of Psychiatry*, 1967, 113, 53–73.

19. Gerard, H. B. The anchorage of opinions in face-to-face groups. *Human Relations*, 1954, 7, 313–325.

20. Goldstein, A. P. *Therapist-patient expectancies in psychotherapy*. New York: Pergamon Press, 1962.

21. Gordon, R. L. Interaction between attitude and the definitions of the situation in the expression of opinion. *American Sociological Review*, 1952, 17, 50–58.

22. Heller, K. Experimental analogues of psychotherapy: The clinical relevance of laboratory findings of social influence. *Journal of Nervous and Mental Disease*, 1963, 137, 420–426.

23. Hemingway, P. Expectancy effects in a behavior therapy situation. Unpublished doctoral dissertation, University of Saskatchewan, 1969.

24. Hoehn-Saric, R., Frank, J. D., Imber, S. D., Nash, E. H., Jr., Stone, A. R., & Battle, C. C. Systematic preparation of patients for psychotherapy. I. Effects on therapy behavior and outcome. *Journal of Psychiatric Research*, 1964, 2, 267–281.

25. Jones, E. E. & Thibaut, J. W. Interaction goals as bases of inference in interpersonal perception. In R. Taguiri & L. Petrullo (Eds.), *Person perception and interpersonal behavior*. Stanford: Stanford University Press, 1958. Pp. 151–178.

26. Katahn, M., Strenger, S., & Cherry, N. Group counseling and behavior therapy with test anxious college students. *Journal of Consulting Psychology*, 1966, 30, 544–549.

27. Kiesler, D. J. Some myths of psychotherapy research and the search for a paradigm. *Psychological Bulletin*, 1966, 65, 110–136.

28. Klein, M. H., Dittmann, A. T., Parloff, M. B., & Gill, M. M. Behavior Therapy: Observations and reflections. *Journal of Consulting and Clinical Psychology*, 1969, 33, 259–266.

29. Krapfl, J. E. & Newas, M. M. The client-therapist relationship factor in systematic desensitization. University of Missouri, 1968, mimeographed.

30. Krasner, L., Weiss, R. L., & Ullmann, L. P. Responsivity to verbal conditioning as a function of awareness. *Psychological Reports*, 1961, 8, 523–538.

31. Lang, P. J., Lazovik, A. D., & Reynolds, D. J. Desensitization, suggestibility and pseudotherapy. *Journal of Abnormal and Social Psychology*, 1965, **70**, 395–402.

32. Lazarus, A. A., Davison, G. C., & Polefka, D. A. Classical and operant factors in the treatment of a school phobia. *Journal of Abnormal Psychology*, 1965, **70**, 225–229.

33. Levin, S. M. The effects of awareness on verbal conditioning. *Journal of Experimental Psychology*, 1957, **13**, 33–36.

34. Libo, L. The projective expression of patient-therapist attraction. *Journal of Clinical Psychology*, 1957, **13**, 33–36.

35. Libo, L. *Picture impressions: A projective technique for investigating the patient-therapist relationship.* Baltimore: University of Maryland Medical School, 1959.

36. Mahl, G. F. Disturbances and silences in the patient's speech in psychotherapy. *Journal of Abnormal and Social Psychology*, 1956, **53**, 1–15.

37. Mahrer, B. A. *Principles of psychopathology: An experimental approach.* New York: McGraw-Hill, 1966.

38. Melamed, B. & Lang, P. J. Study of the automated desensitization of fear. Paper presented at Midwestern Psychological Association, Chicago, 1967.

39. Meyer, V. & Gelder, M. G. Behavior therapy and phobic disorders. *British Journal of Psychiatry*, 1963, **109**, 19–28.

40. Moran, G. Dyadic attraction and orientational consensus. *Journal of Personality and Social Psychology*, 1966, **4**, 94–99.

41. Murray, E. J. & Jacobson, L. I. The nature of learning in traditional and behavioral psychotherapy. In A. E. Bergin & S. L. Garfield (Eds.), *Handbook of psychotherapy and behavior change.* New York: Wiley, 1970.

42. Patterson, C. H. *Theories of counseling and psychotherapy.* New York: Harper & Row, 1966.

43. Paul, G. L. *Insight versus desensitization in psychotherapy: An experiment in anxiety reduction.* Stanford: Stanford University Press, 1965.

44. Postman, L. & Jarrett, R. F. An experimental analysis of "learning without awareness." *American Journal of Psychiatry*, 1952, **65**, 244–255.

45. Rasmussen, G. & Zander, A. Group membership and self-evaluation. *Human Relations*, 1954, **7**, 239–251.

46. Ritter, B. The group desensitization of children's snake phobias using vicarious and contact desensitization procedures. *Behaviour Research and Therapy*, 1968, **6**, 1–6.

47. Rotter, J. B. *Social learning and clinical psychology.* Englewood Cliffs, N.J.: Prentice Hall, 1954.

48. Rotter, J. B. Generalized expectancies for internal versus external control of reinforcement. *Psychological Monographs*, 1966, Whole No. 609.

49. Sapolsky. A. Effect of interpersonal relationships upon verbal conditioning. *Journal of Abnormal and Social Psychology*, 1950, **60**, 241–246.

50. Sarason, I. G. Interrelationships among individual difference variables, behavior in psychotherapy, and verbal conditioning. *Journal of Abnormal and Social Psychology*, 1958, **56**, 339–344.

51. Sarason, S. B. & Mandler, G. Some correlates of test anxiety. *Journal of Abnormal and Social Psychology*, 1952, **47**, 810–817.

52. Schachter, S. Deviation, rejection and communication. *Journal of Abnormal and Social Psychology*, 1951, **46**, 190–207.

53. Spielberger, C. D. The role of awareness in verbal conditioning. In C. W. Eriksen (Ed.), *Behavior and awareness*. Durham: Duke University Press, 1962. Pp. 73–101.

54. Spielberger, C. D., Levin, S. M., & Shepard, M. The effects of awareness and attitude toward the reinforcement on the operant conditioning of verbal behavior. *Journal of Personality*, 1962, **30**, 106–121.

55. Truax, C. B. Depth of intrapersonal exploration on therapeutic process in group psychotherapy with and without vicarious therapy pretraining. Wisconsin Psychiatric Institute, 1963, mimeographed.

56. VanBergen, A. & Koekebakker, J. Group cohesiveness in laboratory experiments. *Acta Psychologica*, 1959, **16**, 81–98.

57. Walsh, G.S. & Dahlstrom, G. W. (Eds.) *Basic readings on the MMPI in psychology and medicine*. Minneapolis: University of Minnesota Press, 1956.

58. Wilson, G. T., Hannon, A. E., & Evans, W. I. M. Behavior therapy and the therapist-patient relationship. *Journal of Consulting and Clinical Psychology*, 1968, **32**, 103–109.

59. Wolpe, J. Isolation of a conditioning procedure as the crucial psychotherapeutic factor: A case study. *Journal of Nervous and Mental Disease*, 1962, **134**, 316–329.

60. Wolpe, J. & Lazarus, A. A. *Behaviour therapy techniques*. New York: Pergamon Press, 1966.

61. Wolpin, M. & Raines, J. Visual imagery, expected roles and extinction as possible factors in reducing fear and avoidance behavior. *Behaviour Research and Therapy*, 1966, **4**, 25–37.

Chapter III

Trait Structuring

In contrast to direct structuring, in which the attempt was made to alter patient attraction by messages describing his likely feelings after meeting the therapist, trait structuring essentially involves providing the patient with a description of certain of the therapist's characteristics, i.e., those likely to have an influence upon attraction. The earliest social-psychological laboratory research in this area was Asch's (1) study of impression formation. He provided groups of college student subjects with one of two lists of adjectives descriptive of the personal characteristics of an hypothetical individual. The first list consisted of: intelligent, skillful, industrious, warm, determined, practical, and cautious. The second list was identical except "cold" was substituted for "warm." Subjects were instructed to write personality sketches of the two persons described by the trait lists, and also to select from a checklist of pairs of opposite traits those that best fit their impression of each person. Analysis of both the personality sketches and trait selections revealed marked differences in subject's perceptions of the persons structured "warm" versus those structured "cold." Building upon Asch's general finding, Kelly (10) sought to discern the specific effects of trait structuring upon the perception of and behavior towards an actual and not hypothetical person. Kelly's subjects were 55 male college students constituting three sections of a psychology course. None of the subjects knew the stimulus person (a "substitute instructor") used in the experiment. The experimental manipulation involved the experimenter coming to the class with the stimulus person and making the following statement:

> Your regular instructor is out of town today, and since we of Economics 70 are interested in the general problem of how various classes react to different instructors, we're going to have an instructor today you've never had before, Mr. _____. Then, at the end of the period, I want you to fill out some forms about him. In order to give you some idea of what he's like, we've had a person who knows him write up a little biographical note about him. I'll pass this out to you now and you can read it before he arrives. Please read these to yourselves and don't talk about this

48

among yourselves until the class is over so that he won't get wind of what's going on.

Two types of notes were then randomly distributed, the two being identical except that in one the stimulus person was described by a trait list including "very warm," and in the other the phrase "rather cold" was substituted. The specific content of these notes was:

> Mr. _____ is a graduate student in the Department of Economics here at M.I.T. He has had three semesters of teaching experience in psychology at another college. This is his first semester teaching Ec. 70. He is 26 years old, a veteran and married. People who know him consider him to be a very warm (rather cold) person, industrious, critical, practical, and determined.

The stimulus person then appeared and led the class in a 20-minute discussion. The experimenter remained in the classroom during this period and recorded how often each student participated in the class discussion. Following the class, each subject wrote a free description of the stimulus person and rated him on a series of rating scales. Analyses of these data indicated that subjects receiving the warm structuring, as compared to those structured cold, rated the stimulus person as significantly more considerate, informal, sociable, popular, humorous, humane, and better-natured. Furthermore, subjects structured warm participated in the class discussion to a significantly greater degree. These findings accord with Asch's to support Kelley's general conclusion that ". . . such a central quality as 'warmth' can greatly influence the total impression of a personality. This effect is found to be operative in the perception of real persons" (10, p. 435). A large number of investigations have successfully replicated or elaborated upon this basic finding (2, 4, 9, 11, 12, 14). The three investigations of trait structuring to be presented below may be considered analogue studies. Their settings and subjects vary in terms of directness of clinical relevance and thus these studies may be viewed as falling at different points on an analogical bridge.

Trait Structuring—YAVIS Subjects

Our first investigation was conducted by Greenberg (7) who, in broad terms, sought to learn whether subjects perceive and respond to a therapist differently as a function of the therapist being labeled "warm," "cold," "experienced," or "inexperienced." Specifically, we hypothesized that subjects structured "warm" or "experienced" would be more attracted to the therapist and more receptive to his influence attempts than would subjects told the therapist was "cold" or "inexperienced." Interaction effects on these same dependent variables were also predicted, such that warm-experienced should be greater than cold-inexperienced.

Subjects for this investigation were 112 university undergraduates (nonpatients) obtained from Introductory Psychology sections. Each subject was randomly assigned to one of four equal-sized groups: experienced-warm, experienced-cold, inexperienced-warm, or inexperienced-cold. Each group contained 14 men and 14 women. Subjects were run in groups of 12 to 16 at a time. After each group of subjects was seated in the experimental room, a printed page was distributed titled "Biographical Information." The experimenter read the contents of this page aloud as subjects followed along. The information provided was:

> In recent years more and more people experiencing emotional and psychological problems have been seeking help from psychotherapists. We are interested in learning more about psychotherapy and the reactions of people to this treatment. Therefore, we are going to play a tape of part of an actual psychotherapy session that took place in a large city other than Syracuse and ask you for your reaction to it. As you listen to the tape we would like you to put yourself in the place of the patient and imagine how you, as the patient, would react to this particular session. The patient in this session is a college student at a large university who sought help after finding, among other things, that he was having difficulty making decisions.

The additional material provided each subject varied according to his experimental condition. For those structured that the therapist was experienced (warm or cold):

> The therapist has been engaged in the practice of therapy for over 20 years and has lectured and taught at some of the country's leading universities and medical schools. Questionnaires submitted to the therapist's colleagues seem to reveal that he is a rather (warm or cold) person, industrious, critical, practical, and determined. Remember to try and put yourself in the patient's place as you listen to the tape.

For those subjects structured that the therapist was inexperienced (warm or cold), the information provided was:

> The therapist is a student engaged in a required part of his training and this session is one of his first experiences as a therapist. Questionnaires submitted to the therapist's colleagues seem to reveal that he is a rather (warm or cold) person, industrious, critical, practical, and determined. Remember to try and put yourself in the patient's place as you listen to the tape.

Following this structuring of therapist characteristics, all subjects listened to the taped psychotherapy session. The tape played was in reality constructed by us, and was not of a real psychotherapy session. To maximize the probability of discerning the effects on subject's tape reactions of our structuring, the tape was constructed so that it portrayed as moderate a degree of therapist attraction and experience as possible. That is, we sought to have the structuring, and not the tape, pull whatever subject reactions emerged. The tape was prejudged by a group of 13 psychologists to be both a credible representation of a psychotherapy session and as relatively ambiguous with regard to the therapist warmth and experience portrayed.

Immediately after the tape presentation, each subject was asked to complete two questionnaires. The first, the Tape Rating Scale,[1] was a modification of the CPRQ, reflecting the fact that the patient responds to a therapist he has actually met when completing the CPRQ but to one whom he has only heard on a recording and not interacted with on the Tape Rating Scale. Specifically, this Scale consists of 28 items designed to measure each subject's attraction toward the taped therapist, items intended to measure subject receptivity to the taped therapist's influence attempts, and two items to serve as an independent check on the warmth and experience manipulations. The second questionnaire was a persuasibility measure[2] designed by us and modeled after the "opinion shift" questionnaires frequently used in social-psychological studies of persuasibility (e.g., 13). It consists of 40 statements describing the presence or absence of various psychological characteristics of the taped patient. Subjects were asked to rate each statement on a seven-point scale in terms of degree of agreement or disagreement regarding the presence or absence of the given characteristic. No information was actually provided in the taped session regarding any of these characteristics of the taped patient. Subjects were told that the taped therapist had also filled out this questionnaire and that his answers were included on their copy of the questionnaire so that they could compare their answers with his. On a randomly selected 20 of the 40 items on this questionnaire the therapist's "answers" were indicated as falling within the slightly agree to slightly disagree range. The other 20 items were "rated" by the therapist at the extremes, i.e., strongly agree or strongly disagree. Note that since no information about the patient, relevant to these items, was actually provided on the tape, uninfluenced patient answers to all items on this questionnaire have a high a priori probability of falling in the middle

---

[1] See Appendix I, pp. 201-203.
[2] Ibid., pp. 204-210.

response categories. Subjects were scored in terms of the extent of agreement between their responses and those of the therapist on those 20 items purportedly rated at the extremes by the therapist. The greater the agreement, the greater, it was assumed, was the subject's persuasibility vis à vis the therapist.

Finally, subjects were also presented with a Willingness to Meet form[3] stating that the Psychology Department, after many inquiries regarding problems of students, was considering asking the taped therapist to come to the university to discuss such problems with students. Subjects were then asked to indicate whether or not they were willing to meet the taped therapist if he indeed came to the campus.

Prior to testing the study's hypotheses, the data derived from the two questions included as a check on the warmth and experience manipulations were examined. These analyses revealed that subjects structured warm rated the taped therapist as significantly warmer than did subjects structured cold ($t = 10.51$, $df = 110$, $p < .001$), and subjects structured experienced, in contrast to those told the therapist was inexperienced, rated him as sounding significantly more experienced ($t = 5.98$, $df = 110$, $p < .001$). Thus both the warmth and experience manipulations appear to have been successful. The mean attraction, receptivity to influence, and persuasibility scores are presented in Table 3.1.

Table 3.1

Mean Attraction, Receptivity, and Persuasibility Scores
for University Sample

	Attraction		Receptivity		Persuasibility	
	Warm	Cold	Warm	Cold	Warm	Cold
Experienced	118.24	83.18	39.46	27.21	103.54	99.43
Inexperienced	105.43	66.68	32.86	20.57	101.96	93.86

Separate analyses of variance applied to those three sets of scores demonstrated, as predicted, that subjects structured warm, rather than cold, were more attracted to the therapist ($F = 50.68$, $df = 1, 104, p < .001$), more receptive to his influence ($F = 28.15$, $df = 1, 104, p < .001$), and more persuaded by his ratings ($F = 7.06$, $df = 1, 104, p < .01$). Also, as predicted, subjects structured experienced were more

[3] See Appendix I, p. 211.

attracted ($F = 8.00$, $df = 1$, 104, $p < .01$) and receptive ($F = 8.21$, $df = 1$, 104, $p < .01$) to the therapist than were subjects structured inexperienced. No significant difference emerged on the persuasibility measure as a function of experience structuring. It will be recalled that interaction effects on these variables were also predicted. Scheffe tests applied to these data revealed the warm-experienced group to be more attracted ($p < .001$), receptive ($p < .001$), and persuaded ($p < .05$) by the taped therapist than the cold-inexperienced group. Also, subjects were more attracted (but not receptive or persuaded) under warm-inexperienced than cold-inexperienced structuring. On the final study measure, Willingness to Meet, a chi square analysis revealed that a significantly larger number of subjects structured warm ($N = 42$) than cold ($N = 30$) stated willingness to meet the taped therapist ($X^2 = 4.71$, $df = 1$, $p < .05$). Also, as predicted, more subjects structured warm-experienced ($N = 23$) than cold-inexperienced ($N = 14$) stated willingness to meet the therapist ($X^2 = 5.10$, $df = 1$, $p < .05$). No significant experienced-inexperienced difference was obtained on this variable. In all, we take these several findings to represent a robust and consistent demonstration of the effects of certain classes of trait structuring on therapy-relevant variables in an analogue context. At minimum, these results serve as clear impetus for a further step toward a psychotherapeutic context along our analogical bridge. Our next investigation took just this step.

Trait Structuring—NON-YAVIS Subjects

Subjects for this second study (8) were 60 male psychiatric inpatients at a Veterans Administration psychiatric hospital. Their mean age was 43; the age range was 19 to 56. All of these patients had functional psychotic diagnoses, predominantly schizophrenia. Most had been hospitalized for many years. It was our assumption that most of these patients would, without special interventions, find it difficult to establish a favorable psychotherapeutic relationship. With three major exceptions, the experimental design employed for this investigation replicated that used for our earlier trait structuring study with college students (7). One such exception, as noted above, was the use of psychotic patients and not college student nonpatients as subjects. This alteration permitted us to move a step further in relevance toward clinical practice. A different taped therapy session, one more germane to the concerns of psychotic inpatients was constructed, satisfactorily piloted, and then employed for this investigation. A final alteration was responsive to the fact that in the earlier study no control for the effects of structuring per se was included. Furthermore, although students structured warm or experienced yielded higher dependent variable scores than those structured cold or inexperienced, we have no information regarding the direction of change. For example, the significant difference between warm and cold structured subjects on attraction could have resulted because subjects structured warm became more attracted than they would have if no structuring were provided while those structured cold responded as if no structuring were provided, or warm-inexperienced, and cold-inexperienced. Patients were randomly those structured cold decreased in attraction toward the therapist, or "warm" could have led to an increase simultaneous with "cold" leading to a decrease.

To obtain some directionality information, therefore, we included an unstructured control group in the present investigation. The experimental groups, as before, were warm-experienced, cold-experienced, warm-inexperienced, and cold-inexperienced. Patients were randomly assigned to one of these five equal-sized conditions. The five conditions were run, in groups of 12 patients each, on two consecutive days. The structuring information provided patients assigned to the four experimental groups was identical in all essential respects to that delivered to the college student subjects. Patients run in the no structuring control condition received only the prefatory biographical information about the therapist. After listening to the (simulated) psychotherapy session, all patients completed the same attraction, receptivity, and persuasibility measures used in the earlier investigation.

The data derived from the CPRQ questions included as a check on the warmth and experience inductions were examined prior to testing

Table 3.2

Mean Attraction, Receptivity, and Persuasibility
Scores for Hospital Sample

	Attraction		Receptivity		Persuasibility	
	Warm	Cold	Warm	Cold	Warm	Cold
Experienced	114.92	112.00	43.75	40.17	101.83	95.42
Inexperienced	118.58	97.17	42.42	34.33	103.17	98.17
Control	95.75		33.08		105.50	

our main hypotheses. This analysis revealed that patients structured warm rated the taped therapist as significantly warmer than did either patients structured cold ($t = 2.40$, $df = 46$, $p < .05$) or unstructured patients ($t = 3.64$, $df = 34$, $p < .05$). The latter two conditions did not differ significantly on rated warmth. No significant between-condition differences emerged on the experience check. The mean attraction, receptivity, and persuasibility scores are presented in Table 3.2.

Separate analyses of variance were computed on these three sets of scores. In addition, on each dependent variable, a Dunnett's Test for Comparison with a Control (5) was used to compare the unstructured control group with the structured groups. On patient attraction to the taped therapist, patients structured warm yielded significantly higher scores than did unstructured patients ($t = 2.67$, $df = 34$, $p < .05$). No other between-condition comparisons on the attraction variable reached statistically significant levels. The analysis of variance for patient receptivity to therapist influence demonstrated a significant main effect of warm and cold structuring ($F = 4.09$, $df = 1$, 44, $p <$ .05), as well as significant comparison effects for both warmth ($t = 2.58$, $df = 34$, $p < .05$) and experience ($t = 2.27$, $df = 34$, $p < .05$) over the no structuring condition. No experience-inexperience effect emerged. Finally, on the measure of persuasibility, none of the possible comparisons among the five study conditions reached acceptable levels of statistical significance.

Though not as widespread in its effects as was true for the college student sample, the structuring of warmth and experience is thus demonstrated to have a significant effect upon the interpersonal perceptions of our psychotic patient sample. This conclusion follows in particular from our receptivity to influence findings, although both receptivity and attraction were enhanced by warm structuring as compared to no structuring. With all the tentativeness inherent in analogue designs in mind, we would propose that these findings suggest a marked influence upon patient early-therapy behavior of messages communicated to him regarding his prospective psychotherapist during the pretherapy or candidacy stage of his treatment career. We have reported elsewhere (6) a significant effect of referral source on patient confidence in the treatment clinic. Patients referred to a psychiatric clinic by a psychiatrist, psychologist, social worker, or those self-referred display greater confidence than did those referred by general medical practitioners, nonpsychiatric medical specialists, parents, or friends. It seems possible that our present study provides a likely explanatory basis for these earlier findings in that the confidence-engendering referral sources were primarily mental health personnel, i.e., persons perhaps more likely than the general practitioner, friend, etc., to include in their referral messages material of the "warmth" and "experience" type.

A final observation seems appropriate regarding the persuasibility findings from these first two analogue studies, an observation particularly relevant to movement toward in-therapy designs. It seems likely that an important aspect of the extrapolatory process, as one begins to move from laboratory to clinic, concerns the differential impact on results of subject characteristics. In our study using college student subjects, there did emerge a significant effect of warm over cold structuring on the opinion shift measure of persuasibility. This finding failed to replicate in the psychotic patient sample. The persuasibility measure came last in the test battery for all subjects. It was the experimenter's impression that the attention span of which most of the psychotic sample were capable was simply too truncated for this test battery. A further possible basis here for the failure to obtain a persuasibility effect is provided by Buss and Lang's (3) examination of psychological deficit in schizophrenia. Their distillation of many investigations of cognitive functioning in schizophrenia suggests a number of processes accounting for the less adequate performance of such patients in this regard as compared to normal subjects. One such process is associative interference, i.e., ". . . a promising hypothesis is that affective stimuli (censure, human, symbolic, taboo) elicit more associations from schizophrenics and that these associations interfere with performance." A second process of likely relevance is overinclusion, i.e., ". . . the tendency to include irrelevant and extraneous aspects in responding to stimuli." We would propose that processes akin to associative interference and overinclusion may in part be responsible for the normal subject-psychotic subject disparity of results of persuasibility, and that such subject differences may prove to be a major factor to be considered in the extrapolatory process.

Trait Structuring—Adolescent Subjects

Our final analogue investigation of trait structuring was conducted by Gable. Our experimental design here sought to examine the effects of warm-cold structuring in both normal and disturbed adolescent populations. In addition, in response to the social-psychological literature dealing with the attraction-relevant consequences of attitude similarity (see Chapter IX), we structured conditions leading the subject to believe that the taped therapist was similar or dissimilar to the subject on a dimension of past personal problem and treatment history. Concretely, we employed a 2 x 2 factorial design nested within type of subject (normal high school student versus disturbed adolescent in a residential treatment center) and involving the factors: (a) trait structuring (warm versus cold), and (b) background structuring (therapist had had major problems as an adolescent versus therapist had not had major problems as an adolescent).

The normal subjects were 40 students randomly selected from grades 10, 11, and 12 in a local high school. There were two restrictions placed on the random selection process. All students being seen for counseling by the school's guidance director, or, to his knowledge, involved elsewhere for counseling or psychotherapy then or in the past, were eliminated from the subject pool. The second restriction was on sex of subject, selection being such that half were male and the other half female. Their age range was 15 to 18.

Forty adolescents were also randomly selected from the treatment center, 20 males and 20 females. All were currently being seen in psychotherapy. They ranged in age from 13 to 18. All were also students in an ungraded high school on the treatment center campus.

The procedures and materials for this investigation paralleled directly those used in our college student and psychotic patient studies of trait structuring, with minor alterations being made in the structuring, tape, and dependent variable measure to reflect the age and circumstances of the adolescent subjects. The one major change involved the structuring for background similarity-dissimilarity. One of the following two phrases was added to our structuring for this purpose:

The counselor does most of his work with high school students. He, himself, saw a counselor regularly to discuss personal problems during his last two years of high school.

The counselor does most of his work with high school students. He, himself, had never seen a counselor during his high school days.

The first phrase above implements background similarity for the treatment center sample and dissimilarity for the high school subjects, with the converse being implemented by the second phrase. All subjects were randomly assigned to the study's eight experimental conditions. Following structuring, they listened to the taped psychotherapy session constructed for this study and then completed a modified (for adolescents) form of the Tape Rating Scale—our dependent measure of attraction and receptivity to influence.

Analysis of variance conducted on the attraction and receptivity data revealed a significant main effect for warm-cold structuring on attraction, but no such effect for receptivity. The significant effect on attraction ($F = 15.29$, $df = 1, 72$, $p < .01$) permitted us to conduct post hoc cell comparisons. This analysis, operationalized in terms of a series of Tukey (a) tests, revealed that high school subjects structured to believe the taped therapist was both warm and similar to themselves in problem and treatment history were significantly more attracted to him than were either high school subjects structured cold and dissimilar or treatment center subjects structured cold and dissimilar. Furthermore, treatment center subjects structured warm-similar were also significantly more attracted to the taped therapist than were cold-dissimilar structured subjects from the treatment center.

A significant type of subject by background similarity interaction effect also emerged on our attraction measure ($F = 8.83$, $df = 1, 72$, $p < .05$). Post hoc analysis revealed that high school-similar subjects were significantly more attracted to the taped therapist than were treatment center subjects structured to believe they were dissimilar to the taped therapist in treatment history.

This investigation thus provides further demonstration for the generality of the attraction-enhancing effects of trait structuring, as well as some suggestive evidence pointing to related effects for one dimension of perceived similarity. The findings from this investigation combine with those of our two other trait structuring studies to clearly suggest the next appropriate investigative step. These analogue findings must be put to direct test in an in-therapy design, a design involving patients about to begin psychotherapy. Just such an investigation is reported in Chapter VII.

References

1. Asch, S. E. Forming impressions of personality. *Journal of Abnormal and Social Psychology*, 1946, **41**, 258–290.

2. Beilin, H. Effects of set upon impression formation. Presented at American Psychological Association, Chicago, 1960.

3. Buss, A. H. & Lang, P. J. Psychological deficit in schizophrenia: I. Affect, reinforcement and concept attainment. *Journal of Abnormal Psychology*, 1965, **70**, 2–24.

4. DiVesta, F. J. & Bossart, P. The effects of sets induced by labeling on the modification of attitudes. *Journal of Personality*, 1958, **26**, 379–387.

5. Edwards, A. L. *Experimental design in psychological research*. New York: Holt, 1960.

6. Goldstein, A. P. & Shipman, W. G. Patient expectancies, symptom reduction and aspects of the initial psychotherapeutic interview. *Journal of Clinical Psychology*, 1961, **17**, 129–133.

7. Greenberg, R. P. Effects of pre-session information on perception of the therapist and receptivity to influence in a psychotherapy analogue. *Journal of Consulting and Clinical Psychology*, 1969, **33**, 425–429.

8. Greenberg, R. P., Goldstein, A. P., & Perry, M. A. The influence of referral information upon patient perception in a psychotherapy analogue. *Journal of Nervous and Mental Disease*, 1970, **150**, 31–36.

9. Jackson, D. N. The measurement of perceived personality trait relationships. Research Bulletin, No. 3, Pennsylvania State University, July, 1960.

10. Kelley, H. H. Warm-cold variable in first impressions. *Journal of Personality*, 1950, **18**, 431–439.

11. Luchins, A. S. Forming impressions of personality: A critique. *Journal of Abnormal and Social Psychology*, 1948, **43**, 318–325.

12. Mensh, I. N. & Wishner, J. Asch on "Forming impressions of personality: Further evidence." *Journal of Personality*, 1947, **16**, 188–191.

13. Silverman, I. Differential effects of ego threat upon persuasibility for high and low self esteem subjects. *Journal of Abnormal and Social Psychology*, 1964, **69**, 567–572.

14. Wishner, J. Reanalysis of "impressions of personality." *Psychological Review*, 1960, **67**, 98–112.

Chapter IV

Therapist Structuring

In our introductory chapter we proposed that the responsibility for the poor quality therapeutic relationship which develops in many therapist-patient pairs lies as much or more with the therapist as with the patient. This appears to be particularly true, we feel, in those therapeutic mismatches involving what we have termed a NON-YAVIS patient and a YAVIS-preferring therapist. The therapist, we noted earlier, may hide behind the process of labeling such patients as "resistive" or "unsuitable," rather than more appropriately pointing to our general lack of therapeutic skills available for assisting such patients and his own affective reactions of dislike for the patient, a sense of inadequacy in contemplating his treatment, and so forth. The rapid termination of treatment by the patient so highly characteristic of such mismatches may well represent a highly adaptive and wholly appropriate decision on the part of the patient. Koegler and Brill (20) comment in this regard:

> . . . the selection for treatment of more psychologically-minded middle-class patients may be based on some need in the therapist, and the assumption that these patients are more likely to respond to treatment may serve as a rationalization for the selection procedure. It is true that there are many individuals who are not suited for psychotherapy *as it is frequently practiced.* However, it is not the patient who should be blamed for not responding, but rather the psychiatrists for not being more flexible in their techniques. It is essential to recognize that some patients may be helped just as much by supportive methods as other patients are by 'insight-therapy.' Ideally, the therapist should be comfortable treating a wide variety of patients by various techniques. (20, p. 114) (italics theirs)

A therapist's humanness may mean warmth, interpersonal sensitivity, patience, perceptiveness, depth of understanding, and a broad array of other protherapeutic virtues. This same humanness, however, is also likely to mean a preference for others who share our values, an ability to communicate best with others who "speak our language," an ability to empathize most fully with those who share our basic assumptions about mental disturbance and its treatment, and discomfort in the presence of those whose life style overlaps little with one's own. Thus to note that psychotherapists hold biases, engage in stereotyping behavior, or are in some ways xenophobic is simply to comment upon their humanness.

When major therapist-patient differences exist on such dimensions as values (25, 27, 36), expectancies (2, 13, 14, 22), social class (6, 8, 20, 24, 28), or race (1, 5, 17, 30, 39), the implications for treatment outcome are markedly negative. One broadly promising approach for discrepancy reduction involves the innovative use of therapeutic procedures other than those subsumed under the rubric "verbal, insight-oriented therapy." Hoehn-Saric *et al.* (18), using their Role Induction Interview procedure, have demonstrated that treatment in such discrepant therapist-patient pairings will proceed well if expectational discrepancies are reduced. Lennard and Bernstein (22) have reported concurring findings. Koegler and Cannon (21) have demonstrated that when middle-class therapists become interested in working with patients from lower socioeconomic levels, they have as much therapeutic success as they do with middle-class patients. Baum *et al.* (3) report similar findings. Gould (15) has demonstrated considerable success with "blue collar" patients when his treatment approaches were responsive to the assumptions such patients hold regarding the nature of emotional disturbance. A similar notion is inherent in the writings of other therapists (e.g., 23, 26), seeking to treat in accord with the patient's life style, who champion more directive therapies involving advice, suggestion, role playing, behavioral rehearsal, and other action - oriented techniques. Other discrepancy - reducing approaches to individual psychotherapy have been developed by Eissler (9), Gendlin (11), Slack (31), and Strean (32). Yamamoto and Goin (38) speak of group psychotherapy from this same perspective. The major movement now developing toward the therapeutic use of paraprofessional, nonprofessional, or indigenous psychotherapists is but a further example of "discrepancy reduction by innovation." Here, similarity of ethnic or community background and life style provides a nondiscrepant therapist-patient pair who share the same values, basic assumptions, and levels of communication. As this and the several other dimensions of the community mental health movement continue to expand and develop, our field can anticipate a growing variety of means for effectively reducing therapist-patient discrepancies of the types we have been discussing.

Relationship enhancement attempts, to ultimately succeed, must go beyond concern with just patient characteristics and discrepancies in the therapist-patient match. We must directly face and deal with the third wellspring of relationship inhibition, namely, therapist bias. In addition to the very substantial number of clinical papers discussing the existence and operation of therapist biases of diverse types (e.g., 6, 20, 26, 28, 30), several relevant research reports have recently appeared. Yamamoto et al. (39) report that therapists high on ethnocentricity see ethnic-minority patients less frequently and for fewer sessions than do therapists low on ethnocentricity. Moore et al. (24) note that the therapists in his study were more likely to treat, and to treat successfully, those patients who viewed their disturbance in psychological rather than physical or social terms. Fiedler and Senior (10) report that their therapists expressed greater attraction toward those patients who expressed themselves freely and had unfavorable feelings toward those expressing little feeling. Therapist bias against treating patients of lower socioeconomic status has been independently documented by numerous investigators (1, 3, 8, 15, 19, 23, 24, 26, 38). Harrison et al. (16) have reported data indicating that such social class biases even extend to child psychotherapy. In an investigation summarizing much of the foregoing, and also capturing the spirit of Schofield's YAVIS designation, Strupp and Wallach (35) found that, "Patients who are considered well-motivated for therapy, whose prognosis is considered good, who are said to have reasonably great ego strength, emotional maturity, capacity for insight, and whose social adjustment is rated favorably, are individuals toward whom therapists tend to feel positively disposed" (35, p. 124). As these investigators note, and as is generally the case for the therapist bias studies noted above, the direction of causation remains unspecified in much of this research. The therapist's attitude toward the patient, Strupp and Wallach suggest, cannot be considered antecedent to his clinical evaluations. Nor, they add, can one conclude that therapists feel more positively toward certain patients *because* they appear to be better prospects for therapy.

Since such a large proportion of research in this domain is of this correlational nature, we set out in the study that follows to investigate the directional nature of therapist bias. In a manner analogous to our "warm-cold" investigations of trait structuring of patients, it will be noted that we kept constant the therapy input to our subjects, varying only the pre-input label provided to the subjects. Should such labeling yield reliable dependent variable differences, the direction of the therapist bias-clinical evaluation relationship is thus demonstrated. Finally, we sought in this study to go beyond a straightforward examination of the presence or absence of therapist bias, and investigated the effects of such bias upon certain crucial dimensions of therapist "in-therapy" behavior.

A Study of Therapist Bias

Subjects for this investigation, conducted by Beal (4), were 135 advanced graduate students in clinical psychology, drawn from 14 universities in the northeastern United States. Their mean age was 25.5; 65 percent were males, 35 percent females; and the median number of hours of clinical experience was 250. Thus it is clearly the neophyte psychologist to whom this study's results may be generalized. Although a sample of more experienced therapists may have been desirable, such a sample was not available to us. It should be noted, however, that several investigators have reported that the types of patients to which our research is oriented are most likely, in clinical settings, to be assigned to the least experienced staff members. Therefore, in a naturalistic sense, generalizations from results with neophytes may well possess greater external validity than findings based upon study of experienced psychotherapists.

In broad overview, nine experimental conditions were constituted. Subjects in *all* conditions viewed the same movie of a purported psychotherapy session. Prior to movie viewing, subjects were provided an "Intake Staff Report," a report which was systematically varied by condition in terms of the movie patient's purported diagnosis and level of motivation for treatment. Postviewing ratings on the movie patient were obtained from all subjects on such dimensions as attraction, prognosis, and willingness to treat. Regular pauses in the movie permitted subjects to indicate what they would say to the patient at various points in the session. These therapist responses were subsequently content-analyzed for empathy and warmth, and the postratings provided the desired data on the presence or absence of bias elicited by the diagnostic and motivational labels. The content analysis for empathy and warmth provided information indicating some of the channels through which therapist bias, if present, may be expressed. With this overview behind us, we will now turn in greater detail to the specific predictions, procedures, and results of this investigation.

Predictions

Beal hypothesized that therapists led to believe that a (film) patient is neurotic, as opposed to therapists structured that the patient is psychopathic, will:

(a) be more favorably disposed toward the patient (attraction, prognosis, willingness to meet),

(b) provide higher levels of what Truax and Carkhuff (37) have termed therapeutic conditions (empathy and warmth), and

(c) be more likely to perceive the patient as similar to themselves (age and social class).

Her second set of predictions, on the same dependent variables, hypothesized more favorable effects when the patient is described as highly motivated, in contrast to having low motivation for psychotherapy. Interaction effects on these postratings, conditions offered, and perceived similarity were also predicted, such that the most favorable effects should follow from the combined neurotic-high motivation labeling, and the least favorable from psychopathic-low motivation structuring.

Procedures

The nine experimental conditions constituted were three levels of diagnosis (neurotic, psychopathic, not stated) by three levels of patient motivation for psychotherapy (high, low, not stated). The experimental subjects, randomly assigned to these nine conditions, were told by E at the beginning of the experimental session that the study in which they were about to participate concerned psychotherapists and what they do in the process of interviewing and evaluating patients. The broad aim of the research was described as obtaining objective data on the techniques used by different therapists. Each subject was given a comprehensive booklet containing all the forms necessary for their participation: Introductory Instructions, Biographical Information Sheet, Film Responding Instructions, Intake Staff Report, Film Response Sheets, Prognosis Scale, Therapist Personal Reaction Questionnaire, and Clinic Face Sheet.

Introductory Instructions. This page reiterated for subjects the supposed nature of the study, briefly outlined the three parts of the procedure (Biographical Questionnaire, Film viewing, and Postratings), and in general sought to provide subjects with an appropriate set for participation.

Biographical Information Sheet. This form obtained from subjects such demographic information as age, sex, marital status, type of graduate program enrolled in, anticipated date of degree, and number of hours of clinical experience. These data served several study purposes: to add credibility to the purported intent of the study, as a check on the eligibility of individual subjects, to determine whether significant initial differences existed among subjects assigned to different experimental conditions (check on randomization), and for use in those study hypotheses relating to perceived similarity.

Film Responding Instructions. These instructions, modeled after Strupp (33) briefly described the film that subjects were about to see, and sought to structure the subjects in the appropriate viewing and responding set. The subject was asked to assume that he was the therapist and was interviewing the patient in the film. Of particular importance in these instructions is the statement:

> In order for you to 'participate' in this interview, we have developed the following procedure. After you have had a chance to read the staff report that the doctor had received, we will start the film and you will meet the doctor and the patient. As usual, the patient will talk, and the doctor will ask questions or make observations. At various points the interview will be interrupted to give you a chance to tell us what you would do if you were the therapist seeing the patient.

Specific response instructions were then provided, along with response examples. Spontaneity was encouraged.

Intake Staff Report. Through a series of pilot studies, nine Intake Staff Reports representing the study's nine experimental conditions were developed. These were, of course, this study's independent variable manipulations. The first two paragraphs of this Report were identical across experimental conditions and contained factual information about the patient, his reason for coming to the clinic, and why he was seen by the intake staff. The third paragraph varied by condition and contained the appropriate diagnostic and motivational information. The final paragraph summarized and reiterated this latter material. In the experimental conditions involving absence of diagnostic and/or motivational structuring, such information was simply excluded from the Report. The following example is the Intake Staff Report given to all subjects assigned to the neurotic-high motivation experimental condition.

Intake Staff Report

This man was seen briefly at intake staff for purposes of making an initial evaluation, and determining eligibility for treatment. He has not previously sought psychiatric help, and was found to be eligible for treatment at this clinic.

The patient is a middle-aged, heavy-set man who appeared for the interview neatly dressed in a business suit. He came to the clinic for help with a drinking problem. His responses to questions were logical and coherent, and he was correctly oriented for time, place, and person. He denied delusions or hallucinations, and none could be elicited.

He displayed an appropriate range of affect during the interview, although the predominant tone seemed rather unhappy and sad. He seemed to have a lot of ambivalent feelings, and apparently experienced some difficulty during the interview in expressing himself definitely on anything. He seemed caught in a morass of indecision and guilt and appears to have a chronically negative self-image. The staff felt that his behavior and demeanor were typically neurotic in nature. He seemed highly motivated to explore his difficulties with someone, and was anxious to know when his first therapy appointment would be. It was decided that the usual procedure of arranging a personal interview with a therapist would be followed, letting the therapist decide whether he would accept the patient for treatment on the basis of his personal evaluation of the case.

In summary, the staff felt that the patient's motivation for psychotherapy is high. The official diagnosis is: neurosis.

Film Response Sheets. Following structuring, and for use during movie viewing, these sheets contained space for subject responses, numbered to correspond to the stopping points in the film.

Prognostic-Evaluation Scale.[1] This prognosis measure, used meaningfully by Strupp (33) in related contexts, consists of 11 multiple-choice items dealing with the subject's impressions of and predictions for the film patient. Prognosis, ego-strength, anxiety, and emotional maturity are among the traits included.

Therapist Personal Reaction Questionnaire. This measure was our index in this investigation of therapist (subject) attraction toward the film patient. Two items were added to this instrument in order to obtain from subjects an estimate of their willingness to treat the film patient.

Clinic Face Sheet. The final page of the booklet sought information from the subjects regarding the patient's diagnosis and motivation (as a check on the experimental manipulations), as well as subjects' impressions of the patient's age, income, occupation, religion, marital status, and other demographic information—information to match against the subject's own demographic characteristics for measurement of perceived similarity.

Film. The film employed was selected from the series of psychother-

[1] See Appendix I, pp. 212-213.

apy films developed by Strupp[2] and his associates (34). While it was described to our subjects as an actual initial interview by a psychiatrist and a male patient, both men (for purposes of confidentiality) were actors. Their statements, however, were an exact transcription of an actual psychiatric interview. The camera focuses almost exclusively on the patient, with occasional glimpses of the back of the doctor's head. The patient talks considerably more than does the doctor. The patient is a short, stocky man in his forties who identifies his problem with the single word "whiskey." He is rather terse in the opening minutes of the interview, but quickly begins describing his life situation and his feelings about it in some detail. Little, if any, direct information is provided by patient or doctor regarding the patient's motivation for psychotherapy or the specific nature of his psychopathology. This quality of ambiguity was one of our major criteria in selecting the film. Our pilot studies indicated that it did not appear to contradict the information provided in any of our nine Intake Staff Reports. The film contained seven stopping points, each 30 seconds in duration, during which time "WHAT WOULD YOU DO?" appeared on the screen. The total running time of the film was 16 minutes.

Empathy and Warmth. It will be recalled that our predictions held that, in addition to their effects on postratings, the diagnostic and motivational structuring would find dependent variable expression in the quality of subjects' statements made "to" the film patient at the selected stopping points during the film. Truax and Carkhuff (37) have impressively demonstrated the therapeutic potency, across a wide variety of patient samples, of therapist empathy and warmth. It was in response to their evidence that we decided to operationalize our interest in quality of subjects' statements on these two dimensions. Two judges were extensively trained on the Truax and Carkhuff Empathy and Warmth Scales, reaching interjudge reliability (Pearson r) of .82 for their empathy ratings and .82 on warmth.[3] Empathy was rated on a nine-point scale ranging from "(1) The therapist seems completely unaware of even the most conspicuous of the client's feelings," to "(9) The therapist unerringly responds to the client's full range of feelings in their exact intensity" (3, p. 57). Warmth was rated on a five-point scale, described by Truax and Carkhuff as ". . . ranges from a high level where the therapist warmly accepts the patient's experience as part of that person, without imposing conditions; to a low level

[2] The assistance and cooperation provided us by Dr. Strupp throughout the preparatory phases of this investigation were an important contribution to its
[3] The full rating scales for empathy and warmth appear in Appendix II, pp. 234-239.

where the therapist evaluates a patient or his feelings, expresses dislike or disapproval, or expresses warmth in a selective or evaluative way" (37, p. 58).

Results

Diagnosis.   A series of two-way analyses of variance across the study's several dependent variables revealed a significant main effect for diagnosis on attraction, empathy, and warmth, and a significant diagnosis-motivation interaction effect on prognosis. More concretely, the neurotic label pulled significantly greater attraction ($F = 4.12$, $df = 2, 126$, $p < .02$), empathy ($F = 5.15$, $df = 2, 126$, $p < .01$) and warmth ($F = 3.19$, $df = 2, 126$, $p < .05$), than did the psychopathic label. In each instance, scores from subjects provided no diagnosis fell in an intermediate position. No significant main effects for diagnosis were obtained on willingness to meet, perceived similarity, or prognosis. Post hoc comparisons, however, revealed a significant interaction effect such that prognosis scores from subjects assigned to the neurotic-high motivation condition were significantly more favorable than were prognoses from psychopathic-low motivation condition subjects.

Motivation. No significant main effects or interaction effects were obtained for motivation on the attraction, empathy, or warmth variables. Significant main effects for motivation were obtained, however, on prognosis, willingness to treat, and perceived similarity. Specifically, the high motivation label pulled significantly more favorable prognostic estimates ($F = 3.85$, $df = 2, 126$, $p < .02$), greater willingness to treat the patient ($F = 3.02$, $df = 2, 126$, $p < .05$), and greater perceived similarity between the patient's age (but not social class) and the subject's age ($F = 3.18$, $df = 2, 126$, $p < .05$) than did the low motivation label. As was analogously true for our results on diagnosis, here the "no motivation stated" condition scores on each dependent variable fell in an intermediate position.

These results demonstrate, in a highly substantial manner, that therapist biasing or stereotyping behavior occurs, and that such behavior finds overt expression, at least in the present analogue context, in the quality of therapeutic communications. Remembering that *all* therapist-subjects saw the *same* movie patient, we can only conclude that the intake labels (and *not* the patient per se) were responsible for the several effects upon postratings and quality of response. How might we summarize this effect? It is clearly a therapist-expectancy effect, the type of effect which we have also demonstrated in other contexts to have a major impact upon the course and outcome of psychotherapy (13, 14). It seems to be an expectancy effect of a self-fulfilling prophecy type, an effect which obviously underscores that attention to enhancing patient attraction alone, without at least equal concern with augmenting the favorableness of the therapist's disposition toward the patient, is likely to have only modest psychotherapeutic benefit at best. In the broadest sense, we take this demonstration of therapist bias and its effects to suggest that in many contemporary clinical settings, psychotherapy ends rather than begins at the intake interview.

References

1. Adams, W. A. The Negro patient in psychiatric treatment. *American Journal of Orthopsychiatry*, 1950, **20**, 305–310.

2. Apfelbaum, D. *Dimensions of transference in psychotherapy*. Berkeley: University of California Press, 1958.

3. Baum, O. E., Felzer, S. B., D'Zmura, T. L., & Shumaker, E. Psychotherapy dropouts and lower socioeconomic patients. *American Journal of Orthopsychiatry*, 1966, **36**, 629–635.

4. Beal, A. Biased therapists: The effects of prior exposure to case history material on the therapists' attitudes and behavior toward patients. Unpublished doctoral dissertation, Syracuse University, 1969.

5. Bernard, V. W. Psychoanalysis and members of minority groups. *Journal of the American Psychoanalytical Association*, 1953, **1**, 256–267.

6. Carlson, D. A., Coleman, J. V., Errera, P., & Harrison, R. W. Problems in treating the lower-class psychotic. *Archives of General Psychiatry*, 1965, **13**, 269–274.

7. Chance, E. *Families in treatment*. New York: Basic Books, 1959.

8. Cole, N. J., Branch, C. H. H., & Allison, R. B. Some relationships between social class and the practice of dynamic psychotherapy. *American Journal of Psychiatry*, 1962, **118**, 1004–1012.

9. Eissler, K. R. Some problems of delinquency. In K. R. Eissler (Ed.), *Searchlights on delinquency*. New York: International Universities Press, 1949. Pp. 3–25.

10. Fiedler, F. E. & Senior, K. An exploratory study of unconscious feeling reactions in fifteen patient-therapist pairs. *Journal of Abnormal and Social Psychology*, 1952, **47**, 446–453.

11. Gendlin, E. T. Initiating psychotherapy with "unmotivated" patients. *Psychiatric Quarterly*, 1961, **35**, 1–6.

12. Goldstein, A. P. Therapist and client expectation of personality change in psychotherapy. *Journal of Counseling Psychology*, 1960, **7**, 180–184.

13. Goldstein, A. P. *Therapist-patient expectancies in psychotherapy.* New York: Pergamon Press, 1962.

14. Goldstein, A. P. Prognostic and role expectancies in psychotherapy. *American Journal of Psychotherapy*, 1966, **20**, 35–44.

15. Gould, R. E. Dr. Strangeclass: Or how I stopped worrying about the theory and began treating the blue-collar worker. *American Journal of Orthopsychiatry*, 1966, **36**, 78–86.

16. Harrison, S. J., McDermott, J. F., Wilson, P. T., & Schrager, J. Social class and mental illness in children. *Archives of General Psychiatry*, 1965, **13**, 411–417.

17. Heine, R. W. The Negro patient in psychotherapy. *Journal of Clinical Psychology*, 1950, **6**, 372–376.

18. Hoehn-Saric, R., Frank, J. D., Imber, S. D., Nash, E. H., Stone, A. R., & Battle, C. C. Systematic preparation of patients for psychotherapy. I. Effect on therapy behavior and outcome. *Journal of Psychiatric Research*, 1964, **2**, 267–281.

19. Hollingshead, A. B. & Redlich, F. C. *Social class and mental illness.* New York: Wiley, 1958.

20. Koegler, R. R. & Brill, N. Q. *Treatment of psychiatric outpatients.* New York: Appleton-Century-Crofts, 1967.

21. Koegler, R. R. & Cannon, J. A. Treatment for the many. In *Emergency psychiatry and brief therapy,* Issue of *International Psychiatry Clinics.* Boston: Little, Brown, 1966.

22. Lennard, H. L. & Bernstein. A. *The anatomy of psychotherapy.* New York: Columbia University Press, 1960.

23. McMahon, J. T. The working class psychiatric patient: A clinical view. In F. Reissman, J. Cohen, & A. Pearl (Eds.), *Mental health of the poor,* New York: Free Press, 1964. Pp. 283–302.

24. Moore, R. A., Benedek, E. P., & Wallace, J. G. Social class, schizophrenia and the psychiatrist. *American Journal of Psychiatry*, 1963, **20**, 149–154.

25. Ortmeyer, D., Welkowitz, J., & Cohen, J. Interaction effects of value system convergence: Investigation of patient-therapist dyads. *Proceedings of the 74th convention,* Washington, D.C.: American Psychological Association, 1966. Pp. 193–194.

26. Reissman, F., Cohen, J., & Pearl, A. (Eds.) *Mental health for the poor.* New York: Free Press, 1964.

27. Rosenthal, D. Changes in some moral values following psychotherapy. *Journal of Consulting Psychology*, 1955, **19**, 431–436.

28. Schaffer, L. & Myers, J. K. Psychotherapy and social stratification. *Psychiatry*, 1954, **17**, 83–93.

29. Schofield, W. *Psychotherapy, the purchase of friendship.* Englewood Cliffs, N.J.: Prentice-Hall, 1964.

30. Seward, G. *Psychotherapy and culture conflict.* New York: Ronald Press, 1956.

31. Slack, C. W. Experimenter-subject psychotherapy. *Mental Hygiene,* 1960, **44,** 238–256.

32. Strean, H. S. Difficulties met in the treatment of adolescents. *Psychoanalytical Review,* 1961, **48,** 69–80.

33. Strupp, H. H. *Psychotherapists in action: Explorations of the psychotherapists' contribution to the treatment process.* New York: Grune & Stratton, 1960.

34. Strupp, H. H. & Jenkins, J. W. The development of six sound motion pictures simulating psychotherapeutic situations. *Journal of Nervous and Mental Diseases,* 1963, **136,** 317–328.

35. Strupp, H. H. & Wallach, M. S. A further study of psychiatrists' responses in quasi-therapy situations. *Behavioral Science,* 1965, **10,** 113–134.

36. Strupp, H. H. & Williams, J. V. Some determinants of clinical evaluations of different psychiatrists. *Archives of General Psychiatry,* 1960, **2,** 434–440.

37. Truax, C. B. & Carkhuff, R. R. *Toward effective counseling and psychotherapy.* Chicago: Aldine, 1967.

38. Yamamoto, J. & Goin, M. K. On the treatment of the poor. *American Journal of Psychiatry,* 1965, **122,** 267–271.

39. Yamamoto, J., James, Q. C., Bloombaum, M., & Hattem, J. Racial factors in patient selection. *American Journal of Psychiatry,* 1967, **124,** 630–636.

Chapter V

Therapist Status

The studies reported in this chapter are oriented primarily toward investigating the effect of the psychotherapist's status upon patient attraction to him. It is ofttimes both appropriate and necessary in psychological research that one's theory or research strategy be altered or abandoned in response to emerging research findings. At the start of the series of investigations to be discussed in the present chapter, our focus was not upon therapist status, but quite elsewhere. The unpredicted findings of our first study, however, appeared to us to be most reasonably explainable by recourse to the literature on attitude change and communicator status. Thus we followed these findings and systematically reoriented this particular series of studies toward the investigation of the attraction-enhancing effects of therapist status. With the foregoing as an overview, let us turn to what was the initial focus of this group of studies—social-psychological research on inequitable reward.

The Psychology of Inequity

Interest in the effects of inequitable reward grew initially from concern in business and industry with determining fair and appropriate worker compensation. Concretely, what is a fair day's wage for a fair day's work and, in contrast, what wage-work relationships are inequitable? Two classes of considerations are relevant—inputs and outcomes. In an industrial context, inputs are the worker's contribution to the work-for-wage exchange, and would include the degree of effort he expends on the job, his education, skill, seniority, etc. Adams (2), the major contributor to this research area, notes that these inputs are as perceived by their contributor and are not necessarily isomorphic with the perceptions of the other party to the exchange.

On the other side of the exchange are the rewards received by an individual for his inputs. These outcomes, in an industrial setting, might include wages, seniority benefits, and job status. In a manner analogous to inputs, outcomes are as perceived by the parties to the exchange. Adams suggests that while his conceptualizations regarding inequitable exchanges grew primarily from wage inequities, ". . . the theoretical notions advanced are relevant to any social situation in which an exchange takes place, whether the exchange be of the type taking place between man and wife, between football teammates, between teacher and student. . . ." To this list of interpersonal exchange possibilities, we would add the therapist-patient dyad. Noting first that the study of inequity has taken place in the context of cognitive dissonance theory, let us pursue our attempt to understand the effects of inequitable reward by looking further into the exchange characteristics of psychotherapy with the purportedly resistive patient. A low level of verbal participation is frequently the primary input contributed by such a patient to the therapeutic interaction. In the absence of any especially rewarding (to the patient) therapist interventions, the patient's perceived outcomes are minimal. That is, the patient feels he is "getting very little out of coming for therapy." From the patient's perspective, this state of affairs may well be a balanced, consonant, or equitable exchange. Both inputs and outcomes are low, little if any perceived inequity exists, and thus little if any cognitive dissonance[1] is aroused. However, as our first study in this series sought to approximate, should the therapist provide such "low input" patients with "high outcomes," an inequitable exchange has occurred and cognitive dissonance is aroused in the patient. One means of dissonance reduction in this context would be an increase in patient input. These formulations will, perhaps, gain in clarity if at this point in our discussion we examine social-psychological research on inequitable reward.

Adams and Rosenbaum (4) predicted that when a person is inequitably rewarded (by overcompensation) in relation to others, he will reduce the resultant feelings of inequity by increasing his inputs. Their subjects were university students hired to serve as opinion interviewers. Two experimental groups were formed: overcompensation and equitable compensation. All subjects were paid at the *same* hourly rate, but the overcompensated subjects were led to feel markedly unqualified to earn at this rate because of purported lack of experience and training. Equitably compensated subjects were led to feel qualified to earn the same wage. They were informed that they were more skilled than census takers and that general education and intelligence were the primary requisites for successful interviewing. The prediction that overcompensated subjects would seek to increase their inputs

---

[1] See Chapter VI for a more complete statement of the relevance of cognitive dissonance theory to the "resistive" patient.

could not find concrete expression by their seeking to obtain more training or experience. Their major potential avenue of dissonance reduction, therefore, was to increase their productivity. Results clearly supported this prediction. Overcompensated subjects obtained significantly more interviews per unit of time than did subjects led to feel equitably compensated.

Building upon Adams and Rosenbaum's findings, Arrowood (8) has reported an even more powerful demonstration of the augmenting effect of inequitable outcomes on inputs. Arrowood reasoned that Adams and Rosenbaum's overcompensated subjects may have worked harder not because of overcompensation per se, but because the induction of overcompensation led them to feel generally unqualified and unsure of holding their jobs. (All subjects thought they were going to be employed as interviewers for several weeks.) If this assumption was correct, Arrowood proposed, the same results might not have emerged if subjects were convinced that their employer would have no knowledge of their productivity. On the other hand, if the effect of overcompensation on inputs is not artifactual, overcompensated subjects should produce more than equitably compensated subjects whether or not they thought their employer would learn of their productivity. Arrowood's experimental groups and procedures were identical to Adams and Rosenbaum's, except that the overcompensated subjects were split into two subgroups—public and private. The public were led to believe that their employer would be aware of their interview productivity, i.e., their work was submitted directly by them to the employer. Work done by the private overcompensated subjects was mailed, by the subjects, in preaddressed envelopes to a firm in a distant state. Thus these subjects believed their direct employer would never learn of their productivity rate. In *both* public and private overcompensation conditions, subjects produced significantly more than equitably paid subjects.

A further demonstration of the inequity effect, in a very different context, is provided by Day (11). His subjects were children who were given training trials in which they pushed a plunger to obtain M&M candies. The number of candies received on each trial varied between one and six, and was a direct function of the pressure exerted on the plunger. After response level had been stabilized, 25 M&Ms were given to each subject on each of five trials, regardless of the pressure exerted. A significant number of subjects responded to the increased reward by increased pressure on the overrewarded trials. In terms of the inequity model, the children were comparing their inputs (pressure) and outcomes (M&Ms) during the overcompensation trials with those exchanged during the base rate trials. These latter trials had defined for the subjects what constituted an equitable exchange, and thus the subsequent overpayment was perceived as inequitable. Increased effort was then forthcoming as a means of restoring an equitable or consonant relationship between inputs and outcomes.

Other investigations have added further confirmation to the existence of an inequity effect and, furthermore, have demonstrated that not only quantity of production, but quality too may be altered by subjects in seeking to restore the equity of an exchange (1, 3, 19).

Inequitable Reward in the Initial Interview

In response to the investigative findings presented above, Deysach (12) conducted an investigation designed to discern the effects of inequitable reward in an interview context. In particular, he sought to learn whether the cognitive dissonance aroused by a "high outcome" provided by an interviewer would result in an increase in interviewee inputs. The input examined was perceived attraction toward the interviewer. Subjects were 52 university undergraduates who had sought vocational counseling at our University Counseling Center. Assignment to both the four experimental conditions and to the two participating counselors was randomly conducted. The counselors were trained for the behaviors they would enact, behaviors comprising the study's independent variable manipulation, but were not informed as to the study's other procedures, rationale, or hypotheses.

The counselor met with the client for an initial counseling interview. The study's independent variable manipulations took place during this interview, approximately five minutes before its end. Since such manipulation was conducted by the counselor, procedures were instituted to avoid the possibility that counselor knowledge of the client's experimental condition would influence the nature of the first 45 minutes (premanipulation) of the interview. When approximately five minutes remained in the interview, the counselor opened the client's clinic folder and looked on the back of the Counseling Request Card the client had filled out earlier. A notation made by E on the back of this card indicated which experimental condition was to be enacted at that point.

Inequitable Reward Condition. The counselor, without prefactory explanation to the client, picked up his office telephone, dialed a number and said, purportedly to the Center's secretary:

> Do you people up front have some coffee and doughnuts for yourselves today? How about bringing a doughnut and a cup back

here? You don't mind doing me a favor just once, do you? . . . No, it's not for myself; I just thought I'd like to buy one for (client's first name). . . . Okay, could you check and see how long it will take? (Then to the client) I've never tried this before and I think I took her by surprise. I just felt you might like some refreshments, but it. . . . (To secretary:) What? How long will it take? (Counselor looks at office clock) I guess we'll have to forget about it then. Thanks a lot anyway. (To client:) I wish I had called earlier. Now, where were we. . . .

Thus, in this condition, the counselor seeks to lead the client to believe an attempt has been made to single him out for an admittedly small but perhaps overcompensatory reward which is an unusual if not unique counselor behavior instituted in the client's behalf.

Equitable Reward Condition. Procedures applied to clients assigned to this condition were identical to those described above, except that the counselor sought to communicate the usualness (and equitableness) and not uniqueness of the reward procedure; e.g., "I've made it a practice with everyone of the clients I see to finish our session with some coffee and a doughnut if I can."

Reverse Reward Condition. This condition was included in Deysach's (12) experimental design for exploratory purposes. Its implementation was similar to that used in the Equitable Reward Condition in terms of the purported usualness of the procedures involved, but in this instance it was made clear that the coffee and doughnut were for the counselor, and not the client. Concretely, the telephone statement made was:

Do you people up front have some coffee and doughnuts for yourselves today? How about bringing a doughnut and a cup back here for me? You know how much I enjoy those doughnuts you bring in. . . . Okay, could you check and see how long it will take? No, no, don't bother to wait 'til I'm through here; just bring it back as soon as the coffee's ready. (Pause) Not 'til then? Okay, I'll be down after the session. Thanks a lot anyway. (To client:) I wish I had called earlier. Now, where were we. . . .

Control Condition. No experimental procedures were administered to subjects assigned to this condition. The counselor simply continued the initial session to completion without interruption.

Deysach's predictions were that clients exposed to the inequitable reward procedure would be more attracted to their counselors and more productive in their subsequent testing behavior for their counselor, than would clients assigned to the study's three other conditions.

At the close of the initial interview, clients in all conditions were instructed to go to the University's Testing Center at their earliest opportunity to take the battery of tests he and his counselor had selected as relevant during the interview. When the client appeared at the Testing Center, and before taking the selected vocational tests, he took two other tests whose purpose was measurement of the study's dependent variables—attraction and productivity. The attraction to counselor measures was the Client's Personal Reaction Questionnaire (9). After completing the CPRQ, the study's productivity measure was administered. A deck of 30 thematic cards was presented to the client, consisting of the four cards of the Picture Impressions Test and 26 Thematic Apperception Test cards.[2] The client was instructed with reference to this thematic card deck:

> At the beginning of this semester our counselor asked us to administer this test to their clients whenever we had an opportunity, and we like to do so as often as our work load permits. The results of this test, unlike your counseling tests, won't mean anything to you personally. Rather, they are useful only to our counselor to help him organize your other test materials without as much effort on his part. Your cooperation here is really a special service to him alone and not to yourself.

Following standard TAT story-writing instructions, and the request that the order of stories follow the order of cards as presented, the client was further instructed:

> Since there are so many cards, and they do take time and effort on your part, you are not expected to write stories for all of them. We require only that you complete the first four. But remember, the more you are able to write beyond that, the more work you can save your counselor. The number of stories you complete beyond the first four and the length of each is up to you.

Client stories resulting from this test were not utilized in the usual diagnostic manner in which such projective tests are typically employed. Instead, number and length of stories were used as indices of client productivity.

A comparison of the inequitably and equitably rewarded clients on these productivity indices revealed a strong tendency ($p < .06$) for those clients provided high outcomes (Inequitable Reward) to choose to respond to a greater number of thematic cards than equitably rewarded clients. The analogous comparison in terms of number of words written was in the same direction, but was not as strong. Thus we are provided with at least suggestive evidence that cognitive disso-

[2] Numbers 1, 2, 4, 5, 10, 11, 14, 15, 19, 20, 3BM, 3GF, 6BM, 6GF, 7BM, 7GF, 8BM, 8GF, 9BM, 9GF, 17BM, 17GF, 18BM, 18GF, 12M, 12F.

nance aroused by inequitable reward may have an impact upon productivity in an interview context analogous to its impact in the social-psychological laboratory.

An analysis of variance on the CPRQ attraction data yielded positive but unpredicted findings. The significant overall F for treatments ($F = 3.39$, $df = 3, 44$, $p < .05$) permitted us to make direct comparisons between cell means. Using Tukey (a) tests for these comparisons (28), it was found that while the means for both client reward conditions (inequitable $= 33.9$; equitable $= 36.2$) were approximately equal to the control group mean (36.8) the mean of the reverse Reward Condition (53.7) was greater than that for the inequitably rewarded clients ($p < .05$), equitably rewarded clients ($p < .07$), and control clients ($p < .07$). Furthermore, a comparison of the mean attraction to counselor score obtained from reverse reward clients with the combined mean of client attraction in the three other conditions yielded results of even greater reliability ($p < .01$). Our post hoc speculations regarding the bases for these unpredicted findings relied primarily on the position that the procedures involved in the reverse reward condition enhanced the generalized importance of the counselor in the client's eyes, i.e., a "status-spread effect." Our subsequent studies in this series were responsive to this speculation, and thus were all concerned with testing more directly the attraction-enhancing effects of high levels of therapist status.

Communicator Status and Attitude Change

Before presenting our further studies of therapist status, it is important to note that there exists a body of social-psychological research literature of relevance to this area of investigation. A number of studies have demonstrated that characteristics of the source of persuasive messages influence the degree to which such messages are accepted. Several of these characteristics appear relevant to the dimension of status. Hovland and Weiss (14), for example, report an investigation in which they varied source credibility through the use of communicators differing in trustworthiness. Their general procedure consisted of presenting an identical communication to two groups of subjects, in one case from a source of high credibility and in the other from one of low credibility. Opinion questionnaires were administered before, immediately after, and one month after the communication. One of their communications was, "Should the antihistamine drugs continue to be sold without doctor's prescription?" An affirmative position regarding the issue was presented as emanating from the *New England Journal of Biology and Medicine* (high credibility source) or from a mass circulation monthly pictorial magazine (low credibility source). Results, both in terms of judged trustworthiness and postcommunication attitude change, were significantly greater under high credibility conditions.

Kelman and Hovland (16) had high school students listen to a recording of an educational program in which a speaker advocated extreme leniency in the treatment of juvenile delinquency. Three variations of the speaker's credibility were used. In the High Credibility condition, he was described as a juvenile court judge who was highly trained, well-informed, authoritative, and sincere. In the Low Credibility condition, he was described as someone who had been a delinquent in his youth, who was currently involved in some behavior of questionable legality, and who was currently out on bail on a drug-peddling charge. In a third, Control Condition, the speaker was described as someone who had been chosen at random from the studio audience; no further information was provided. As in the study described above, results of his investigation demonstrated greater attitude change and judgments of greater trustworthiness in the High Credibility condition as compared to Low Credibility, with neutral information yielding intermediate scores.

Masling *et al.* (21) found positiveness of sociometric ratings in a military sample to be highly related to the status of those being rated. Taguiri *et al.* (26) found college students tending to choose high status individuals for roommates. Hurwitz *et al.* (15) report a similar finding, especially for subjects viewing themselves low in status. Pepitone (23), Goranson (13), and others (6, 7, 10, 18) have presented similar results. Thus this general effect of a communicator's credibility and status upon both the manner in which he is evaluated and the degree to which his message is accepted has been well-substantiated. These findings combine to form our extrapolatory rationale for the therapist status studies which follow.

Status Spread in the Initial Interview

Goldstein and Walker, working in a vocational counseling setting, conducted an investigation in which variations in counselor-client status spread were represented in four experimental conditions. Two counselors and 46 clients participated. Client assignment to counselor and experimental condition were randomly conducted. As in Deysach's study, clients participated in an initial interview whose nature was uninfluenced by the research procedures until approximately five minutes before its completion. At this point in the interview, in two of the study's experimental conditions, the counselor pressed a button under his desk that sounded a buzzer in an office down the hall thus activating a research assistant to leave that office and walk down the hall to the counselor's office. In the condition in which we sought to minimize the status differential between client and counselor, i.e., the Interruption Rejected Condition, the interrupted (research assistant) knocked on the door of the counselor's office. The counselor got up from his desk, opened the office door, and the following conversation ensued:

> *Interruptor:* I found a copy of that test referral list. . . .
> *Counselor:* Don't you see I have a client now? (Points to 'Do Not Disturb' sign.) You shouldn't just barge in like this. I thought you would know better. I'll see you later. (Counselor closes door firmly, returns to desk, apologizes to client for interruption.)

A second experimental condition sought to widen the status spread between client and counselor over that present in the condition described above. Thus, in the Interruption Accepted Condition, the following conversation took place between the counselor and the interruptor:

> *Interruptor:* I found a copy of that test referral list. (Hands sheet of paper to counselor.) The Counseling Center has been using this for years. (Counselor studies paper for approximately one minute.)
> *Counselor:* It looks pretty obsolete to me. I don't know why the director hasn't changed it. I think I'll make some changes. Let's add the Minnesota Analogies Test, Thematic Apperception Test, and the California Counseling Inventory. Let's eliminate the Army General Classification Test and the Purdue Pegboard. Is there anything else, John?
> *Interruptor:* No, I was just on my way to my office. (Counselor then closes door, returns to desk, and resumes interview, providing no apology or other reference to the interruption for the client.)

A third experimental condition, spreading even further the client-counselor status differential, was the Interruption Sought Condition. The procedures here were such that the interruptor responded to the buzzer not by knocking on the counselor's door but, instead, by speaking loudly to the Center's secretary while he stood outside this door:

> *Interruptor:* (loudly) Madeline, I'll be in my office for the next hour.
> *Counselor:* (Gets up from desk without excusing self, opens

door) John, have you found a copy of the test referral list?

Interruptor: Yes, I was going to show it to you when you finished
with your client. I happen to have it here. (Hands
sheet of paper to counselor.) The Counseling Center
has been using this for years. (Counselor studies
paper for approximately one minute.)

Counselor: It looks pretty obsolete to me. I don't know why the
director hasn't changed it. I think I'll make some
changes. Let's add the Minnesota Analogies Test,
Thematic Apperception Test, and the California
Counseling Inventory. Let's eliminate the Army General Classification Test and the Purdue Pegboard. Is
there anything else, John?

Interruptor: No, I was just on my way to my office. (Counselor
then closes door, returns to desk, and resumes interview, providing no apology or other reference to the
interruption for the client.)

In addition to these three experimental conditions varying in degree
of status spread, a no-manipulation Control Condition was also run. If
it is indeed the case, as our interpretation of Deysach's study suggests,
that the greater the spread in counselor-client status as the client per-
ceives it, the greater the client's attraction to the counselor, then our
experimental predictions for this study are clear. The experimental
conditions should be arrayed on attraction in the order: Interruption
Sought, Interruption Accepted, Control, Interruption Rejected. Clients
completed postinterview CPRQ's at the University Testing Center.
The mean score for each condition is presented in Table 5.1.

Table 5.1

Client Attraction and Degree of Status Spread

Experimental Condition	Client Attraction to Counselor
Interruption Sought	39.0
Interruption Accepted	43.8
Control	37.2
Interruption Rejected	32.1

An analysis of variance on these data failed to yield a significant,
overall *F*. Thus, while the trend of the data accords with our notion of
an attraction-status spread relationship, this study's findings cannot be
considered as providing clearly supportive evidence.

The Goldstein and Walker study failed to provide evidence that the greater the status spread between client and counselor, the greater will be client attraction to that counselor. Kiesler (17) has cautioned the therapy research community against what he terms the "myth of patient uniformity." He appropriately chides us for not being sufficiently responsive in our experimental designs to the influence of subject variables upon dependent variable measures. Perhaps the Goldstein and Walker study suffered from just this myth, random assignment of clients notwithstanding. Findings from the social-psychological laboratory once again are helpful in this regard, in that evidence exists pointing us more discriminatingly toward predictions of *which* classes of clients are most likely to be responsive on attraction dimensions to wide status differentials.

Adorno *et al.* (5) have described the highly authoritarian individual as a person who readily identifies with authority figures, who is overly concerned with status and power, and who is contemptuous of those of lower status. Their friendship preferences are for individuals of prominent social or economic status. Sanford (25) and Medalia (22) have demonstrated that high authoritarian group members prefer high status leadership and, in general, are more comfortable in leader-centered than in group-centered groups. Thibaut and Riecken (27) report confirming results. Thus it seems possible that there exists a status spread by subject authoritarianism interaction such that high authoritarian subjects are more attracted to high status individuals while low authoritarian subjects are more attracted to low status individuals. This was the prediction our next investigation sought to examine.

Sabalis (24), the principal investigator for this study, administered the California *F* Scale (5) to a population of 325 students taking an Introductory Psychology course. Thirty-eight subjects (19 male, 19 female) whose *F* Scale scores fell in the upper quartile of this population, and 38 representing the lower quartile, were selected for this investigation. To insure that *E* would not know into which group any given subject fell, the actual selection of subjects was conducted by someone other than *E*. All experimental procedures were held constant save for experimenter status. Thus this investigation was operationalized in terms of a 2 x 2 factorial design, i.e., high status *E* versus low status *E* by high authoritarian *S* versus low authoritarian S. Subjects in all conditions were required to take, as the primary task of the experiment, the Picture Impressions Test (20). This task was structured in such a way that the subject wrote his or her stories, rather than telling them to *E*. Subjects assigned to the High Status Condition were sent a postcard prior to their participation, indicating when their appointment was. The E was indicated on the card as Dr. Robert Sabalis. When S arrived for the appointment, E introduced himself to S as "Dr. Sabalis, a member of the faculty of the Psychology Department." A "Dr. Robert Sabalis" nameplate was on E's desk, and the office itself was a well-furnished, rather large office belonging to a faculty member. E was neatly dressed in a business suit. He explained to S that he wanted S to take the PIT because he (E) was conducting research on the test and its validity. As S began to write his responses to the PIT cards, E opened a textbook and began to jot down notes from it, indicating to S as he did that he was preparing an examination for one of the classes he taught.

In the Low Status Condition, E's name on the postcard and in the introduction of himself upon meeting was "Bob Sabalis." He described himself to S as a senior undergraduate psychology major who was trying to learn how to give the PIT to subjects as a requirement for one of his courses. E's attire was consistent with the typical undergraduate's. He met with S in a very small, sparsely-furnished office. E began to jot down notes, indicating to S as he did that he was studying for a class examination he had to take.

After completion of the PIT, each S was introduced to a second E, who administered a version of the CPRQ to S. CPRQ instructions were such that it was made to appear to be a scale seeking S's evaluation of the PIT and its administration. This form of the CPRQ yielded five separate scores: attraction to tester, attraction to test (the referent in this study being the PIT), attraction to psychological testing in general, attraction to psychological research in general, and subjective effortfulness of participation in the experiment. Separate analyses of variance for these five dependent variables across the status and authoritarianism conditions revealed two significant effects. On the subscale reflecting subject attraction to psychological tests in general, a significant authoritarianism by status interaction effect was obtained ($F = 6.15$, $df = 1$, 64, $p < .05$). The Tukey (a) procedure then utilized to evaluate individual cell means revealed the high authoritarian Ss under the High Status Condition to be significantly more attracted on this dimension than were low authoritarian Ss under the High Status Condition ($p < .05$). A main effect for status emerged on the subjective effort subscale ($F = 4.65$, $df = 1$, 64, $p < .05$). Subjects in the Low Status Conditions rated the experiment as significantly more effortful than did subjects in the High Status Conditions. None of the comparisons on the attraction to tester, test, or research in general subscales reached acceptable levels of statistical significance. An additional analysis of variance was conducted on the subject attraction to interviewer scores derived from the Picture Impressions Test.[3] This analysis revealed no significant effect for status on PIT attraction, and no significant status by authoritiarianism interaction. However, main effects for both authoritarianism and sex were obtained. Low authoritarian Ss were significantly more attracted than high authoritarian Ss ($F = 4.08$, $df = 1, 64$, $p < .05$), and male subjects more than female subjects ($F = 4.08$, $df = 1, 64$, $p < .05$).

In summary of these investigations, we are thus provided with beginning evidence pointing to the relevance for attraction enhancement of status differential within therapy-relevant dyads. Our finding of the interactive role played by authoritarianism in this status-attraction relationship should serve as encouragement to other investigators pursuing this domain to examine related dispositional characteristics.

References

1. Adams, J. S. The measurement of perceived equity in pay differentials. Unpublished manuscript, Behavior Research Service, General Electric Co., May, 1961.

2. Adams, J. S. Toward an understanding of inequity. *Journal of Abnormal and Social Psychology*, 1963, **67**, 422–436.

3. Adams, J. S. & Jacobsen, P. R. Effects of wage inequities on work quality. *Journal of Abnormal and Social Psychology*, 1964, **69**, 19–25.

4. Adams, J. S. & Rosenbaum, W. B. The relationship of worker productivity to cognitive dissonance. *Journal of Applied Psychology*, 1962, **46**, 161–164.

5. Adorno, T. W., Frenkel-Brunswik, E., Levinson, D. J., & Sanford, R. N. *The authoritarian personality*. New York: Wiley, 1966.

6. Arnet, C. E., Davidson, H. H., & Lewis, H. N. Prestige as a factor in attitude change. *Sociology and the Sociological Review*, 1931, **16**, 49–55.

7. Aronson, E. & Golden, B. W. The effects of relevant and irrelevant aspects of communicator credibility on opinion change. *Journal of Personality*, 1962, **30**, 137–146.

8. Arrowood, A. J. Some effects on productivity of justified and unjustified levels of reward under public and private conditions. Unpublished doctoral dissertation, University of Minnesota, 1961.

9. Ashby, J. D., Ford, D. H., Guerney, B. W., Jr., & Guerney, L. Effects on

[3] Interjudge reliability for the scoring of PIT attraction was Pearson $r = .93$.

clients of a reflective and leading type of psychotherapy. *Psychological Monographs*, 1957, **7**, 1–32.

10. Bowden, A. O., Caldwell, F. F., & West, G. A. A study in prestige. *American Journal of Sociology*, 1934, **40**, 193–204.

11. Day, C. R. Some consequences of increased reward following establishment of output-reward expectation level. Unpublished master's thesis, Duke University, 1961.

12. Deysach, R. E. The effects of a counselor favor on client attraction and openness to influence. Unpublished master's thesis, Syracuse University, 1967.

13. Goranson, R. E. Effects of the experimenter's prestige on the outcome of an attitude change experiment. Paper read at Midwestern Psychological Association, Chicago, May, 1965.

14. Hovland, C. I. & Weiss, W. The influence of source credibility on communication effectiveness. *Public Opinion Quarterly*, 1961, **15**, 635–650.

15. Hurwitz, J. I., Zander, A. F., & Hymovetch, B. Some effects of power on the relations among group members. In D. Cartwright and A. Zander (Eds.), *Group dynamics: research and theory*. Evanston, Ill.: Row, Peterson, 1969. Pp. 800–809.

16. Kelman, H. C. & Hovland, C. I. Reinstatement of the communicator in delayed measurement of opinion change. *Journal of Abnormal and Social Psychology*, 1953, **48**, 327–335.

17. Kiesler, D. J. Some myths of psychotherapy research and the search for a paradigm. *Psychological Bulletin*, 1966, **65**, 110–136.

18. Kulp, D. H. Prestige as measured by single-experience changes and their permanency. *Journal of Educational Research*, 1934, **27**, 663–672.

19. Lawler, E. E. & O'Gara, P. W. The effects of inequity produced by underpayment on work output, work quality and attitudes toward the work. Paper presented at American Psychological Association, New York, September, 1966.

20. Libo, L. The projective expression of patient-therapist attraction. *Journal of Clinical Psychology*, 1957, **13**, 33–36.

21. Masling, J., Greer, F. L., & Gilmore, R. Status, authoritarianism, and sociometric choice. *Journal of Social Psychology*, 1955, **41**, 297–310.

22. Medalia, N. Z. Authoritarianism, leader acceptance, and group cohesion. *Journal of Abnormal and Social Psychology*, 1955, **51**, 207–213.

23. Pepitone, A. *Attraction and hostility*. New York: Atherton Press, 1964.

24. Sabalis, R. F. Subject authoritarianism, interviewer status, and interpersonal attraction. Unpublished master's thesis, Syracuse University, 1969.

25. Sanford, F. H. *Authoritarianism and leadership*. Philadelphia: Institute for Research in Human Relations, 1950.

26. Taguiri, R., Kogan, N., & Long, L. M. Differentiation of sociometric choice and status relations in a group. *Psychological Reports*, 1958, 4, 523–526.

27. Thibaut, J. W. & Riecken, H. W. Authoritarianism, status, and the communication of aggression. *Human Relations*, 1955, 8, 95–120.

28. Winer, B. J. *Statistical principles in experimental design.* New York: McGraw-Hill, 1962.

Chapter VI
Effort

A major force underlying a great deal of social-psychological research in recent years has been the development and elaboration of cognitive balance theories (9, 15, 19, 20). Festinger's (9) theory of cognitive dissonance has, perhaps, been the most seminal of these developing theories in terms of the amount and breadth of research to which it has given rise.

In broad terms, cognitive dissonance is defined as a psychological tension having motivational characteristics. The theory speaks primarily about the conditions that arouse dissonance in an individual and the various means by which dissonance reduction may occur. The specific focus of the theory is upon cognitive elements and the relationship between them. Cognitive elements are items of information or cognitions about oneself, one's behavior, and one's environment. Two cognitions are said to be consonant if they are mutually consistent; that is, if one follows from, implies, or is compatible with the other. A patient's cognition that he is markedly reluctant to participate in psychotherapy as the therapist defines it, and participation in a "resistive" manner are consonant elements. Cognitive consonance in psychotherapy may also be represented by the patient's cognition of high attraction toward the therapist and behaviors displaying openness to the therapist's influence attempts. Cognitive dissonance is said to exist when two cognitive elements, occurring together, are mutually inconsistent; that is, one follows from the obverse of the other or is incompatible with the other. A high level of patient attraction to the therapist, simultaneous with participation in a "resistive" manner are dissonant elements. A low level of patient attraction to the therapist would be dissonant with a high level of responsiveness to therapist influence attempts. As noted above, cognitive dissonance is defined as a psychological tension having motivational characteristics. More fully, the central hypothesis of the theory holds that the presence of dissonance gives rise to pressure to reduce that dissonance, and that the magnitude of this pressure is a direct function of the magnitude of the existing dissonance. The nonintrospective, nonpsychologically-minded, guidance-oriented patient discussed earlier indeed has cognitive dissonance aroused when confronted with the "rules of psychotherapy" from a YAVIS-preferring psychotherapist. As we also noted earlier, over half of such patients reduce such dissonance by promptly terminating psychotherapy. To find the rules of the game ill-fitting and to decide not to play are consonant behaviors.

However, an alternate channel of dissonance reduction exists. Festinger and Carlsmith (10) propose that "when an organism obtains an insufficient reward relative to a particular expenditure of energy, there will be a tendency to discontinue the effortful activity or to attribute additional value to the activity or to its goal consequences" (10, p. 203). Thus dissonant elements may be brought into closer harmony not only by leaving the field (e.g., quitting psychotherapy) but also by altering one of the dissonant cognitions. The patient may reevaluate and then positively revalue the rules of the game. He may make more favorable his view of the likely therapy outcome. In concrete response to our goal of relationship enhancement for such patients, it thus follows that we must attend to (a) arousing cognitive dissonance, so that the patient is dissatisfied with the consonance between his negative view of therapy and his relatively nonparticipatory in-therapy behavior, and (b) maximizing the likelihood that the channel of dissonance reduction chosen is attraction enhancement and not termination.

In the investigations discussed below, the specific procedures utilized for dissonance-arousal purposes all sought to manipulate patient effort. We will examine first the social-psychological laboratory studies of effort and attraction enhancement, and then turn to our own investigations on these dimensions in psychotherapy-relevant contexts.

Laboratory Studies of Effort

Aronson and Mills (3) report an investigation dealing with the effects of severity of initiation on attraction. Their subjects were college women who had volunteered to participate in discussion groups. Three experimental conditions were constituted: (a) a severe (High Effort) initiation into the group, (b) a mild (Low Effort) initiation condition, and (c) No Initiation Effort control condition.

As a precondition to joining the group, the high effort Ss were required to read aloud material likely to cause feelings of marked embarrassment. Ss assigned to the Low Effort Condition read material unlikely to cause embarrassment. No preadmission procedures were required of control Ss. Each S then listened to a tape recording which appeared to be an ongoing discussion being conducted by the group, and then completed a questionnaire evaluating the discussion and the group members. Results provided clear support for their hypothesis. Ss in the severe initiation condition perceived the group as significantly more attractive than did either mild initiation or control Ss.

In a very different context, Aronson (2) again demonstrated a strong, positive influence of the degree of effort expended by Ss on an experimental task upon the attractiveness of that task. He predicted that an individual striving for a goal unsuccessfully would experience cognitive dissonance; that is, the cognition that he was expending effort would be dissonant with the cognition of being unrewarded. One means of reducing dissonance in this context, Aronson held, would be for S to find something about the situation (other than goal attainment) to which he could attach value. Aronson varied the degree of effort (effortful versus easy) required of S in his attempts at goal attainment. On each trial all Ss obtained a container. On rewarded trials the containers were red and contained money. On unrewarded trials the containers were green and empty. All Ss were required to rate the relative attractiveness of the two colors both before and after the experimental trials. Note that each time an S received an unrewarded container under effortful conditions, his cognition that it was empty was dissonant with his cognition that he had exerted effort to obtain it. Thus it was predicted that, in order for dissonance reduction to occur, S would attach value to the color of the unrewarded container. Results clearly supported this prediction. A large, significant difference emerged between effortful and easy conditions in relative preference for the two colors. Ss working under the easy set shifted in preference toward red, the rewarded color. Ss in the effortful set shifted toward green, the unrewarded color.

Zimbardo (24) has reported concurring results. He had 20 university students, all of whom were very much in favor of a numerical grading system, read a statement which consisted of a series of arguments against such a grading system. Half of the Ss read the report under high effort conditions, half under low effort conditions. Degree of effort was manipulated, respectively, in terms of a relatively long or a very brief period of delayed auditory feedback while reading the report. Postreading measurement of attitudes toward the grading system revealed that high effort Ss became significantly more opposed to the numerical system than did the low effort Ss. Thus the augmenting effect of effort on attraction receives further support.

Other studies yield additional positive evidence. Wright (22) reported a series of investigations demonstrating, with children as Ss, that preference for an object is greater when the object is less accessible than when it is easy to reach. In a series of animal experiments, Lewis (17) found that rats expending the greatest effort during trials developed the strongest preference for the stimulus involved. Further support for both the robustness and generality of this effort-attraction effect is provided by Aiken (1), Cohen (8), and Yaryan and Festinger (23).

Patient Effort and the Psychotherapy Relationship

The potential relevance for psychotherapy of the laboratory research just examined becomes apparent when one notes the wide variability across psychotherapies in the hurdles over which the patient-to-be must pass on his way from candidate status to that of bona fide patient. As was true for the laboratory studies, in which effort was operationalized in several different ways, therapy-associated patient effort varies in both amount and kind. Such effort may be primarily physical, and thus involve traveling a considerable distance at regular intervals to the therapist's office.[1] Related to this, but more complexly, such effort may be psychophysiological, involving a broad array of autonomic responsiveness to the potential threats of psychotherapy. One may also speak of initiation effort—reflecting the fact that some candidates are transformed into patients by the act of a telephone call (11); others must pass through a lengthy initiation involving psychological testing, intake interview(s), and trial or diagnostic therapy sessions (5), while yet others experience procedures at intermediate points on this effort continuum. Initiation effort appears to reflect an admixture of the physical effort involved in presenting oneself for these various procedures and what we might term intrapsychic effort. It is this last domain, intrapsychic effort, that may well be most relevant to both the laboratory research cited earlier and the concerns of the psychotherapist. Subsumed under intrapsychic effort would be discomfort associated with finding one's guidance expectations unmet, anxiety attendant on therapist-instigated pressures to inspect one's defenses, and, more generally, the array of difficulties experienced by all patients when seeking to overcome resistances and engage in the difficult work of intrapersonal exploration.

Intrapsychic Effort via Tape Distortion

In the studies described in the remainder of this chapter, Ss were

[1] It is of interest in this regard that Frank (12) notes that ". . . except for the original cures, Lourdes has failed to heal those who live in its vicinity. . . . On arrival at Lourdes after an exhausting, even life-endangering journey, the sufferer's expectation of help is further strengthened." (Pp. 54-55)

psychotherapy patients or vocational counseling clients who had voli-
tionally sought assistance at our University Counseling Center. Since
so very many psychotherapy patients terminate after their initial interview, we sought to investigate procedures instituted at this crucial
juncture, i.e., between the first and second therapy sessions.

Subjects in our first investigation were 30 university undergraduates
who had sought psychotherapy at our University Counseling Center.
Most presented problems of an essentially psychoneurotic nature. No
special intake procedures were instituted for this study. During the
candidacy or preadmission stage, therefore, all that was requested of
these patients was that they complete a brief form to provide identi-
fying and referral source information. In this investigation, as in all of
our in-therapy studies, patients were assigned to psychotherapists randomly, with the only restriction on randomization that each therapist
saw an equal number of patients in each experimental condition.
Patients then met for their initial psychotherapy session. Immediately
after this session, each patient filled out a CPRQ. This initial measure
of patient attraction to the therapist provided us with base rate information, information necessary to discern the effects of our subsequent
manipulations.

At this point in time, at the close of the first session, assignment to
three experimental conditions was randomly conducted. The therapist
said to the patient, "I want to see about scheduling for you," opened
his desk drawer, and removed an envelope from the top of a stack
placed there by E. If the number "0" appeared on the slip in the
envelope, the therapist simply set up his next therapy session with the
patient and arranged for postsession testing (CPRQ). If the number
"2" was on the slip, the therapist structured the patient not only for
testing but also for returning to the Center before his next therapy session. The actual structuring is presented below. Note, however, that
this procedure prevented the therapist from knowing to which of the
two "return-to-Center" conditions a patient had been assigned.
Patients assigned to the No Effort condition thus received no interven-
ing manipulation by us. They simply left the Center after completing
their first session and CPRQ and returned one week later for their next
therapy and testing sessions. Moderate Effort condition patients, just
before being introduced to the tester by their therapist at the end of
the first session, were told:

> I have decided that I would like you to listen to the tape of this
> session two times before seeing me again. We have done this in the
> past and found it to be helpful. It is important that you listen

quite attentively. Mr. _____ (tester) will set up the appointment for you.

Thus it is the therapist himself who initiated the effort manipulation.

Patients assigned to the High Effort condition received identical structuring and thus also returned to the Center twice between their first and second therapy sessions to listen (alone) to the tape of their first session. However, prior to their first such tape listening session, we rerecorded their first therapy session tape, filtering white noise into the audio system, thus making the tape difficult to understand. In this regard, these patients were told that, "through no one's fault but the manufacturer's, the tape had a lot of interference."

The CPRQ was administered to each patient four times: immediately after the first therapy session ($CPRQ_1$), immediately before the second therapy session ($CPRQ_2$),[2] immediately after the second session ($CPRQ_3$), and immediately after their fifth therapy session ($CPRQ_4$). The first testing was used as premanipulation base rate information.

Analyses of variance on the resultant difference scores (e.g., $CPRQ_2$-$CPRQ_1$) across conditions were then performed. These analyses revealed a significant effect of our manipulations on attraction as measured after the second interview ($CPRQ_3$-$CPRQ_1$) ($F = 4.34$, $df = 2, 34, p < .05$), but no such effect either before this interview ($CPRQ_2$-$CPRQ_1$) or following the fifth therapy session ($CPRQ_4$-$CPRQ_1$). Post hoc comparisons on the $CPRQ_3$-$CPRQ_1$ data revealed that both High and Moderate Effort condition patients were significantly more attracted than were No Effort patients. In addition to this demonstration of the effects of effort on attraction, inspection of the study's data revealed that on all occasions of measurement, the Moderate Effort patients reported (nonsignificantly) higher levels of attraction than did *both* High and No Effort patients. This consistent and unpredicted trend appeared to us to be worthy of further study.

Perhaps the effects of effort on attraction are curvilinear, i.e., perhaps task-relevant effort beyond a certain point becomes noxious and thus attraction decreasing. There are other potential bases for the possible superior effectiveness of our Moderate Effort condition. One of these concerns the perceived relevance of the effortful activity to the patient's definition of the task. It may well have been that Moderate Effort condition patients perceived coming to the Center twice to listen to their own tape (Moderate Effort condition) as relevant to the goals

---

[2] That is, after the second tape listening session (High and Moderate Effort patients) or one-week wait period (No Effort patients).

of their psychotherapy, but those listening under conditions of white noise (High Effort) may have perceived such effortfulness as irrelevant to their purpose in being there. It was this possible basis for the consistent trend of moderate effort having a more substantial effect on attraction than high effort which our next study sought to investigate.

Before turning to our investigation of effort relevance, an additional finding from the present study is of interest. The tape recordings of the first and second therapy sessions for patients in all conditions were subjected to a timing analysis according to procedures developed by Mahl (18). This analysis yields a silence quotient (SQ), an index representing how much the patient spoke during the session in relation to the amount of time available for him to speak. A comparison of changes in each patient's silence quotients against increments in attraction over sessions demonstrated, as was true in our initial study of direct structuring, that the more attracted the patient becomes, the more he talks. Concretely, the correlation between $(SQ_2\text{-}SQ_1)$ and $(CPRQ_3\text{-}CPRQ_1)$ was -.32; between $(SQ_3\text{-}SQ_1)$ and $(CPRQ_4\text{-}CPRQ_1)$ was -.50.

Relevance of Effort

Subjects for this investigation were 45 college undergraduates who had requested vocational counseling at our University Counseling Center. Three experimental conditions were constituted to which clients were randomly assigned. In the Relevant Effort Condition, the initial counseling session appointment was for two hours. Upon arriving for this appointment, the client was informed by the intaker that the first hour was to be spent taking a battery of tests. Since our intent in this study was to keep effort constant across conditions, while varying the perceived relevance of the effortful task, we needed a test battery unfamiliar to the typical client, i.e., a battery which could be perceived as both relevant to and irrelevant to vocational counseling. The tests chosen for this purpose were from French's (13) cognitive battery, i.e., Inference, Simile Interpretations, Gestalt Transformation, Finding A's, and Hidden Patterns. The specific statement made by the intake worker to clients in the Relevant Effort Condition was:

> There are a number of tests we want you to take for your counseling. Here they are. (Intaker hands client a test folder labeled 'Counseling Test Battery.') They take one hour to complete. Be sure to sign them and return them to me before you meet with Mr. _____. We'll get them scored along with any other tests he asks you to take and turn them over to him.

Procedures for the 15 clients assigned to the Irrelevant Effort Condition were identical to those described above, save for the structuring message which was:

> There are a number of tests we want you to take. We are doing some research for a testing company and they need results from people who come for counseling. While these tests have nothing to do with your counseling, and your counselor won't even see them, we'd like you to take them anyhow so we can fulfill this research contract. (Intaker hands client a folder labeled 'Research Test Batery.') You'd probably like the results but, I'm sorry, we mail them back unscored. No need to even sign them.

Clients in this condition then completed the same test battery as Relevant Effort clients. Fifteen additional clients were assigned to a No Testing Control Condition. They simply came to the Center for counseling and were treated as nonresearch clients typically were. All clients then participated in their initial counseling interview. Client assignment to the three counselors used in this study was randomly conducted, with each counselor seeing an equal number of clients in each condition. Following the session, each client completed a CPRQ and each counselor filled out a Therapist's Personal Reaction Questionnaire.

Analysis of the CPRQ data failed to yield support for this study's predictions. A one-way analysis of variance on the attraction data across conditions failed to reach an acceptable level of statistical significance.[3] Similarly negative results were obtained regarding the effects of effort relevance in a follow-up investigation conducted by Perry (21).

Our studies of effort relevance thus provide no evidence to suggest that moderate effort in our third study appeared to be the superior attraction-enhancer because of the irrelevance to psychotherapy of the white noise taping procedure. Perhaps the trend toward superiority of moderate effort over *both* high effort (white noise) and no effort was a function not of effort alone, but instead, effort plus the fact that in the Moderate Effort Condition, patients had the greatest opportunity to actually hear their first session and react to it without distraction. In a recent clinical paper, Geocaris (14) has described his use of "interposed tape review sessions." He asked a small number of his psychotherapy patients to return to his office regularly between sessions to listen (alone) to the tape of the just preceding session. Geocaris felt such interposed review experiences led to the patient's forgetting less material between therapy hours, to their becoming aware of character

---

[3] The single significant finding emerging from this study, unrelated to its major concern with effort, was a significant correlation between CPRQ and TPRQ scores ($r = .42$, $df = 44$, $p < .01$).

defenses more quickly, and, more generally, that the course of therapy was accelerated. Barcai (6) reports similar impressions using this technique, i.e., greater continuity of themes, more meaningful material introduced earlier, quicker recognition of defenses, and a positive effect of feedback about progress on motivation for treatment. We would summarize the opportunity provided by such tape review sessions under the term "consolidation." Patients undergoing such an experience have at hand the possibility of considering with some perspective the events of the preceding therapy session, inspecting their defenses, gains, and setbacks more closely, observing as it were the behaviors of their therapist and more generally consolidating any budding insights or gains which emerged in the session itself.

The clinical reports just cited suggest that, in our in-therapy study, the attraction enhancement may have been due at least in part to the opportunity for consolidation provided the patient by the effort-manipulation procedures. Our next investigation, therefore, sought to compare directly the attraction-enhancing effects of effort versus effort plus the opportunity for consolidation.

Effort and Opportunity
for Consolidation

Seventy-eight patients participated in this three condition study. As before, assignment to condition and therapist was randomly conducted. Also, as in the study reported earlier, there was a control condition in which patients did not return to the Center between their first and second therapy sessions, and two experimental conditions in which they returned to the Center twice. In one of these, the Own Tape Condition, the patient listened twice to the tape recording of his own initial session, thus providing *both* an opportunity for consolidation as well as intrapsychic effort. In the Other Tape Condition, the patient listened to two different tape recordings, recorded by E, describing various aspects of contemporary psychotherapy in the United States. This material was drawn from recent texts by Frank (12) and Cameron (7) and discussed the types of patients who seek psychotherapy, by whom and where it is administered, the training of psychotherapists, etc. These discussion tapes possessed the advantage of constituting a credible task for new psychotherapy patients, of demanding a measure of physical effort to come to the Center twice to hear them, but of providing no opportunity for consolidation.

The CPRQ was administered to all patients by the clinic intake worker immediately after the initial interview ($CPRQ_1$), immediately before the second interview (and thus *after* the tape listening sessions) ($CPRQ_2$), and immediately after the second interview ($CPRQ_3$). One-way analyses of variance across conditions for the two attraction change scores of relevance to the study's predictions ($CPRQ_2$-$CPRQ_1$; $CPRQ_3$-$CPRQ_1$) revealed no differential change in attraction across conditions from initial interview to pre-second interview (postmanipulation), and (consistent with our first effort study) a significant differential effect from postinitial interview to post-second interview ($F = 5.60$, $df = 2, 77$, $p < .05$). Scheffe tests performed on these data revealed the attraction increment for Own Tape (consolidation opportunity) subjects to be significantly greater than that for No Tape (control) subjects, and than that for No Tape and Other Tape combined. There was no significant difference between those cells representing Other and Own Tapes.

A second finding deriving from this investigation is of interest. In this study, as well as all of our other attempts to enhance *patient* attraction, the independent variable manipulations were directed toward the patients involved. The participating therapists were unaware of the study's hypotheses and in no instance were patients assigned to them on any but a random basis. Thus there should be no *a priori* basis for anticipating a systematic difference in therapist attraction to the patient. Yet this is precisely what this investigation found. Using difference scores derived from the second session TPRQ minus first session TPRQ, a significant effect across conditions emerged ($F = 4.29$, $df = 2, 35$, $p < .05$). Scheffe tests on these data revealed that therapists were significantly more attracted to Own Tape Condition patients than to either Other Tape or No Tape patients. This finding largely parallels that found for patient attraction to the therapists, thus suggesting further support for the notion of reciprocal affect (16) and the law of Talion.

To this point, therefore, our series of studies has begun to yield an additional procedure for attraction enhancement in a psychotherapeutic context. Our first study involving tape playback sessions pointed not only to an effort effect, but also to a possible consolidation explanation of the attraction-enhancing effect of such tape listening. The present study is open to a similar dual interpretation. Further investigation oriented toward clarifying the basis for this attraction-enhancing procedure thus appears worthwhile. In addition, the relationship implications of those dimensions of psychotherapy-relevant effort described by us earlier as physical, psychophysiological, or as associated with initiation into treatment remain untouched investigative domains.

References

1. Aiken, E. G. The effort variable in the acquisition, extinction, and spontaneous recovery of an instrumental response. *Journal of Experimental Psychology*, 1957, **53**, 47–51.

2. Aronson, E. The effect of effort on the attractiveness of rewarded and unrewarded stimuli. *Journal of Abnormal and Social Psychology*, 1961, **63**, 375–380.

3. Aronson, E. & Mills, J. The effects of severity of initiation on liking for a group. *Journal of Abnormal and Social Psychology*, 1959, **59**, 177–181.

4. Ashby, J. D., Ford, D. H., Guerney, B. G., Jr., & Guerney, L. Effects on clients of a reflective and a leading type of psychotherapy. *Psychological Monographs*, 1957, **71**, Whole No. 453.

5. Bach, G. R. *Intensive group psychotherapy.* New York: Ronald Press, 1954.

6. Barcai, A. But who listens—Therapeutic values of replayed tape recorded interviews. *American Journal of Psychotherapy*, 1967, **21**, 286–294.

7. Cameron, N. *Personality development and psychopathology.* Boston: Houghton Mifflin, 1963.

8. Cohen, A. R. Communication discrepancy and attitude change: A dissonance theory approach. *Journal of Personality*, 1959, **27**, 386–396.

9. Festinger, L. *A theory of cognitive dissonance.* Stanford: Stanford University Press, 1957.

10. Festinger, L. & Carlsmith, J. M. Cognitive consequences of forced compliance. *Journal of Abnormal and Social Psychology*, 1959, **58**, 203–210.

11. Fink, H. K. Some therapeutic departures in group therapy. *Psychological Newsletter*, 1956, **8**, 1–11.

12. Frank, J. D. *Persuasion and healing.* Baltimore: Johns Hopkins University Press, 1961.

13. French, J. Kit of reference tests for cognitive factors. Princeton, N.J.: Educational Testing Service, 1963.

14. Geocaris, K. The patient as listener. *Archives of General Psychiatry*, 1960, **2**, 81–88.

15. Heider, J. *The psychology of interpersonal relations.* New York: Wiley, 1958.

16. Jones, E. E. & Thibaut, J. W. Interaction goals as bases of inference in interpersonal perception. In R. Taguiri & L. Petrullo (Eds.), *Person perception and interpersonal behavior.* Stanford: Stanford University Press, 1958. Pp. 151–178.

17. Lewis, M. Psychological effect of effort. *Psychological Bulletin*, 1965, **64**, 183–190.

18. Mahl, G. F. Disturbances and silences in the patient's speech in psychotherapy. *Journal of Abnormal and Social Psychology*, 1956, **53**, 1–15.

19. Newcomb, T. M. The prediction of interpersonal attraction. *American Psychologist*, 1956, **11**, 575–586.

20. Osgood, C. E. & Tannenbaum, P. H. The principle of congruity in the prediction of attitude change. *Psychological Review*, 1955, **62**, 42–45.

21. Perry, M. A. The effects of effort and perceived consensus of others on change in self-concept. Unpublished master's thesis, Syracuse University, 1969.

22. Wright, H. F. The influence of barriers upon strength of motivation. *Contributions to Psychological Theory*, 1937, **1**, Whole No. 3.

23. Yaryan, R. & Festinger, L. Preparatory action and belief in the probable occurrence of future events. *Journal of Abnormal and Social Psychology*, 1961, **63**, 603–606.

24. Zimbardo, P. G. Involvement and communication discrepancy as determinants of opinion change. *Journal of Abnormal and Social Psychology*, 1960, **60**, 86–94.

Chapter VII

Interaction Effects: Structuring-Status-Effort

The investigation[1] to be reported in this chapter had two primary goals. Throughout our entire research program, a major concern has been the parameters or limits of extrapolation from the social-psychological laboratory. We have been reasonably successful in extrapolating laboratory attraction findings derived from young, attractive, verbal, intelligent, and successful college student subjects to similarly YAVIS individuals seen in a college counseling center or in the context of therapy-analogue experimental designs. In several earlier chapters we have sought to extrapolate more broadly to NON-YAVIS psychiatric patients and have had rather mixed extrapolatory success. The present investigation represents our most complete attempt at such extended extrapolation of structuring, status, and effort-based procedures for attraction enhancement.

Earlier chapters have presented research examining the attraction-enhancing consequences of a series of procedures, each procedure tested singly. The present factorial investigation sought to discern the effects of these procedures acting in combination. Thus we designed a 12-condition experiment, involving two levels of trait structuring (warm, cold), two levels of interviewer status (high, low), and three levels of patient effort or opportunity for consolidation (Own Tape, Other Tape, No Tape). One hundred and sixty-eight psychiatric outpatients at a community psychiatric clinic were randomly assigned to these 12 conditions. All study manipulations occurred during the intake phase of each patient's treatment career. Upon arrival at the clinic for the initial interview, each patient was provided a structuring sheet by the clinic secretary, and urged to read it carefully before the interviewer arrived. These structuring sheets provided our warm-cold and high status-low status structuring. For example, the warm-high status and cold-low status structurings were as follows:

[1] Co-investigators for this investigation were Robert Sabalis, Joseph Himmelsbach, Roger Greenberg, and the present writer.

(Warm-High Status)
Intake Interview Background

In recent years more and more people have been coming to St. Joseph's Hospital seeking help for many types of problems.

The interview you are about to have is called an intake interview. Its purpose is to help us get a better idea of your problems and how we might best assist you.

It has been found helpful, in the past, for the patient to know something about his intake interviewer. He is a doctor who has studied at some of the country's leading universities and medical schools. He has had considerable experience working with patients.

Patients who have seen this interviewer seem to feel that he is a rather warm person, industrious, practical, and determined.

You may observe his warm, interested manner during your interview with him.

(Cold-Low Status)
Intake Interview Background

In recent years more and more people have been coming to St. Joseph's Hospital seeking help for many different types of problems.

The interview you are about to have is called an intake interview. Its purpose is to help us get a better idea of your problems and how we might best assist you.

It has been found helpful, in the past, for the patient to know something about his intake interviewer. He is a student engaged in a required part of his training. He has had limited experience working with patients.

Patients who have seen this interviewer seem to feel that he is a rather cold person, industrious, practical, and determined.

You may observe his formal, businesslike manner during your interview with him.

Each patient then met with the interviewer for an individual intake interview which lasted no less than 20 minutes and no more than 30 minutes. The interview format was moderately structured, each interview revolving around the following series of questions:

INTERVIEW SCHEDULE

1. What brings you to the clinic?
2. How long have you felt this way?
3. Describe what it feels like.
4. How has your family reacted?
5. What other problems have developed?
6. What caused you to come in *now?*
7. How has it affected your work?
8. How has it affected other aspects of your life?

9. How do you feel we can help you?
10. What is *your* idea of what psychotherapy is?

Although the interviewer was attired and introduced (and self-labeled) as "Doctor" or "Mister" depending upon status condition, we were unable to vary the interview setting as we had done in our earlier status investigation (4). Thus all interviews were conducted in the same office. Three intake interviewers were used over the two-year period of data collection for this study. While each saw a different total number of patients, within each interviewer's patients there were an equal number per condition. Each interview was tape-recorded. Following the interview, the interviewer completed a TPRQ and the patient participated in one of three effort manipulations. In the Own Tape Condition, the patient listened (alone) to the recording of his just completed interview. Other Tape patients listened to a 20-minute tape, recorded by the present writer, which broadly discussed contemporary psychotherapy in the United States. Following tape listening for patients in these two sets of conditions, and following the interview for No Tape patients, a brief test battery was administered. Since our earlier studies had suggested that both patient authoritarianism (see Chapter V) and patient-therapist compatibility (see Chapter IX) were important influences upon patient attraction to the therapist, we felt it important that we include measures of these variables in order to later covary out their effects, thus more adequately discerning the effects of our manipulations on our dependent variables. Therefore, our test battery consisted of the *F* Scale (1) as our authoritarianism measure, Schutz's (5) FIRO Scale as our compatibility measure, and the CPRQ as our measure of attraction. The intake interviews were content-analyzed[2] following Ashby *et al.*'s (2) procedures for openness and guardedness.[3]

Our hypotheses were that on our dependent variable measures of attraction (CPRQ, TPRQ) and patient interview behavior (openness, guardedness), warm structuring would yield more positive scores than cold structuring, high status more than low status, and Own Tape more than Other or No Tape. Interactional predictions were also formulated such that combinations of two or more manipulations, which singly were hypothesized to enhance attraction, should lead to greater attraction than combinations involving fewer such manipulations; e.g., warm structuring and high status should have a more positive effect than warm structuring plus low status.

[2] Interjudge reliability (Pearson r) = .87.
[3] See Appendix II, pp. 227-231.

Results

The CPRQ item dealing with interviewer warmth was used as the check upon our warm-cold manipulation. Patients structured to believe that the interviewer was warm perceived him significantly more positively on this item than did patients structured for a cold interviewer ($t = 5.00$, $df = 165$, $p < .01$).

A series of covariance analyses were then performed, covarying out the effects of patient authoritarianism and patient-therapist compatibility. No significant main effects were obtained. That is, viewed singly, neither trait structuring, structured interviewer status, nor our effort-consolidation manipulations significantly influenced any of our four dependent measures. In addition, no interaction effects emerged on any of the several comparisons involving the CPRQ, openness, or guardedness scores. With regard to therapist attraction to the patient, however, a moderate number of significant interactions were obtained. Under conditions of cold structuring, our subsequent Scheffe test indicated that patients who are to hear their own tape are significantly more attractive to the interviewer than are those who are to hear no tape. This finding emerged with both F and FIRO covaried out ($F = 4.87$, $df = 2, 119$, $p < .01$), with just F controlled ($F = 5.16$, $df = 2$, 119, $p < .01$), and with only FIRO controlled ($F = 4.81$, $df = 2, 119$, $p < .01$). While a relatively small number of significant F tests from a considerably larger pool of those computed must be viewed with great tentativeness, it should be noted that the foregoing finding replicates the TPRQ result obtained in our final effort study conducted at our Counseling Center. There, too, therapists were significantly more attracted to those patients who were to have what we termed a consolidation opportunity, in contrast to those listening to no tape.

A small series of significant three-way interactions was also obtained. Scheffe tests on these data revealed that our interviewers were significantly less attracted to the patient to whom, in terms of our manipulations (and predictions!), we gave the least. That is, in comparison to *all* other 11 cells, the patients falling in that cell defined by cold structuring, low-status structuring, and no tape were significantly least liked. This finding held with both F and FIRO covaried out ($F = 3.11$, $df = 2, 119$, $p < .05$), with only F controlled ($F = 3.17$, $df = 2, 119$, $p < .05$), and with just FIRO controlled ($F = 3.54$, $df = 2, 119$, $p < .05$). Rosenthal's (3) extensive research on experimenter bias may be relevant here. It appears possible that, functioning as a self-fulfilling prophecy, the interviewer's anticipation that such patients would perform "less well" on our dependent measures (including, relevant to our reciprocity findings, attraction to the interviewer) may have negatively influenced their level of attraction to the patient. This speculation may be relevant in an explanatory sense not only to these three-way interactions, but also to the two-way interactions discussed above.

Perhaps most significant about the results of this investigation, however, is the general absence of significant results and the implications of this paucity of findings for our broad concern with the limits of extrapolation from the social-psychological laboratory. Trait structuring, status manipulations, and the expenditure of effort all function to enhance interpersonal attraction in the laboratory setting. In large measure, the studies reported in earlier chapters indicate that analogous manipulations yield similar attraction enhancement in moderately disturbed college students seen for treatment in a counseling center. While our analogue studies with psychotic inpatients demonstrated attraction enhancement following trait structuring, and, to a lesser extent, direct structuring, such an effect has not been demonstrated to follow from the three types of manipulations in the present study, involving psychiatric outpatients seeking treatment at a community clinic. It is not only in the domains of structuring, status, and effort, however, that we have tested the limits of our extrapolatory strategy. In the chapters that follow, laboratory techniques for attraction enhancement based upon modeling (Chapter VIII), matching (Chapter IX), and role playing (Chapter X) with NON-YAVIS patients will be examined. Following this presentation, we will be in a more complete position to draw firmer conclusions regarding the parameters and limits of extrapolation.

References

1. Adorno, T. W., Frenkel-Brunswik, E., Levinson, D. J., & Sanford, R. N. *The authoritarian personality.* New York: Harper, 1950.

2. Ashby, J. D., Ford, D. H., Guerney, B. G., Jr., & Guerney, L. Effects on clients of a reflective and a leading type of psychotherapy. *Psychological Monographs,* 1957, **46**, 1–32.

3. Rosenthal, R. *Experimenter effects on behavioral research.* New York: Appleton-Century-Crofts, 1966.

4. Sabalis, R. F. Subject authoritarianism, interviewer status, and interpersonal attraction. Unpublished master's thesis, Syracuse University, 1969.

5. Schutz, W. C. *The FIRO scales, test and manual.* Palo Alto, Calif.: Consulting Psychologists Press, 1957.

Chapter VIII

Modeling

Imitative behavior has long been a focus of psychological research. The concepts involved to describe and explain the modification of an individual's behavior following his exposure to a model have included matched-dependent behavior, copying, and same-behavior (30); empathic learning (33); observational learning (13); identification (27); vicarious learning (10); and, perhaps most convincingly, modeling (9). A very substantial number of investigations combine to demonstrate that modeling is an effective, reliable, and, relative to other response acquisition procedures, rapid technique for the development of novel responses and the strengthening or weakening of previously acquired responses. The wide array of studies supporting this conclusion have been fully reviewed and integrated by Bandura (3, 9), Mowrer (33), and Flanders (14). Behaviors experimentally demonstrated in these laboratory investigations to be alterable by modeling techniques are numerous and varied, and have included aggression (9), altruism (11), moral judgments (8), speech patterns (19), career planning (23), emotional arousal (40), dependency (9), sexual anxiety (9), sexual assertiveness (44), delay of gratification (31), and self-reward and self-punishment (7).

The earliest clinical uses of modeling procedures occurred in largely informal research attempts, and focused primarily on children. Jones (22) sought to modify phobic reactions by exposing the phobic child to other children who were interacting with the feared object in a fearless manner. Not only was her attempt successful, but she also was able to demonstrate that such fears may be acquired through a modeling process. Chittenden (12), Jack (4), and Page (36) each provided an early demonstration that children's aggressive behavior could be successfully modified by use of modeling techniques. More recently, Lovaas (26) has reported successful modification of both the verbal and nonverbal behavior of schizophrenic children by use of modeling procedures. Both Gula (18) and Sarason (38, 39) report similarly positive outcomes in their modeling attempts to alter the acting-out behavior of delinquent adolescent boys, and Bandura *et al.* (6) have provided a rigorous demonstration of the usefulness of modeling to reduce phobic behavior in nursery school children. Phobic behavior in adult patients also has been successfully modified by modeling procedures (4, 5, 16).

A few investigations are perhaps even more closely relevant to interview types of psychotherapy. Truax (42, 43) developed a 30-minute tape recording consisting of excerpts of "good" within-therapy patient behaviors. Truax notes, "The tape itself illustrates in a very concrete manner how clients explore themselves and their feelings. It provides both cognitive and experiential structuring of 'how to be a good client'" (42, p. 863). Experimental patients listened to this tape; control patients did not but were treated as were the experimental patients in all other major respects. A series of comparisons of the early session behavior of these two groups of patients revealed that those undergoing the modeling procedure showed significantly higher levels of intrapersonal exploration and significantly greater symptomatic change.

Myrick (34), in an investigation building upon Truax's findings, sought somewhat more complexly to augment the level of client self-reference by use of modeling procedures. He developed a script of a counseling session in which the client (model) gradually shifted in his verbalizations away from discussion of others toward increasing focus upon himself. The script was both video- and tape-recorded. Ninety clients were randomly assigned to either video-modeling, tape-modeling, or control conditions. After viewing and listening to the interview (Video Condition), listening to it (Tape Condition), or a brief wait period (Control Condition), all clients met for an individual, 30-minute interview with the counselor to whom they had been randomly assigned. A content analysis of these interviews revealed significantly more self-references in both experimental conditions as compared to the (no modeling) control clients. Friedman (15), Marlatt (28, 29), and Whalen (45) have similarly reported significant modeling effects in the context of interview or interview-analogue investigations.

Schwartz and Hawkins (40) report findings even more directly relevant to psychotherapy as currently practiced. They constituted a pool of schizophrenic inpatients into three psychotherapy groups. Two patients assigned to the first group were individuals who frequently verbalized affective statements. Two assigned to the second group quite infrequently offered such affective verbalizations. These four patients were designated by the investigators as models displaying the presence (Group I) or absence (Group II) of affective verbal behavior. No such models were assigned to the third group. Each group met for 16 sessions, during which the group leader endeavored to reinforce all affective statements. As the investigators had predicted, significant within-group difference emerged. From early to late psychotherapy sessions, Groups I and III increased significantly in the number of affective statements made across all group members (except the models). Group II decreased significantly in this regard. This investigation combines with those presented earlier to indicate that modeling procedures have, in at least a small way, already begun to yield consistent behavior change effects in psychotherapy-relevant contexts. Our own investigations of modeling and attraction enhancement, presented below, sought to achieve further progress in this direction.

Modeling and Attraction Enhancement—YAVIS Subjects

Much of the research on modeling behavior has sought to identify subject characteristics which serve to augment or lessen the amount of modeling which occurs. One such characteristic is subject self-esteem. DeCharms and Rosenbaum (13), Gelfand (17), and Rosenbaum *et al.* (37) have all demonstrated that low self-esteem subjects model an array of behaviors significantly more than do subjects evidencing high self-esteem. This finding is bolstered by related evidence indicating significantly greater persuasibility in low self-esteem subjects (20, 24). examine not only the effects of modeling on attraction enhancement, but also the interaction of any such modeling effects with subject self- Since low self-esteem is a particularly salient characteristic of most psychotherapy patients, we chose in the investigation that follows to esteem. Thus we designed a factorial investigation involving two levels of subject self-esteem by two levels of displayed patient attraction to a therapist. Our predictions were that subjects hearing a model (taped patient) display high attraction toward a taped therapist would themselves report significantly higher attraction toward the therapist than subjects hearing a model who expressed negative feelings; that low self-esteem subjects would model significantly more than high self-esteem subjects; and that there would be a tape by subject interaction such that low self-esteem subjects hearing the High Attraction tape would be most attracted to the taped therapist. Analogous predictions were made for the dependent variables, persuasibility, and willingness to disclose.

Orenstein (35), the principal investigator for this study, administered DeCharms and Rosenbaum's Value Profile (13) to a pool of 417 female Introductory Psychology students. This test administration took place two months before the experiment was actually run. DeCharms and Rosenbaum (13) and Rosenbaum, Horne, and Chalmers (37) have provided adequate evidence for the Value Profile as a measure of self-esteem in college populations. Across samples, and within a possible score range of 10 to 70, these investigators report a grand mean on the Value Profile of 48. Our population mean was 45.2. Our high self-esteem subjects, representing the upper quartile from our distribution of scores, all had scores of 54 or higher; low self-esteem subjects (lower quartile) scored 38 or lower. Forty of each of the two types of subjects were randomly selected, and then half of each group was randomly assigned to the High or Low Attraction Tape Conditions. The attraction tapes were designed for this investigation. Each presented the same 25-minute segment of a psychotherapy session. Therapist verbalizations were identical on the two tapes as were, with one major series of exceptions, patient verbalizations. On the High Attraction tape, 16 statements were made by the taped patient expressing positive feelings toward the therapist, e.g., "I bet you know what I mean; you seem the type that would understand that." "You know, I think you really know your business." "Good, I like that [the chance to see the therapist for another session] because, well, I really feel comfortable talking to you." Patient statements expressing low attraction were substituted for the foregoing on our Low Attraction tape, e.g., "You're really pushing me, aren't you?" "I don't know why I'm telling you all this." "Do you think it would be possible to arrange to have someone else see me? I mean, I wasn't too comfortable talking to you today." Following consensus from a panel of psychologists that these tapes were credible as psychotherapy sessions and that high and low levels of patient attraction were satisfactorily portrayed, the tapes were played to a pilot sample of 21 female college undergraduates. These pilot subjects completed CPRQ's after hearing the tapes, seeking as they did to represent what they viewed as the taped patients' feelings. The High Attraction tape pulled a significantly higher level of patient attraction in this pilot sample ($t = 6.90, df = 20, p < .01$).

Subjects were run in groups of approximately seven each. Pretape structuring paralleled that provided in our other tape analogue investigations, and essentially sought to provide the subjects with the appropriate set for evaluating a taped psychotherapy session. After listening to either the High Attraction or Low Attraction tape, each subject completed a CPRQ, the Persuasibility Questionnaire we had used earlier in our investigations of trait structuring (see Chapter III), and a Willingness to Disclosure Questionnaire (41). As employed by us, this last measure sought to learn from the testee what she would be willing to disclose to the taped therapist if they had the opportunity to meet and interact. The areas of possible self-disclosure covered by this questionnaire are:

(a) attitudes and opinions,
(b) tastes and interests,
(c) work or studies,
(d) money,
(e) personal concerns, and
(f) feelings about one's own body.

Research conducted by Simonson (41) has revealed that the last two areas examined, personal concerns and feelings about one's body, are the two areas of the questionnaire most responsive to pretherapy manipulations of the type under investigation here. Since both of these subareas are particularly central to the psychotherapeutic interaction, they form our primary concern with regard to the issue of self-disclosure.

An analysis of variance on the CPRQ data revealed a highly significant main effect for tape modeling ($F = 75.44$, $df = 1, 79$, $p < .01$), no significant main effect for subject self-esteem, and no significant tape by subject interaction effects. Post hoc analyses [Tukey (a) tests] revealed that both high and low self-esteem subjects exposed to the High Attraction tape were significantly more attracted to the taped therapist than either high or low self-esteem subjects hearing the Low Attraction tape. A similar modeling effect emerged on the personal concerns subscores of the Willingness to Disclose measure ($F = 4.12$, $df = 1, 79$, $p < .05$), but not with reference to scores reflecting feelings about one's body. Here, low self-esteem subjects exposed to the Low Attraction tape were significantly less willing to discuss their personal concerns than were subjects in all other cells. A main effect for self-esteem also was obtained on this subscale, such that high self-esteem subjects were more willing to disclose on this dimension than were low self-esteem subjects ($F = 8.19$, $df = 1, 79$, $p < .01$). Finally, on our measure of persuasibility, no tape or interaction effects emerged but low self-esteem subjects were significantly more persuasible than high self-esteem subjects ($F = 5.40$, $df = 1, 79$, $p < .05$). Post hoc comparisons revealed low self-esteem subjects exposed to either tape were each significantly more persuasible than high self-esteem subjects hearing either tape.

Thus this study's results provide a robust demonstration that attraction enhancement via modeling procedures occurs, and that such enhancement appears to influence, at least in a minor way, a consequent of interpersonal attraction, i.e., willingness to discuss personal concerns. No evidence was obtained in support of the notion that the level of subject self-esteem influences or interacts with the degree of attraction-modeling which takes place. Self-esteem does, however, appear to be casually related to other psychotherapy-relevant variables. High self-esteem subjects are significantly more willing to be open about their personal concerns; low self-esteem subjects are significantly more persuasible. Such findings combine to clearly permit an investigative step further on an analogical bridge toward psychotherapeutic practice. The investigation reported below represents just such a step.

Modeling and Attraction Enhancement—NON-YAVIS Patients

The broad aim of this investigation, for which Liberman (25) was the major investigator, was to test for the presence of modeling effects on attraction and disclosure in a live, therapy-like interview with NON-YAVIS patients. Subjects were 84 male alcoholic inpatients in a state hospital for alcoholic patients. Their median age was 43; median length of hospitalization was 23 days. None had concomitant diagnoses of organicity, and all were sober at the time of their experimental participation. A complete range of socioeconomic levels was represented in this sample. All study patients were participating in intensive (15 hours per week) short-term group psychotherapy.

Six experimental conditions were constituted—four modeling conditions and two control conditions. The modeling conditions were operationalized in terms of four tapes of initial psychotherapy interviews constructed for this investigation. These tapes depicted an alcoholic patient who expressed either (a) high attraction-high disclosure, (b) high attraction-low disclosure, (c) low attraction-high disclosure, or (d) low attraction-low disclosure. Therapist statements were identical on all four tapes. Our pilot procedures revealed these tapes to be credible as psychotherapy sessions and satisfactory depictions of the various attraction-disclosure combinations. Our two control conditions may be described as the Neutral Tape and No Tape Conditions. The Neutral Tape Condition consisted of a discussion between two (unidentified) people about the nature of psychotherapy, what kinds of people typically receive it, the professionals offering it, etc. This tape sought to control for the attraction-disclosure manipulations combined. This tape and the four modeling tapes were identical in length. The No Tape Condition sought to control for attentional and related aspects of the act of tape listening.

The study's predictions were that patients exposed to a high attraction model would later display greater attraction to their own interviewer than would patients exposed to either a low attraction model, a neutral tape, or no tape. Similarly, exposure to a high-disclosing model was predicted to lead to greater disclosure in an actual interview than was exposure to a low-disclosing model, a neutral tape, or no tape.

The 84 patients were randomly assigned to the study's six conditions. For patients assigned to the four modeling conditions, experimental procedures began by each patient being given (by an E unaware of the study's hypotheses) the following instructions:

> In recent years, more and more people experiencing emotional and psychological problems related to alcoholism have been obtaining help from psychotherapists. We are interested in learning more about psychotherapy and the reactions of alcoholics to this form of treatment.
>
> In order to obtain information concerning alcoholics' reactions to therapy, we are going to play a tape of part of an actual psychotherapy session that took place in another state. This recording is from an initial therapy session with an alcoholic patient that took place in a hospital. By the way, it's important to mention that this patient has given us his permission to use his tape for these purposes. Here is some of his background:
>
> This patient was in his mid-to-late thirties, and before coming to the hospital he was just about at the end of his rope. His family had threatened to leave him; he was losing his job; and he was about one step removed from total social and economic ruin. However, since this recording of his initial therapy session was made, he has shown great improvement. He has since been discharged from the hospital; he has obtained a well-paying job, and one which he says he enjoys; he has been able to stay dry, according to him, 'without too much trouble;' and he's reported lately that he's beginning to get back with his family.
>
> This history of the patient you are about to hear on the tape is true, but we know that 'success stories' like this don't happen every day. Nevertheless, we would like to find ways of treating alcoholism so that these successes will happen more often.
>
> One way to begin to find out why this patient was so successful in therapy is to start by looking at his first therapy session.
>
> As you listen to the tape, we would like you to put yourself in the place of a patient and imagine how you, as a patient, would react to a similar situation.

These pretape instructions sought to optimize the patient's perceptions of the model as being similar to him in background and personality, as being rewarded for his behavior, and as being successful in his efforts—in response to the frequent finding in the modeling research literature that reward consequences to the model influence the amount of observer-modeling which occurs. Each subject then listened to the taped therapy session appropriate for his experimental condition. The same procedure held for the Neutral Tape Condition patients, except that their pretape instructions were:

> In recent years, more and more people experiencing emotional and psychological problems related to alcoholism have been obtaining help from psychotherapists. We are interested in learning more about psychotherapy and the reactions of alcoholics to this form of treatment.
>
> In order to obtain information concerning alcoholics' reactions to therapy, we are going to play a tape in which two people talk about psychotherapy. Please listen carefully.

No Tape Condition patients participated in none of the above procedures, and began their study participation with the second (interview) phase of the investigation. For these patients and, after tape listening, for patients in the five tape conditions, E introduced the interviewer (another E) who stated:

> I would like to ask you some questions about yourself and I would like you to answer them as honestly and as truthfully as you can. As you can see, what we say in here will be tape-recorded. However, the recordings will be held in strictest confidence. No one else here in the hospital will hear what you say unless you request it. OK?

Each study patient then participated in an individual intake-like interview during which he was asked exactly the same questions which had been addressed to the patient on the four modeling tapes. These questions were:

> a. I wonder if you could tell me what you see as the causes of your drinking problem?
> b. Now, try to describe to me what you see as your strong points and your weak points.
> c. Now I'd like you to tell me the kinds of things that get you angry. . . . What are some of the things you do about your anger; how do you handle it?
> d. What about the kinds of things that get you anxious, or fearful?
> e. Now, I'd like you to tell me what your parents were like. . . . If you had a choice, in what way would your parents be different?
> f. There's one more question I'd like to ask. Most people have some sort of sexual problem. I wonder if you could tell me what sort of difficulties you've had in this area?

Following this interview, the first E administered a CPRQ to each patient. This completed the study's experimental procedures.

The tape-recorded interviews were content-analyzed for disclosure following Ashby *et al.*'s (1) content-analysis procedures.[1] These data and the CPRQ attraction data constituted the study's dependent variable information. Preliminary to data analysis relevant to the study's hypotheses, a correlational analysis was performed between the study's dependent variable data and an array of demographic information obtained on each patient. The purpose of this analysis was to identify any variables usable for adjustment purposes in a covariance analysis. One such variable, IQ, was identified as a significant premanipulation correlate of subsequent attraction scores (Pearson $r = .23$, $df = 82$, $p < .05$). The subsequent analysis of covariance on attraction scores, however, failed to reveal any significant main or interaction effects. Thus, in contrast to Orenstein's (35) successful demonstration with YAVIS subjects, this study failed to find an attraction enhancement effect by modeling with NON-YAVIS patients. Analysis of variance on the study's disclosure data, in contrast, did yield a significant overall effect ($F = 2.36$, $df = 5, 78$, $p < .05$). Tukey (a) tests performed on all possible cell comparisons revealed that patients exposed to the high disclosure model were significantly more disclosing in their own interview than were patients exposed to the low disclosure model, but only when both models displayed low attraction toward the taped therapist. In addition, high disclosure modeling led to significantly greater patient disclosure than did no tape listening.

The results of the Orenstein and Liberman investigations demonstrate the likely viability of modeling procedures when used for psychotherapy-relevant purposes. However, as seems the case with regard to most other means of attraction enhancement examined in our research program, such viability appears much more substantial for YAVIS-like subjects or patients. Liberman's disclosure-modeling results do, however, contrast with those emerging when the attraction enhancement procedure being examined was direct structuring, trait structuring, status or effort manipulations—all of which were essentially unsuccessful with NON-YAVIS populations. We would suggest, therefore, that further investigation of the usefulness of modeling procedures in psychotherapeutic contexts involving patients analogous to Liberman's appears to be a potentially fruitful endeavor.

[1] Interjudge reliability (Pearson r) = .93.

References

1. Ashby, J. D., Ford, D. H., Guerney, B. G., Jr., & Guerney, L. Effects on clients of a reflective and a leading type of psychotherapy. *Psychological Monographs*, 1957, 7, 1–32.

2. Bandura, A. Behavior modification through modeling procedures. In L. Krasner and L. P. Ullmann (Eds.), *Research in behavior modification*. New York: Holt, Rinehart & Winston, 1965. Pp. 310–340.

3. Bandura, A. Vicarious processes: A case of no-trial learning. In L. Berkowitz (Ed.), *Advances in experimental social psychology*. Vol. 2. New York: Academic Press, 1965. Pp. 3–57.

4. Bandura, A. Modeling approaches to the modification of phobic disorders. Ciba Foundation Symposium. *The role of learning in psychotherapy*. London: Churchill, 1968.

5. Bandura, A., Blanchard, E. B., & Ritter, B. The relative efficacy of desensitization and modeling approaches for inducing behavioral, affective, and attitudinal change. *Journal of Personality and Social Psychology*, in press.

6. Bandura, A., Grusec, J. E., & Menlove, F. L. Vicarious extinction of avoidance behavior. *Journal of Personality and Social Psychology*, 1967, 5, 16–23.

7. Bandura, A. & Kupers, C. J. The transmission of patterns of self-reinforcement through modeling. *Journal of Abnormal and Social Psychology*, 1964, 69, 1–9.

8. Bandura, A. & McDonald, F. J. Influence of social reinforcement and the behavior of models in shaping children's moral judgments. *Journal of Abnormal and Social Psychology*, 1963, 67, 274–281.

9. Bandura, A. & Walters, R. H. *Social learning and personality development*. New York: Holt, Rinehart & Winston, 1963.

10. Berger, S. M. Incidental learning through vicarious reinforcement. *Psychological Reports*, 1961, 9, 477–491.

11. Byron, J. H. & Test, M. Models and helping: Naturalistic studies in aiding behavior. *Journal of Personality and Social Psychology*, 1967, 6, 400–407.

12. Chittenden, G. E. An experimental study in measuring and modifying assertive behavior in young children. *Monographs Social Research in Child Development*, 1942, 7, No. 31.

13. DeCharms, R. & Rosenbaum, M. E. The problem of vicarious experience. In D. Willner (Ed.), *Decisions, values and groups*. New York: Pergamon Press, 1960. Pp. 267–277.

14. Flanders, J. P. A review of research on imitative behavior. *Psychological Bulletin*, 1968, 69, 316–337.

15. Friedman, P. H. The effects of modeling and role playing on assertive behavior. Unpublished doctoral dissertation, University of Wisconsin, 1968.

16. Geer, J. & Turteltaub, A. Fear reduction following observation of a model. *Journal of Personality and Social Psychology*, 1967, **6**, 327–331.

17. Gelfand, D. M. The influence of self-esteem on rate of verbal conditioning and social matching behavior. *Journal of Abnormal and Social Psychology*, 1962, **65**, 259–265.

18. Gula, M. Boy's House—The use of a group for observation and treatment. *Mental Hygiene*, 1944, **28**, 430–437.

19. Hingtgen, J. N., Coulter, S. K., & Churchill, D. W. Intensive reinforcement of imitative behavior in mute autistic children. *Archives of General Psychiatry*, 1967, **17**, 36–43.

20. Hovland, C. I., Janis, I. L., & Kelley, H. H. *Communication and persuasion*. New Haven: Yale University Press, 1953.

21. Jack, L. M. An experimental study of ascendant behavior in preschool children. *University of Iowa Studies in Child Welfare*, 1934, **9**, 7–65.

22. Jones, M. C. The elimination of children's fears. *Journal of Experimental Psychology*, 1924, **7**, 383–390.

23. Krumboltz, J. D. & Schroeder, W. W. Promoting career planning through reinforcement. *Personnel and Guidance Journal*, 1965, **44**, 19–26.

24. Lesser, G. S. & Abelson, R. P. Personality correlates of persuasibility in children. In I. L. Janis & C. I. Hovland (Eds.), *Personality and persuasibility*. New Haven: Yale University Press, 1959. Pp. 187–206.

25. Liberman, B. The effect of modeling procedures on attraction and disclosure in a psychotherapy analogue. Unpublished doctoral dissertation, Syracuse University, 1970.

26. Lovaas, O. I. Some studies on the treatment of childhood schizophrenia. In J. Schlein (Ed.), *Research in psychotherapy*. Vol. 3, Washington, D.C.: American Psychological Association, 1968.

27. Maccoby, E. E. & Wilson, W. C. Identification and observational learning from films. *Journal of Abnormal and Social Psychology*, 1957, **55**, 76–87.

28. Marlatt, G. A. Exposure to model and task ambiguity as determinants of verbal behavior in an interview. Paper presented at Western Psychological Association, San Diego, 1968.

29. Marlatt, G. A. Vicarious and direct reinforcement control of verbal behavior in an interview setting. Unpublished doctoral dissertation, Indiana University, 1968.

30. Miller, N. E. & Dollard, J. *Social learning and imitation*. New Haven: Yale University Press, 1941.

31. Mischel, W. Father-absence and delay of gratification: Cross-cultural

comparisons. *Journal of Abnormal and Social Psychology*, 1961, **63**, 116–124.

32. Mowrer, O. H. *Learning theory and personality dynamics.* New York: Ronald Press, 1950.

33. Mowrer, O. H. *Learning theory and behavior.* New York: Wiley, 1960.

34. Myrick, R. D. Effect of a model on verbal behavior in counseling. *Journal of Counseling Psychology*, 1969, **16**, 185–190.

35. Orenstein, R. The influence of self-esteem on modeling behavior in a psychotherapy analogue. Unpublished master's thesis, Syracuse University, 1969.

36. Page, M. L. The modification of ascendant behavior in preschool children. *University of Iowa Studies in Child Welfare*, 1935, **12**, 1–69.

37. Rosenbaum, M. E., Horne, W. C., & Chalmers, D. K. Level of self-esteem and the learning of imitation and non-imitation. *Journal of Personality*, 1962, **30**, 147–156.

38. Sarason, I. G. Verbal learning, modeling, and juvenile delinquency. *American Psychologist*, 1968, **23**, 254–266.

39. Sarason, I. G. & Gazer, V. J. Social influence techniques in clinical and community psychology. In C. D. Spielberger (Ed.), *Current topics in clinical and community psychology.* New York: Academic Press, 1969. Pp. 1–66.

40. Schwartz, A. N. & Hawkins, H. L. Patient models and affect statements in group therapy. *Proceedings of the 73rd Annual Convention of the American Psychological Association.* Washington, D.C.: American Psychological Association, 1965. Pp. 265-266.

41. Simonson, N. R. Self-disclosure and attraction in psychotherapy. Paper presented at Eastern Psychological Association, Philadelphia, 1969.

42. Truax, C. B. The process of group psychotherapy. *Psychological Monographs*, 1961, **25**, Whole No. 511.

43. Truax, C. B. & Wargo, D. G. Effects of vicarious therapy pretraining and alternate sessions on outcome in group psychotherapy with outpatients. *Journal of Consulting and Clinical Psychology*, 1969, **33**, 440–447.

44. Walters, R. H., Bowen, N. V., & Parke, R. D. Experimentally induced disinhibition of sexual responses. Unpublished manuscript, University of Waterloo, 1963.

45. Whalen, C. The effects of a model and instructions on group's verbal behavior. *Journal of Consulting and Clinical Psychology*, 1969, **33**, 509–521.

Chapter IX

Matching

In our introductory chapter we began to examine the broadly negative consequences for the psychotherapeutic interaction of an ill-matched therapist-patient pair. Our focus at that point was upon divergencies in psychological-mindedness, role expectations, and locus of responsibility for psychotherapeutic change. In the present chapter, we will focus upon certain other psychological dimensions of therapist-patient similarity and dissimilarity relevant to optimal pairing. Our extrapolatory base for this effort will be social-psychological studies of dyadic compatibility. Ours, however, is far from the first attempt to discern the effects upon psychotherapeutic variables of matching of patient and therapist. Thus it is instructive that we examine first the existing literature on the therapeutic implications of therapist-patient similarity and dissimilarity.

Studies of Therapist-Patient Matching

Tuma and Gustad (57) predicted that the degree of patient growth in self-awareness over the course of therapy would be positively associated with the degree of therapist-patient personality similarity. Therapist-patient personality similarity was examined in terms of manifest anxiety (55), authoritarianism (2), and the scale dimensions of the California Personality Inventory (23).[1] Their prediction was clearly confirmed on the dimensions of therapist and patient dominance, social presence, and social participation, with supporting trends in the areas of anxiety and self-acceptance. Thus, with regard to this investigation, we note a series of personality dimensions on which therapist-patient similarity is relevant to patient change, as well as several dimensions on which similarity appears unrelated to growth in patient self-awareness. In an independent investigation, Vogel (58) confirmed one of Tuma and Gustad's findings in that he, too, found no relationship between the similarity of therapist and patient authoritarianism and patient change. Rosenthal (42) and Welkowitz et al. (59) have

---

[1] Tolerance, flexibility, dominance, social participation, social presence, impulsivity, self-acceptance, good impression.

reported positive relationships between patient change and similarity in patient and therapist values. These findings, however, may well represent effect more than cause. Value and change measures were *both* obtained in these two studies after therapy was well underway. Thus it seems likely that these studies do not suggest that initial value similarity enhances patient change, but instead (as Rosenthal proposes) that, over the course of successful psychotherapy, patients' values tend to converge with those of their therapists. Pepinsky and Karst (39) have independently demonstrated this convergence phenomenon.

On other dimensions of personality, investigators have predicted that more favorable therapeutic consequences would follow from therapist-patient dissimilarity or, more exactly, complementarity. Bare (4) tested this notion on the need dimensions of self-abasement, dominance, aggression, original thinking, and exhibitionism. Need measurement was conducted pretherapy, change measurement posttherapy. Her results were basically confirmatory, and were most robust on the dimensions of original thinking and aggressiveness. Snyder (52) has independently reported related results in substantiation of a need-complementarity position. Bare comments that, "Dissimilarity, rather than similarity was much more frequently associated with high ratings of success. Similarity in an interpersonal relationship can have a negative effect by pulling reciprocal responses" (p. 422). This reciprocity effect suggested by Bare has indeed been demonstrated in independent studies by Russell (44) and Heller *et al.* (25).

Yet a third predictive position has appeared in the psychotherapy research literature regarding optimal therapist-patient matching. The most favorable therapeutic consequences will follow, this position holds, when therapist and patient characteristics of a given kind are neither highly similar nor highly dissimilar. Carson and Heine (17) reasoned that if ". . . psychotherapeutic success depends upon the therapist being able to achieve an optimum balance between empathy and objectivity in dealing with his patient, then the relationship between patient-therapist similarity and therapeutic success might well be of curvilinear form" (17, p. 38). The investigators determined the degree of pretherapy similarity in the MMPI profiles of 60 therapist-patient pairs, and then related these similarity indices to supervisor ratings of outcome. Their prediction of a significant, curvilinear relationship was substantiated. It should be noted, however, that Carson and Lewellyn (18) were unable to replicate this finding—although it remains unclear whether the failure to replicate was due to the unreliability of the finding per se or the fact that the outcome ratings in the second study came not for the supervisors but from the therapists themselves.

Mendelsohn and his co-workers (34, 35, 36, 37) have reported a series of relevant investigations. In each of these studies, both therapists and patients completed the Myers-Briggs Type Indicator (47), a personality test which yields scores on four Jungian dimensions: extroversion-introversion, sensation-intuition, thinking-feeling, and judgment-perception. In all three investigations, results indicated that moderate similarity between therapist and patient on these dimensions was most highly associated with therapy duration. Dissimilarity was a consistent predictor of early termination. High similarity, in partial contrast, was associated with variable lengths of treatment. Some high similarity patients remained in therapy as long as those evidencing moderate similarity with their therapist; other high similarity patients terminated very rapidly. The investigators speculate that high levels of therapist-patient similarity may have resulted in the therapist prematurely exploring highly conflictual material or, alternatively, may have led the patient to feel overly transparent. In Carson and Heine's (17) terms, the necessary relationship between objectivity and empathy was likely not present. Thus, while in highly dissimilar pairs the decision to terminate was usually made jointly, patients in highly similar pairs either remained in therapy for an extended time or unilaterally terminated very early.

What broad conclusions can be drawn from these several investigations? A wide array of personality dimensions are represented, rarely the same ones in two different studies. Similarity, dissimilarity, and curvilinearity predictions were tested, each type of prediction finding only partial support. In a manner which, interestingly, is highly consistent with what others have concluded from investigations of mate selection in courtship and marriage (32, 56), it seems clear that the least appropriate conclusion one might draw from this research is that any single orientation is comprehensively valid. The conclusions most appropriate are very likely trait-specific, such that on certain dimensions a high level of similarity is facilitative, on others complementarity augments therapeutic progress, and on yet others a moderate degree of therapist-patient similarity is most optimal for matching purposes. One could build, perhaps, toward a rather complex pattern analysis in which findings from research such as that examined above were distilled, combined, and weighted in such a manner that therapist-patient pairings were made on the basis of similarity on several traits, dissimilarity or complementarity on several others, and moderate similarity on yet others. Such a composite matching index, even if possible, would be of questionable practicality in clinical settings and, furthermore, is currently largely an abstraction in terms of the relative paucity of relevant research. An approximation to such a complete instrument does exist, however. It is an instrument whose psychometric structure reflects *both* similarity and complementarity. The interpersonal dimensions upon which it focuses are the very dimensions others have held to be central to the psychotherapeutic interaction (20, 33, 52). Its predictive usefulness has been demonstrated in a wide variety of nonpsychotherapeutic contexts and on a large number of diverse "outcome" criteria. Furthermore, we would predict, these criteria are of substantial extrapolatory relevance for purposes of therapist-patient matching. We refer here to the Fundamental Interpersonal Relations Orientation Scale (FIRO) developed by Schutz (48, 49).

Fundamental Interpersonal
Relations Orientation

Schutz's goal in developing the FIRO was to construct an instrument useful for pairing people for maximum compatibility in a wide variety of interpersonal exchange contexts. He postulated three types of needs as central to such exchanges: inclusion, control, and affection. The more two people are similar in the importance these needs have for them, Schutz holds, the more compatible they will be. Compatibility, he adds, also requires complementarity with regard to how much the members of the dyad wish to originate or receive the behaviors representing the need. Thus dyadic compatibility based upon the FIRO reflects both interpersonal similarity and complementarity on the three need dimensions. Concretely, therefore, the FIRO consists of six subscales, i.e., expressed and wanted behavior in the areas of inclusion, control, and affection.

Schutz defines the interpersonal need for *inclusion* as the need to establish and maintain a satisfactory relationship with people with respect to interaction and association. Positive inclusion in an interpersonal relationship is reflected by such terms as associate, interest, belong, pay attention to, companion, and join. Negative inclusion is connoted by exclude, isolate, lonely, detached, abandon, ignore. On the FIRO Scales, expressed (originator) inclusion behavior is represented by such items as "I make efforts to include other people in my activities and to get them to include me in theirs." And, "I try to belong, to join social groups, to be with people as much as possible." Wanted (receiver) inclusion is reflected, for example, in, "I want other people to include me in their activities and to invite me to belong, even if I do not make an effort to be included."

The need for *control* is defined as the need to establish and maintain a satisfactory relationship with people with respect to power and control. Schutz notes that control behavior refers to the decision-making process in dyads. Terms associated with positive control are power, authority, dominance, influence, superior, and leader. Negative control is connoted by follower, resistance, submissive, rebellion, henpecked. Test items representing expressed control behavior include, "I try to exert control and influence over things" and, "I take charge of things and tell other people what to do." On the receiving pole (wanted control) are such items as, "I want others to control and influence me" and, "I want other people to tell me what to do."

The interpersonal need for *affection* is the need to establish and maintain a satisfactory relationship with others with respect to love and affection. Positive connotations of this need are love, like, emotionally close, personal, friend, and intimate. Negative connotations include hate, cool, dislike, emotionally distant, and rejecting. On the FIRO, expressed affection is exemplified by, "I make efforts to become close to people" and, "I express friendly and affectionate behavior and try to be personal and intimate." Wanted behavior in this need area is exemplified by, "I want others to express friendly and affectionate feelings toward me and to try to become close to me."

Using the six FIRO scores, four compatibility indices may be determined for any two individuals. The more each person's expressed behavior on the three need dimensions matches the other person's wished-for behavior, the greater is their *reciprocal compatibility*. *Originator compatibility* is determined by comparing the degree to which each member of the dyad likes to originate versus receive behavior in each of the three need areas. Such compatibility is diminished if both persons prefer to originate behaviors or to receive behaviors in the three need areas. The more two people agree on how involved they want to become in each of the need areas, not just in dyads but also more broadly (as in group contexts), the greater the *interchange compatibility*. Reciprocal, originator, and interchange compatibility scores are summed to yield a *total compatibility* index.

In the course of constructing and seeking validational evidence for the FIRO, Schutz and his co-workers conducted a number of investigations relevant to our present extrapolatory efforts. Each of the studies examined below had as its intent the examination of behavioral or interpersonal consequents of FIRO-determined dyadic compatibility. Alexander *et al.* (3), in one of these validational studies, administered the FIRO and a sociometric instrument to a sample of fraternity members. Each type of compatibility score for all possible dyads was determined and related to several types of sociometric choices. These sociometric dimensions included choice of roommate, traveling companion, house manager, etc. As the investigators had predicted, a series of highly significant relationships emerged between the sociometric choices made and each of the four types of compatibility indices. In two related but independent investigations, Bennis and Peabody (5) and Gross (24) demonstrated similarly significant associations between level of dyadic compatibility in small groups and the group's level of cohesiveness.

In addition to examination of such attraction-relevant consequences of interpersonal compatibility as sociometric choice and group cohesiveness, productivity criteria of different types have been studied. Abelow (1) constituted 100 randomly selected undergraduates into compatible and incompatible five-man groups. Each group met 14 times over a six-week period during which they engaged in a wide variety of tasks, all of which demanded group effort and cooperation for optimal success. Across tasks, the compatible groups were significantly more productive than were groups constituted based upon low FIRO compatibility. Using both different kinds of subjects and tasks, Rudner (43) was able to replicate this finding. Hutcherson (26) determined the interchange and originator compatibility separately on the three need dimensions for eight male junior high school teachers and 747 of their students. He found that academic achievement was positively related to compatibility in the control areas, negatively with regard to inclusion and affection. Focusing on productivity of yet another kind, Sapolsky (45) examined the effects on verbal conditioning of interpersonal compatibility between experimenter and subject. The FIRO was administered to 300 potential subjects, from whom 30 were selected who were either highly compatible or highly incompatible with the five participating experimenters. The conditioning task followed Taffel's (54) procedure in which E used "mmm-hmm" to reinforce sentences which S began with "I" or "We." Dependent variable measurement focused upon the effects of such reinforcement on increasing the use of these personal pronouns. The performance of Ss in compatible S-E pairs was significantly higher than that of Ss incompatible with their Es. When these latter Ss were given the opportunity to respond with their (incompatible) Es not present, they performed at as high a level as Ss in compatible S-E pairs. Thus, the negative effect of incompatible matching was upon performance, and not learning. Sapolsky comments:

Krasner has pointed out the similarity between the verbal reinforcement by E in conditioning procedures and the therapist's use
of "mmm-hmm" in the psychotherapy setting. The findings of the
present study suggest that the subtle cues provided by a therapist's use of "mmm-hmm" are likely to be effective only when the
interpersonal relationship between him and the patient is positive
or compatible. (45, p. 246)

The interpersonal compatibility studies examined thus far constitute
the beginnings of the very type of analogical bridge we discussed in
our introductory chapter. Almost all of these studies were conducted
in a laboratory context, used nonpatient, human subjects, and focused
upon the effects of dyadic compatibility on change processes relevant
to but somewhat removed from psychotherapy. As a group, these studies provide a solid foundation from which further investigative steps
towards direct focus upon psychotherapy may be taken. A second
investigation conducted by Sapolsky (46) takes just such a step.
Moving away from the laboratory, he examined the relationship
between doctor-patient compatibility and patient change. Twenty-five
psychiatric inpatients and the three psychiatric residents to whom they
had been randomly assigned participated in the investigation. Each
participant completed the FIRO at the beginning of the investigation.
Patients remained in the hospital an average of 200 days, during
which time they underwent a variety of treatment procedures, only
one of which was psychotherapy (an hour and one-half per week).
Immediately after discharge, patient improvement ratings were made
for each patient by the supervising psychiatrist. These ratings correlated significantly ($r = .45$, $df = 20$, $p < .05$) with doctor-patient
total compatibility scores from the FIRO. This correlational finding
completes our task of setting the stage for our investigation of FIRO
compatibility and therapist-patient attraction. Sapolsky's contribution
is the important demonstration of a significant relationship between
therapist-patient compatibility and a psychotherapeutic change process. As we noted in our introductory chapter, and as is true of Sapolsky's study, a great deal of the research conducted on the psychotherapeutic relationship permits specification of degree of association, but
yields little or no evidence regarding causation or directionality.
Correlational studies are necessary to the development of a research
area, are often highly illuminating, and frequently are the only kind of
investigation it is practical to conduct in a given setting. But for a
domain to develop fully, manipulative investigations are often vital,
the specification of causation often crucial. It is this sentiment to
which our own research sought to respond.

Interpersonal Compatibility
in Psychotherapy

Gassner (22) predicted that therapists and patients matched for high compatibility based on the FIRO would rate their relationship more favorably than would therapists and patients matched for low compatibility. She also predicted greater behavior change in the patients matched for high compatibility, as compared to low compatibility match or control patients. The therapist population consisted of 24 ministers participating in a 12-week training program in pastoral counseling at a state mental hospital. Twenty-two were men; two were women. Their average age was 27. Prior to selection of the patient sample, a survey of the hospital was conducted in order to identify those patients who were able to read and who were likely to remain hospitalized for the duration of the pastoral training program. The FIRO was administered to the 150 patients thus identified. Testing was conducted on the ward in groups of three to eight patients. At this point in time, the FIRO was also administered to the ministers. Our selection goal was to obtain one high compatible and one low compatible patient for each therapist. The total compatibility score for every possible therapist-patient pair was determined and the most compatible patient and least compatible patient for each therapist were selected. From the remaining 102 patients who had taken the FIRO, 24 were randomly selected to constitute a no treatment control group. Patients in the three conditions (Compatible Match, Incompatible Match, Control) were comparable with regard to age, proportion of males and females, number of years hospitalized, and diagnosis (primarily schizophrenic). Since, with the exception of Sapolsky's (46)

Table 9.1
Test-Retest Reliability Coefficients for the FIRO

Subscale	r
Expressed Inclusion	.93
Wanted Inclusion	.53
Expressed Control	.72
Wanted Control	.95
Expressed Affection	.79
Wanted Affection	.67

study, the FIRO had not been used previously with a psychotic population, we retested 10 randomly selected patients after a two-week period to determine test-retest reliability. The correlations between initial testing and retesting for each FIRO Scale are presented in Table 9.1.

Psychotherapy sessions for each patient-therapist pair were held twice per week for 12 weeks. After the third and eleventh weeks of treatment for each therapist-patient pair, the patient completed a CPRQ and the therapist completed a TPRQ. It will be recalled that, in addition to relationship predictions, Gassner hypothesized greater patient change in the high compatible match than in either patients matched for low compatibility or in control patients. To test this hypothesis, a few days before the patients were scheduled for their first interview the ward nurse most familiar with each patient was asked to rate the patient on the MACC Behavioral Adjustment Scale, Form II (19). This scale consists of 20 questions concerned with mood, cooperation, communication, and social contact. Its demonstrated reliability and validity appear more than adequate. The same nurses rerated each patient after the therapist had seen him for three weeks. Control patients were also rerated at this time.

This investigation's results were as follows. Patients matched for high compatibility with their therapists, in contrast to those matched for low compatibility, evaluated the therapy relationship significantly more favorably after both the third and eleventh weeks of treatment. These results are presented in Table 9.2.

Table 9.2

Relationship Ratings from Patients Matched for
High and Low Compatibility

	After 3 Weeks (CPRQ$_1$)			After 11 Weeks (CPRQ$_2$)		
	X	SD	t	X	SD	t
High Compatibility	52.0	8.05		53.3	6.72	
			2.33*			2.15*
Low Compatibility	45.0	13.69		45.7	15.73	

* $df = 23$, $p < .05$.

The analogous relationship ratings obtained from the therapists yielded no significant between-condition differences. These results are presented in Table 9.3.

The findings presented in Tables 9.2 and 9.3 are based upon total

Table 9.3

Relationship Ratings from Patients Matched for
High and Low Compatibility

	After 3 Weeks (TPRQ₁)			After 11 Weeks (TPRQ₂)		
	X	SD	T	X	SD	t
High Compatibility	128	37.30		134	26.35	
			1.33			.80
Low Compatibility	115	31.81		126	35.40	

compatibility matchings. It is also worthwhile examining the compatibility subscores as they relate to the attraction ratings. These results are presented in Table 9.4.

Table 9.4

Correlation of Relationship Scores with Compatibility Subscores

Relationship Score	Reciprocal Compatibility	Originator Compatibility	Interchange Compatibility
CPRQ₁	— .43*†	— .08	— .39*
CPRQ₂	— .33*	.01	— .34*
TPRQ₁	— .09	.08	— .10
TPRQ₂	— .09	— .02	— .08

* $df = 47, p < .05$.
† Since the lower a dyad's FIRO score, the greater the compatibility, negative correlations are consistent with our hypothesis.

Thus, after both 3 and 11 weeks of therapy, reciprocal and interchange compatibility relate significantly to patient relationship ratings. No analogous significant relationships existed between the compatibility subscores and the therapists' ratings.

This investigation's final major hypothesis predicted that patients matched for high compatibility with their therapists would evidence more behavior change than patients matched for low compatibility or control patients. In Table 9.5 are presented the mean pretherapy and third week MACC ratings completed on all study patients by the ward nurses.

Although the trend of the change scores is in the predicted direction, none of the within—or between—condition comparisons on the

Table 9.5
Mean MACC Scores

Condition	Pretherapy	Third Week	Difference
High Compatibility	57.6	59.9	2.30
Low Compatibility	52.3	52.7	.36
Control	56.9	56.6	— .03

above data reached acceptable levels of significance. Unfortunately, summer vacations and both personnel turnover and reassignment prevented us from obtaining behavioral ratings at the eleventh week of therapy, when they might well have been considerably more meaningful.

In summary of this investigation, its major result is the demonstration of a significant effect of compatibility matching upon patient attraction to the therapist, a finding clearly consistent with the social-psychological research from which this study grew. The failure to find a similar effect of matching on the therapists' ratings was discussed with the therapists themselves after the study was completed. Their introspections regarding what transpired vis à vis their low compatibility patients suggest the operation of some sort of overcompensatory process. Several of the therapists reported becoming aware of negative feelings toward such patients, experiencing guilt in response to these feelings, and also deciding that if they didn't help such "unlikable" patients, no one would. Thus, they explained, both these feelings toward themselves and toward the patient led them to redouble their therapeutic efforts. And, their TPRQ scores would suggest, also led them to reevaluate their feelings toward the low compatibility patients.

To this point in the present chapter we have examined in our own research and that conducted by others the consequences for attraction enhancement of matching on an array of personality and interpersonal need dimensions. Social psychologists have also devoted considerable research attention to the attraction-enhancement consequences of matching individuals for attitude similarity within both the dyad and small groups. It is this literature to which we will now turn, as well as to our own extrapolatory research which grew therefrom.

Attitude Similarity

In both laboratory and field settings, social psychologists have devoted a great deal of attention to the effects of attitude similarity upon interpersonal attraction. As early as 1937, Winslow (60) reported a high positive relationship between friendship choices and attitude similarity. Richardson (41), in 1940, was similarly able to demonstrate a high degree of relatedness between friendship patterns and similarity of attitudes. A number of other early investigators have reported concurring correlational findings (6, 21, 40, 50, 51). More recent investigations have further substantiated and clarified this relationship. One especially noteworthy characteristic of most of this research, however, is that in the vast majority of studies inquiring into the attitude similarity-attraction relationship, no actual meeting takes place between the subject and the other person whose attitudes are purported to be similar to his. Thus Jones and Dougherty's (27) subjects listened to tape recordings on which the stimulus person described his political orientation; Worchel and McCormick (61) had their subjects overhear the stimulus person talking to someone else in the next experimental booth; Smith (51) and Novak and Lerner (38) gave their subjects attitude scales supposedly filled out by the stimulus person, filled out to be either highly similar or dissimilar to that filled out by the subject. Kiesler and Goldberg (29) simply told each subject, after he had completed an attitude scale himself, that he was similar or dissimilar to a person he would hear on a tape and evaluate. In each of these "no meeting" studies, a significant relationship was obtained between perceived attitude similarity and subject attraction to the stimulus person.

These characteristics, i.e., no contact between subject and stimulus person, and positive findings, are also typically the case in the extensive research in this area conducted by Byrne and his research group (7, 8, 10, 12, 14). Byrne's initial study involved administering a general attitude scale to Introductory Psychology students. Approximately two weeks later, these students were asked to participate in an experiment in which they were given a copy of the same attitude scale purportedly filled out by a student from another class. In actuality, the experimenter had filled out each scale so that it represented attitudes highly similar or dissimilar to those originally expressed by the subjects. Subjects were informed that the purpose of the study was to determine how much they could learn about another person solely on the basis of his attitude scale responses. On a series of postmeasures, results indicated that subjects in the similar attitudes condition were significantly more attracted to the stimulus person than were those led to believe they and the stimulus person held dissimilar attitudes.

Using essentially the same paradigm, Byrne et al. (12) have obtained the same positive results when subjects were Job Corps trainees, or hospitalized surgical, alcoholic, or schizophrenic patients; and across attitude items varying in importance or interest to the subjects. Thus, within the limitations inherent in this "no meeting" design, attitude similarity and interpersonal attraction appear to covary in a consistent and robust manner. The few investigations in which the subject and stimulus person were actually provided with an opportunity to meet and interact following similarity-dissimilarity manipulation have yielded somewhat more equivocal results. While tending to support the attitude similarity-attraction relationship, such results have been considerably less reliable (28, 30). Both types of studies, however, combine to suggest that to the extent that directionality can be specified, attitude similarity *causes* increased interpersonal attraction.

Attitude Similarity and Vocational Counseling

Our first attitude similarity study was conducted at our Vocational Counseling Center. Forty clients were randomly assigned to three experimental conditions, such conditions being defined in terms of the purported percent attitude agreement between client and counselor. Upon arrival at the Center, each client was handed a copy of the Student Opinion Questionnaire (the F Scale) by the intake worker and told: "This is an opinion inventory which we have all of our clients fill out. It helps us see if the amount of opinion similarity between a client and his counselor effects the counseling that goes on between them." After filling out the Questionnaire, and waiting a short time for the intake worker to score it, one of three messages was then communicated to the client:

High Similarity Condition

You and Mr. _____ agree on almost every item, 88 percent. That's rather unusual. If you'll wait here, he'll see you soon.

Moderate Similarity Condition

You and Mr. _____ agree on 50 percent of the items. If you'll wait here, he'll see you soon.

Low Similarity Condition

You and Mr. _____ agree on only 12 percent of the items. That's rather unusual. If you'll wait here, he'll see you soon.

Each client then participated in his initial counseling interview, after which he completed a CPRQ. At this point in time, the counselor filled out a TPRQ. On neither of these dimensions, client attraction to the counselor or counselor attraction to the client, were there any significant between-condition differences.

Similarly negative results emerged in a subsequent study which sought to widen the spread between the similar and dissimilar manipulations. Working in the same Center, with a new sample of 50 clients, three experimental conditions were constituted. High Similarity was represented by 100 percent agreement, Low Similarity by zero percent agreement, and we also included a No Manipulation control group. After completing the Opinion Questionnaire, clients were again asked to wait while the intake worker scored it. This time was used by the intake worker to complete another copy of the Questionnaire in such a manner that, with regard to positiveness or negativeness of response, it agreed 100 or zero percent with that completed by the client. This copy was then handed to the client who was told:

> We find that counseling goes better not only if your counselor has a good idea of what you think about the issues on the Opinion Questionnaire, but also if we give the client a chance to learn how the counselor feels about the same issues. This is the same Questionnaire you filled out, but this one was filled out by your counselor, Mr. _____. Take a few minutes and read it thoroughly.

High and Low Similarity Condition clients then spent seven minutes reading this Questionnaire. This feedback process was omitted for control clients. Following the initial interview, CPRQ and TPRQ measures were obtained. As noted above, no significant between-condition differences were obtained.[2]

Two possible bases for these negative findings may be considered. In both of these investigations, in contrast to the vast proportion of social-psychological laboratory studies in this domain, subject and stimulus person actually meet and interact. While laboratory manipulation of attitude similarity may indeed enhance attraction *in the absence of* an actual meeting between the participants, it seems possible that the effect is not sufficiently powerful to endure in the presence of actual interaction, which at times may provide contrary evidence. Since our clients were assigned randomly to counselors in both of our investigations, it is possible that the nature of their initial interview interactions washed out any attraction-enhancing effects which the experimental manipulations might have had.

A second issue of potential relevance to our findings is that of topic

[2] As has been the case in several of our investigations, a significant correlation ($r = .40$, $p < .05$) emerged between CPRQ and TPRQ scores.

importance. Byrne has argued that agreement or disagreement between subject and stimulus person on a topic felt to be important by the subject will have a stronger effect on attraction than will agreement or disagreement on topics viewed as less important. Evidence in support of this contention is equivocal. In Byrne's original study (7), described earlier, all subjects (at the first testing session) were asked to indicate which 13 items concerned issues of greatest importance to them, and which 13 were of least importance. When the subjects returned after two weeks to be presented with the stimulus person's attitude scale, they were divided into four groups. Two of these groups, high and low similarity, were discussed earlier. The third group received scales containing similar attitudes on the issues they had previously rated important, and dissimilar on those rated unimportant. That procedure was reversed for the final experimental group. Of the six dependent variable measures, three—feelings about the stimulus person, ratings of his adjustment, and ratings of his morality—yielded significant differences favoring the high similarity-on-important-topics group. In two separate investigations, however, Byrne and Nelson (14, 15) failed to replicate this topic-importance effect. It should be noted that our choice of the F Scale as the Opinion Questionnaire in our earlier studies in this area was dictated largely by the apparent credibility of this measure for attitude measurement purposes in a vocational counseling context. Perhaps, however, the negative results of both these studies, as well as Bryne and Nelson's, is in part attributable to the possibility that the attitude dimensions involved were generally of insufficient importance to the participating clients. We sought, therefore, in our next attitude similarity study, to focus upon an attitude dimension of maximal importance to the investigation's subjects. In addition, the study was designed in such a manner as to ascertain both the separate and combined effects on attraction of attitude similarity and topic importance.

Attitude Similarity and
Topic Importance

In broad overview of this investigation, for which Cheney was the principal investigator, premeasures on a group of attitude items dealing with alcoholism as well as a variety of other issues were administered to prison inmates serving sentences for public intoxication. In a psychotherapy analogue design, the inmate subjects were asked to listen to a tape recording of a psychotherapy session. Before doing so, however, each subject was given a copy of an attitude scale purportedly completed by the therapist on the tape. These scales, implementing the attitude similarity-by-topic-importance design of the study, contained either alcoholism-relevant or alcoholism-irrelevant items and were faked to be 90 or 10 percent similar to the scale responses given earlier by the subject himself. A fifth group of inmates served as control subjects. They participated in all experimental procedures but received no information regarding the attitudes of the taped therapist. Following tape listening, all subjects completed measures dealing with their attraction to the psychotherapist. Thus the issue of topic importance is dealt with in this investigation by the presence and absence of attitude items of major importance to the participating subjects. The study's predictions were of a main effect on attraction for attitude similarity, such that the greater the structured similarity the greater the attraction; and an interaction effect on attraction for attitude similarity and topic importance, such that alcoholism items (high importance) under high similarity (90 percent agreement) would result in greater attraction enhancement than either of the other three experimental conditions or the control condition.

Subject and Materials. The study was conducted at a county penitentiary. Male inmates serving sentences for public intoxication constituted the subject pool. Inmates of this type were screened by the prison staff prior to subject selection, and only those who were sufficiently detoxicated were asked to participate in the study. Of the 79 requests thus made for voluntary participation in the study, four inmates refused. The remaining 75 inmates constituted the final subject pool. Subjects participated in the study in groups of two to five, depending on the number available on any given day. Subject assignment to experimental condition was randomly conducted.

A 15-minute tape recording of a simulated psychotherapy session, developed earlier for our investigation of trait structuring, was used for this investigation. The tape contained no statements relevant to any of the issues represented in the attitude scales. As in our other analogue investigations using a taped psychotherapy session, a series of prejudging procedures was utilized during the development of the tape to maximize its credibility as a psychotherapy session.

Items for the attitude scale used in this investigation were drawn from three sources. Twenty-seven items relevant to an array of issues were drawn from the longer scale used by Byrne and Nelson (14). Items selected from this source were those appropriate for an inmate as opposed to college student population, e.g., deleted items concerned behavior on campus, fraternities, etc. Ten items were also selected from each of two attitudes-toward-drinking scales (37, 53). The resultant 47 items were randomly ordered, placed in scale format, and administered to a pilot sample of five randomly selected inmates. The test and posttest inquiry responses of this pilot sample were utilized for final item selection. All items which caused any difficulty in understanding, and all items whose responses failed to yield at least a 60:40 split between agreement and disagreement categories were eliminated. In this manner, 10 items relevant to alcoholism and drinking, and 10 items relevant to general issues—all of which were understandable and had yielded sufficient response variability—were selected as our final item pool constituting our attitude scale.[3]

Dependent variable measurement of attraction in this investigation was operationalized in terms of the CPRQ, and a statement of the subject's willingness to actually meet with the therapist should such an opportunity be available.

Procedure. To minimize the likelihood of subject awareness of the purposes of the study's manipulations, initial procedures sought to lead the subjects to believe they were participating in two independent investigations. We sought to augment this belief by using different experimenters and instructions during what were, in fact, the two phases of this one investigation. In the first phase, subjects were seated in the experimental room and told:

> My name is _____. I'm part of a research project at Syracuse University. We're interested in finding out how different groups in the community feel about a variety of issues. The sheets in front of you are made up of a number of opinions. We would like you to indicate how much you agree or disagree with each of them. You can do this by circling one of the six phrases following each opinion.

Subjects then completed the attitude scale, and were told:

> Thanks a lot. There's something else we'd like you to participate in. I'm not sure what it's all about, but Mr. _____ will be in in a minute to explain it to you. Thanks again.

During the following five minutes, the first experimenter left the room and filled out the attitude scales which were to be given to the subjects, supposedly representing the taped therapist's attitudes. For subjects in the two Topic Important conditions, the bogus scale consisted of the 10 alcohol-relevant items. For subjects in the two Topic Unimportant conditions, the scale items referred to general, nonalcoholism

---

[3] See Appendix I, pp. 216-218.

issues. Within each set of Importance conditions, it will be recalled, one condition was to represent 90 percent agreement with the subject's own responses, the other 10 percent agreement. To accomplish this apparency of attitude similarity or dissimilarity, Byrne's (9) procedure of Constant Discrepancy was utilized, a procedure, which Byrne holds, maximally disguises the relationship between the subject's responses and those of the stimulus person. Thus subjects in the Topic Important-Similar and Topic Unimportant-Similar conditions were to receive scales with 9 of the 10 items marked similar to theirs; the converse was the case for the two dissimilar conditions, and control subjects received no bogus attitude scale.

After bogus scoring was completed the second experimenter entered the experimental room and told the subjects:

> I am Mr. _____ and I'm part of a different research program at Syracuse University. What we're interested in is introducing psychotherapy to various groups of people who might be able to benefit from it. More and more people who are having serious problems in living are finding help through a treatment called psychotherapy. Psychotherapy consists of a person with problems sitting down and discussing these problems with a professional psychotherapist. The psychotherapist has been trained through many years of schooling and experience to understand and help people solve their problems. We want to give you an idea of what goes on during psychotherapy, so we are going to play a tape recording of a typical psychotherapy session.

Subjects in the control condition, who received no bogus attitude scales, were then played the tape. Subjects in the four experimental conditions, however, were given the following additional instructions:

> But before we play the tape we thought it would be good for you to know something about the psychotherapist. Probably the best way to find out about a person is to find out what he thinks about things. We have asked the psychotherapist to fill out a questionnaire about ('a variety of issues' or 'drinking'). We thought this might interest you. You will find a copy of this in the large envelope. It looks like this. Take it out. I will read the statements and I want you to look at how much the psychotherapist agrees or disagrees with them. I think a lot of these statements are like ones you just filled out. (The statements were then read slowly by the experimenter.) Now that you know something about the psychotherapist, we would like you to hear him doing psychotherapy.

The tape of the simulated psychotherapy session was then played and the postmeasures administered.

Results

Preliminary to the study's major data analysis, we felt it necessary to empirically test our assumption that attitude scale items relating to alcohol were of greater importance to the subjects than were general issues items. Control condition subjects were thus asked to select those items from the full, 20-item attitude scale that they would seek to discuss with the therapist if they had the opportunity to meet with him. Analysis of these data revealed that subjects chose significantly more alcohol than general items ($t = 3.27$, $df = 9$, $p < .005$), thus demonstrating, at least in this relative sense, the importance of issues relevant to alcohol.

Analyses of variance performed on the attraction and willingness to meet scores failed to support the predicted main effect for attitude similarity or the predicted similarity-importance interaction effect. That is, attitude similarity failed to enhance attraction beyond that reported by the dissimilar or control subjects ($F = .125$, $df = 1, 70$, $p > .05$), and similarity and topic importance failed to interact to produce the predicted enhancing effect upon attraction ($F = .746$, $df = 1$, 70, $p > .05$). We did not predict a main effect for topic importance, but such was indeed obtained ($F = 4.64$, $df = 1, 70$, $p < .05$). Subjects shown attitude scales, purportedly completed by the taped therapist, which contained alcohol-relevant items were significantly more attracted to the therapist than subjects shown a scale containing alcohol-irrelevant items, independent of whether or not the therapist's attitudes were similar or dissimilar to theirs on these alcoholism items. This finding must be considered in light of its post hoc nature. Independent of attitude similarity, when listening to a therapist whose stated goal is to help people with their problems, subjects are more attracted to him when the attitudes he expresses are *relevant* to this task, as compared to when he expresses task-irrelevant attitudes. It is possible that such expression of relevant attitudes more saliently offers the subject the possibility of treatment and hope of problem resolution.

In this investigation, as well as the two reported earlier in which client and counselor actually met and interacted, no effect of attitude similarity on interpersonal attraction was obtained. This failure is in clear and marked contrast to the consistent findings in the laboratory and field studies from which we are extrapolating here. Perhaps a clue to this discrepancy of result lies in the disparate nature of the goals of the dyadic relationships involved in the laboratory and field studies as compared to our psychotherapy investigations. In a great many of the relevant social-psychological studies, the effects of attitude similarity on attraction have been investigated with regard to *friendship* relationships. The ideally equalitarian nature of such relationships as well as the types of activities in which friends might ideally engage make quite logical the notion that the greater the between-friend attitude similarity the more mutually satisfying the friendship. In friendship relationships, in short, attitude similarity is very likely facilitative—and, therefore, attraction enhancing.

A rather different set of conditions prevails in a psychotherapeutic context. A help-seeker wishes assistance from a help-giver. The help-seeker's motivation may be such that he comes for assistance at least in part because there exist important aspects of his current functioning, self-concept, and view of the world that he rejects, and wishes modified. Such an individual, upon learning that the help-giver shares some of the very views that he, the help-seeker, wishes to modify, may develop a view of the help-giver that involves less, and not greater attraction. In such an instance, in brief, attitude similarity may be *unfacilitative*—and, therefore, not attraction-enhancing. Such a notion is, of course, largely speculative. Our considerations at the beginning of the chapter suggest that one must get beyond gross dimensions of similarity or dissimilarity, and make quite specific differential predictions such that similarity on some dimensions, but dissimilarity on others will be attraction-enhancing. On yet other dimensions, neither similarity nor dissimilarity may be relevant to attraction enhancement. At least with regard to similarity or dissimilarity on the authoritarianism and alcohol-relevant dimensions of our own investigations, we have no evidence that either is relevant to attraction enhancement.

References

1. Abelow, A. The tigers: A study of a street corner gang. Unpublished honors thesis, Harvard University, 1956.

2. Adorno, T. W., Frenkel-Brunswik, E., Levinson, J. D., & Sanford, R. N. *The authoritarian personality.* New York: Harper, 1950.

3. Alexander, W., Gonzales, R., Herminghaus, J., Marwell, G., & Wheeless, L. Personality variables and predictability of interaction patterns in small groups. Unpublished paper, Massachusetts Institute of Technology, 1957.

4. Bare, C. Relationship of counselor personality and counselor-client personality similarity to selected counseling success criteria. *Journal of Consulting Psychology,* 1955, **19,** 239–245.

5. Bennis, W. & Peabody, D. The relationship between some personality dimensions and group development. Unpublished paper, 1956.

6. Bonney, M. E. A sociometric study of the relationship of some factors to mutual friendships on the elementary, secondary and college levels. *Sociometry*, 1946, 9, 21–47.

7. Byrne, D. Interpersonal attraction and attitude similarity. *Journal of Abnormal and Social Psychology*, 1961, 62, 713–715.

8. Byrne, D. Response to attitude similarity-dissimilarity as a function of affiliation need. *Journal of Personality*, 1962, 30, 164–177.

9. Byrne, D. Attitudes and attraction. In L. Berkowitz (Ed.), *Advances in experimental social psychology*. Vol. 4, New York: Academic Press, 1969.

10. Byrne, D. & Clore, G. L. Predicting interpersonal attraction toward strangers presented in three different stimulus modes. *Psychonomic Science*, 1966, 4, 239–240.

11. Byrne, D. & Griffitt, W. A developmental investigation of the law of attraction. *Journal of Personality and Social Psychology*, 1966, 4, 699–702.

12. Byrne, D., Griffitt, W., Hudgins, W., & Reeves, K. Attitude similarity-dissimilarity and attraction: Generality beyond the college sophomore. *Journal of Social Psychology*, in press.

13. Byrne, D., London, O., & Reeves, K. The effects of physical attractiveness, sex and attitude similarity on interpersonal attraction. *Journal of Personality*, 1968, 36, 259–271.

14. Byrne, D. & Nelson, D. Attraction as a function of attitude similarity-dissimilarity: The effect of topic importance. *Psychonomic Science*, 1964, 1, 93–94.

15. Byrne, D. & Nelson, D. The effect of topic importance and attitude similarity-dissimilarity on attraction in a multi-stranger design. *Psychonomic Science*, 1965, 3, 449–450.

16. Byrne, D. & Wong, T. J. Racial prejudice, interpersonal attraction and assumed dissimilarity of attitudes. *Journal of Abnormal and Social Psychology*, 1962, 65, 246–253.

17. Carson, R. C. & Heine, R. W. Similarity and success in therapeutic dyads. *Journal of Consulting Psychology*, 1962, 26, 38–43.

18. Carson, R. C. & Lewellyn, C. Similarity in therapeutic dyads. *Journal of Consulting Psychology*, 1965, 30, 458.

19. Ellsworth, R. B. *The MACC behavior adjustment scale*. Los Angeles: Western Psychological Services, 1957.

20. Ford, D. H. Research approaches to psychotherapy. *Journal of Counseling Psychology*, 1959, 6, 55–60.

21. Forsyth, E. & Katz, L. A matrix approach to the analysis of sociometric data: Preliminary report. *Sociometry*, 1946, 9, 340–347.

22. Gassner, S. M. The relationship between patient-therapist compatibility and treatment effectiveness. Unpublished doctoral dissertation, Syracuse University, 1968.

23. Gough, H. G. *California psychological inventory: Test and manual.* Palo Alto, Calif.: Consulting Psychologists Press, 1956.

24. Gross, E. F. An empirical study of the concepts of cohesiveness and compatibility. Unpublished honors thesis, Harvard University, 1957.

25. Heller, K., Myers, R. A., & Kline, L. V. Interviewer behavior as a function of standardized client roles. *Journal of Consulting Psychology,* 1963, **27**, 117–122.

26. Hutcherson, D. E. Relationships among teacher-pupil compatibility, social studies grades, and selected factors. Unpublished doctoral dissertation, University of California, Berkeley, 1963.

27. Jones, E. E. & Dougherty, B. N. Political orientation and the perceptual effects of an anticipated interaction. *Journal of Abnormal and Social Psychology,* 1959, **59**, 340–349.

28. Kaufmann, H. Similarity and cooperation received as determinants of cooperation rendered. *Psychonomic Science,* 1967, **9**, 73–74.

29. Kiesler, C. E. & Goldberg, G. N. Multidimensional approach to the experimental study of interpersonal attraction: Effect of a blunder on the attractiveness of a competent other. *Psychological Reports,* 1968, **22**, 693–705.

30. Krauss, R. M. Structural and attitudinal factors in interpersonal bargaining. *Journal of Experimental Social Psychology,* 1966, **2**, 42–55.

31. Leary, T. *Interpersonal diagnosis of personality.* New York: Ronald Press, 1957.

32. Levinger, G. Note on need complimentarity in marriage, *Psychological Bulletin,* 1964, **61**, 153–157.

33. Lorr, M. & McNair, D. M. An interpersonal behavior circle, *Journal of Abnormal and Social Psychology,* 1963, **67**, 68–75.

34. Mendelsohn, G. A. Effects of client personality and client-counselor similarity on the duration of counseling. *Journal of Counseling Psychology,* 1966, **13**, 228–234.

35. Mendelsohn, G. A. & Geller, M. H. Effects of counselor-client similarity on the outcome of counseling. *Journal of Counseling Psychology,* 1963, **10**, 71–77.

36. Mendelsohn, G. A. & Geller, M. H. Structure of client attitudes toward counseling and their relation to client-counselor similarity. *Journal of Consulting Psychology,* 1965, **29**, 63–72.

37. Mendelson, F., Wexler, D., Kubzonsky, P., Harrison, R., Leiderman, G., & Solomon, P. Physician's attitudes toward alcoholic patients. *Archives of General Psychiatry,* 1964, **11**, 392–399.

38. Novak, D. W. & Lerner, M. J. Rejection as a consequence of perceived similarity. *Journal of Personality and Social Psychology,* 1968, **9**, 147–152.

39. Pepinsky, H. B. & Karst, T. O. Convergence, a phenomenon in counseling and in psychotherapy. *American Psychologist,* 1964, **19**, 333–338.

40. Precker, J. A. Similarity of valuings as a factor in selection of peers and near-authority figures. *Journal of Abnormal and Social Psychology*, 1952, **47**, 406–414.

41. Richardson, H. M. Community of values as a factor in friendships of college and adult women. *Journal of Social Psychology*, 1940, **11**, 303–312.

42. Rosenthal, D. Changes in some moral values following psychotherapy. *Journal of Consulting Psychology*, 1955, **19**, 431–436.

43. Rudner, R. Small group problem solving. Unpublished paper, Harvard University, 1953.

44. Russell, P. D. Counselor anxiety in relation to clinical experience and hostile or friendly clients. Unpublished doctoral dissertation, Pennsylvania State University, 1961.

45. Sapolsky, A. Effect of interpersonal relationships upon verbal conditioning. *Journal of Abnormal and Social Psychology*, 1960, **60**, 241–246.

46. Sapolsky, A. Relationship between patient-doctor compatibility, mutual perception, and outcome of treatment. *Journal of Abnormal and Social Psychology*, 1965, **70**, 70–76.

47. Saunders, D. Preliminary discussion of the Myers-Briggs Type Indicator. Unpublished paper, Princeton, N.J.: Educational Testing Service, 1958.

48. Schutz, W. C. *The FIRO scales, test and manual.* Palo Alto, Calif.: Consulting Psychologists Press, 1957.

49. Schutz, W. C. *FIRO: A three-dimensional theory of interpersonal behavior.* New York: Holt, Rinehart & Winston, 1958.

50. Shapiro, D. Psychological factors in friendship choice and rejection. Unpublished doctoral dissertation, University of Michigan, 1953.

51. Smith, A. J. Similarity of values and its relation to acceptance and the projection of similarity. *Journal of Psychology*, 1952, **43**, 251–260.

52. Snyder, W. U. *The psychotherapy relationship.* New York: Macmillan, 1961.

53. Strassburger, F. & Strassburger, Z. Measurement of attitudes toward alcohol and their relation to personality variables. *Journal of Consulting Psychology*, 1965, **29**, 440–445.

54. Taffel, C. Anxiety and the conditioning of verbal behavior. *Journal of Abnormal and Social Psychology*, 1955, **51**, 496–501.

55. Taylor, J. The relationship of anxiety to the conditioned eyelid response. *Journal of Experimental Psychology*, 1951, **41**, 81–92.

56. Tharp, R. G. Psychological patterning in marriage. *Psychological Bulletin*, 1963, **60**, 97–117.

57. Tuma, A. H. & Gustad, J. W. The effects of client and counselor personality characteristics on client learning in counseling. *Journal of Consulting Psychology*, 1957, **4**, 136–143.

58. Vogel, J. L. Authoritarianism in the therapeutic relationship. *Journal of Consulting Psychology*, 1961, **25**, 102–108.

✗ 59. Welkowitz, J., Cohen, J., & Ortmeyer, D. Value system similarity: Investigation of patient-therapist dyads. *Journal of Consulting Psychology*, 1967, **31**, 48–55.

60. Winslow, C. N. A study of the extent of agreement between friends' opinions and their ability to estimate the opinions of each other. *Journal of Social Psychology*, 1937, **8**, 433–442.

61. Worchel, P. & McCormick, B. Self-concept and dissonance reduction. *Journal of Personality*, 1963, **31**, 588–599.

Chapter X
Role Playing

Role playing has been defined by Mann (21) as "a situation in which an individual is explicitly asked to take a role not normally his own, or if his own in a setting not normal for the enactment of the role" (21, p. 227). Unlike the majority of the social-psychological research domains examined elsewhere in this book, the use of role playing for behavior modification not only has a long and substantial laboratory history, but has also received considerable usage in clinical contexts. We will in this chapter briefly summarize first the laboratory underpinnings of our extrapolatory attempts; then we will consider in somewhat greater depth a number of the uses of role playing in psychotherapeutic settings; and, finally, we will turn to our own investigation of role playing as a means of enhancing psychotherapeutic attraction.

Laboratory Investigations

A number of the laboratory studies oriented toward examining the attitude-change consequences of role-play participation have utilized essentially the same experimental paradigm. A sample of subjects are premeasured on one or more salient attitude dimensions. Subjects are then randomly assigned to either a role-play condition, some type of exposure condition and a control group. The role-play subjects are requested to make a speech or other public statement championing a position *counter* to their initial attitude. Exposure condition subjects passively listen to such statements, while control subjects neither present nor hear the counter-attitudinal statement. Postmeasurement on the relevant attitude is then obtained. This design, or a variant of it, has repeatedly yielded results indicating significantly greater attitude change in the direction of the counter-attitudinal position in role play versus both exposure and control subjects (5, 10, 12, 17, 26). Furthermore, this effect has emerged across a wide variety of attitudinal dimensions. Beyond these studies demonstrating the basic change potential of role-play procedures, several investigators have sought to identify parameters of the role enactment or its structuring to subjects which serve to augment or diminish the degree of subsequent attitude change. Attitude change will be greater, the greater the subject's,

(a) degree of perceived *choice* regarding whether to participate in role playing (6),

(b) *commitment* to the counter-attitudinal position in the sense that his enactment is public rather than private, or otherwise difficult to "undo" (4),

(c) degree of *improvisation* in enacting the counter-attitudinal role (17), and

(d) *reward*, approval, reinforcement, or other means of stabilizing the role-played position (27).

These major role-play parameters—choice, commitment, improvisation, and reward—were maximized in our role-play study, which involved particularly resistive patients, as a means of providing the most optimal test possible of the role playing—therapeutic attraction relationship.

One laboratory investigation in particular deserves closer examination, especially just prior to our consideration of psychotherapeutic applications of role playing. It very powerfully demonstrates both the attitudinal and behavioral consequences of role playing in a domain quite relevant to the concerns of many contemporary psychotherapists. Janis and Mann (13), in response to their suspicion that habitual behavior that was highly resistant to change would not yield to the usual, cognitively-oriented role-playing procedures, designed an investigation of the effects of what they termed "emotional role playing" on the reduction of smoking. All subjects were asked to improvisationally assume they were medical patients who had just undergone a series of diagnostic tests and were awaiting the results. The experimenter enacted the part of physician. Half of the 26 participating subjects (all women, and all smokers) were asked to play the role of patient (Role-Play Condition); the other 13 subject-"patients" listened to recordings of these role enactments (Exposure Condition). All subjects were premeasured on their attitudes toward smoking, cancer, and their future plans regarding their smoking behavior. The role-play subjects then enacted five scenes with the experimenter-"physician," all of which were designed to be fear-arousing. The scenes included an apprehensive soliloquy in the waiting room in expectation of the diagnostic results, a conversation with the physician during which the patient was told she had lung cancer and that surgery was necessary, enactment of intense concern about the diagnosis and the moderate probability of a favorable outcome, and making hospital arrangements.[1] Immediately following the role-playing session, subject's attitudes

---

[1] Consistent with our discussion in Chapter I of the importance of discerning effective commonalities across psychotherapies as well as across psychothera-

toward smoking were assessed. This measure, as well as information on number of cigarettes smoked per day were also obtained after two weeks. In each instance, the role-play subjects were significantly more negative toward smoking, and smoked significantly fewer cigarettes, than did exposure subjects. This decrease in smoking favoring the role-play subjects was still in evidence on follow-up 18 months later!

Psychotherapeutic Applications

As Krasner (18) has noted, the suggested use of drama for therapeutic purposes can be traced to as early a source as Aristotle. In modern times, but still well before Moreno's (22) psychodramatic movement, Reil (32) in 1803 made use of role-play procedures with institutionalized mental patients. Reil advocated that a special theater be established in mental hospitals in which patients would be urged to portray events from their earlier lives, and in which the hospital staff could serve as judges, prosecutors, etc., and point out to each actor-patient "the folly of his ways." The major early impetus to the psychotherapeutic use of role playing was provided by Moreno, starting in 1911 and continuing as an important therapeutic approach today. While rather little that approximates rigorous research has come from this movement, and its adherents still continue to publish largely claims, counterclaims, and intuitive reports, their use of role-play procedures has been extensive, detailed, and imaginative. In this system, role-play procedures are utilized primarily to act out past or present conflicts. In contrast to this cathartic orientation, Lazarus (19) has relied upon an instrumental learning rationale to promulgate a therapeutic use of role playing which he describes as behavioral rehearsal. Most often, behavioral rehearsal has been used with patients deficient in assertiveness skills, and has focused upon future behaviors anticipated by the patient and associated with high levels of anxiety. Lazarus describes his procedure as follows:

> In this method patient and therapist role-played various scenes which posed assertive problems for the patient . . . expressing disagreement with a friend's social arrangements, asking a favor, upbraiding a subordinate at work, contradicting a fellow employee. . . . Commencing with the less demanding situations, each scene was systematically rehearsed until the most troublesome encounters had been enacted to the satisfaction of patient and therapist. The therapist usually role-played the significant persons in the pa-

---

peutic and nontherapeutic change process, it is of interest to note the major similarities between these laboratory change procedures and both psychodramatic (22) and implosive behavioral (30) approaches to psychotherapy.

tient's life according to descriptions provided by the latter. The patient's behavior was shaped by means of constructive criticism as well as modeling procedures in which the therapist assumed the patient's role and demonstrated the desirable responses. (19, Pp. 209-210)

In addition to assertiveness training, Lazarus (19) has begun to make use of behavioral rehearsal to aid patients in dealing with other specific behavioral patterns. This orientation contrasts to some degree with the related use to which role playing has been put in Kelly's (16) fixed-role therapy, an approach in which considerably greater improvisation in role enactment is required of the patient. Fixed-role therapy too, however, has an instrumental rather than cathartic intent. In using this approach, the initial diagnostic information available on the patient is used by the treatment staff to construct a fixed-role sketch. This sketch is a carefully planned but sparsely detailed role-play script or outline consisting of the types of behaviors it would appear therapeutically desirable for them to assume; that is, to assume temporarily during the weeks of role playing the behaviors, and more permanently to the extent that the role-play experience mediates adoption by the patient of the role-played attitudes and behaviors as "his own." In contrast to both psychodrama and the beginning stages of behavioral rehearsal, fixed-role therapy role playing occurs outside the treatment clinic, thus providing the patient with the opportunity of observing and experiencing interpersonal feedback from his real world in response to his role-played behaviors.

While role playing has been used adjunctively by proponents of almost all psychotherapeutic approaches (2, 3, 8, 9, 23, 28, 29, 31), the three orientations described above are its major psychotherapeutic applications. With the exception of but a few investigations, neither psychodramatic (9, 14, 26), behavioral rehearsal (19), nor fixed-role therapy (7, 25) use of role playing has received substantial experimental scrutiny regarding its efficacy. All three approaches *appear* quite useful, but further evidence must be forthcoming before firmer outcome-relevant conclusions may be drawn.

Role Playing and Attraction Enhancement

Our single investigation of the effects of role playing on attraction enhancement was conducted by Hollander (11). Subjects for this study were 45 male psychiatric inpatients at a VA Hospital located in a small, rural, midwestern city. Almost all were farmers or laborers, and most had only grade school education. Twenty-six of these patients had a primary diagnosis of alcoholism, with most of the remainder diagnosed as having some type of personality or character disorder. Consistent with the traditional experimental paradigm so frequently utilized in this research domain, we constituted three experimental conditions—Role-Play, Exposure, and Control. Prior to assignment to one of these groups, all patients were administered an Attitudes toward Psychotherapy and Psychotherapists Scale (APPS).[2,3] This Scale was designed to serve as a measure of a subject's generalized attitude toward therapists and therapy, i.e., without specific reference to a particular psychotherapist or series of therapy sessions. All patients also completed a Willingness to Disclose Questionnaire (15) at this point. Our intent in obtaining such attitudinal information was to develop a basis on which to adjust in our later covariance analysis of attraction and disclosure data. This initial testing also clearly established that the prevailing disposition of the patient sample as a whole toward therapy and therapists was primarily negative. Following administration of the APPS, subjects were randomly assigned to an experimental condition and given the following instructions (by an E who was unaware of the study's hypotheses):

Role-Play Condition

Hello, I'm Mrs. Helberg. I guess you know we have been trying to learn how you feel about psychiatrists and psychologists. Well, right now we have a patient who is very worried about going to a psychologist, and we wonder if you could tell this man why going to a psychologist is a good thing to do. You can tell him how much psychologists know about mental and nervous problems, how friendly and understanding psychologists are, how psychologists can be trusted, how much better he is going to feel after he has talked with a psychologist, and anything else you can think of. Now, you don't *have* to do this for us, but we'd really appreciate it if you would. OK? Remember, this patient is going to listen to what you've said, so really try to convince him.

Exposure Condition

Hello, I'm Mrs. Helberg. I guess you know we've been trying to learn how you feel about psychiatrists and psychologists. Well, on this tape we have one man's opinion about why going to a psychologist is a good thing. We'd like you to take a few minutes and listen to it. OK?

Control Condition

Hello, I'm Mrs. Helberg. I guess you know we've been trying to learn how you feel about psychiatrists and psychologists. Well,

---

[2] See Appendix I, pp. 219-221.
[3] Test-retest reliability $= .87$ on a sample of 10 VAH patients.

I'll be with you in just a few minutes. Meanwhile, why don't you just relax and listen to music?

Each Exposure Condition patient was yoked, on a random basis, with a patient from the Role-Play Condition such that each of the former actually heard a role enactment performed by one of the latter. It is important to note, with regard to the enactment of the Role-Play Condition, that an effort was made to maximize the four parameters of role playing shown to augment their effect on attitude change in the social-psychological laboratory. Thus the subject was given a *choice* regarding his participation; a high level of *commitment* was established in that he knew another patient would hear his enactment; E provided *reward* in the form of verbal approval to all role-play subjects for their enactment; and at least a moderate level of *improvisation* was required of the patient. With regard to improvisation, pilot work revealed that the role-play instructions could not consist of a fully open script outline calling for maximal improvisation with this patient sample. Their very marked tendency toward concreteness, nonverbalness, and related characteristics precluded such major improvisation and required us to provide a moderately structured role outline. An even more serious consequent of the rather impoverished ideational and verbal level on which almost all of our sample functioned relates to the duration of our experimental variable manipulations. While we had planned to have each Role-Play Condition patient enact a pro-therapy role for 10 minutes, the actual average length of role enactment (and hence also length of exposure and wait period) was two minutes. This occurred in spite of what we view as our almost heroic attempt at coaxing, cajoling, rewarding, and encouraging.

Following the role-play, exposure, or wait periods, each subject took a second APPS, the $APPS_2$-$APPS_1$ difference score representing the effects of our experimental manipulations on generalized attraction to psychotherapy and psychotherapists. Each subject was then introduced to a second (also unaware) E. This E then conducted an interview with the subject, an interview whose specific content consisted of the same intake interview-like questions used in our earlier study (20) of modeling and attraction enhancement.[4] Following each interview, the subject completed a CPRQ and the interviewer filled out a TPRQ. These postinterview-attraction measures were used to discern the effects of our experimental manipulations on attraction enhancement with reference to specific interviewer-interviewee pairs (in contrast to the more general nature of APPS-measured attraction). Each inter-

---

[4] See p. 111, for the interview questions.

view was tape-recorded and later content-analyzed for openness and guardedness following Ashby et al.'s (1) procedures.[5] Eight patients were randomly selected from those assigned to each condition for follow-up purposes. Approximately one week after the initial interview, a second, individual intake-like interview was conducted with each of these 24 patients. This interview was also followed by CPRQ and TPRQ testing, as well as content analysis for openness and guardedness. These data provide information relevant to the issue of how enduring were the effects, if any, of our experimental manipulations. Our predictions were that on these several postmanipulation, post-interview, and follow-up measures of attraction and disclosure, Role-Play patients would have significantly higher scores than would Exposure patients, who, in turn, would exceed Control patients.

No significant effects emerged from our series of covariance analyses. That is, in no instance were there significant differences between the Role-Play, Exposure, and Control groups on any of the attraction or disclosure criteria. While the ordering of means by condition on almost all 10 of these criteria revealed the role-play group to have the most favorable score, the within-group variance in all three conditions was exceedingly large. This characteristic of the array of patient scores within each condition is of interest not so much as an explanation for the nonsignificant covariance results per se, but because very substantial within-group variance has been clearly characteristic of patient scores in *every* study in the present research program which involved NON-YAVIS patients. Covarying out the effects on dependent variable criteria of patient premanipulation attraction and willingness to disclose was appropriate in the present analysis, but it is clear that in studying markedly NON-YAVIS patient samples, even greater experimenter effort must be exercised in the form of experimental and/or statistical controls as a means of dealing more effectively with within-sample heterogeneity.

An additional influence upon the negative results of this investigation appears to relate to the difficulty we experienced in adequately implementing the Role-Play Condition. Our initial goal of a 10-minute duration of role playing for each patient was itself modest in comparison to the time period involved in studies such as Janis and Mann's (13), in which the effects of role playing were powerfully demonstrated. Our actual role-play duration of approximately two minutes contrasts even less favorably with those enactment periods shown to be effective and, as our results suggest, may well have been roughly equivalent to no role playing at all!

[5] Interjudge reliability (Pearson r) = .89.

In spite of this study's absence of findings,[6] we would be reluctant to too strongly conclude that role playing appears to be an ineffective technique for NON-YAVIS patients. Riessman and Goldfarb (24) present a very strong position, based on considerable evidence drawn from developmental psychological research, that in terms of experiential background, life style, and both past and current reinforcement values, techniques such as role playing are likely to be effective for behavior change purposes in individuals whom we have described throughout this book as NON-YAVIS. Thus, at this stage of our investigative knowledge, our position with regard to the effects of role playing on behavior change in NON-YAVIS patients best remains, simply, "not proven."

However, future research in this domain would do well to be responsive to deficiencies in the depth and breadth of the patient's pre-role-playing behavioral repertoire. It seems quite possible, unfortunately largely in retrospect, that the NON-YAVIS patients in Hollander's (11) study simply knew too little about psychotherapy, psychotherapists, and relevant attitudes thereto. One cannot satisfactorily enact an attitudinal or counter-attitudinal position if one's knowledge, familiarity, or experience with the relevant attitudinal domain is minimal. Our pre-role-playing instructions to patients in the form of a broad script outline including examples of what they might say or do in their role enactment provided them with some relevant behaviors, but clearly not enough. Perhaps an approach akin to Lazarus' (19) behavioral rehearsal, consisting of a flexible and repeated interplay of modeling (to establish familiarity with the appropriate repertoire of adaptive behaviors) role playing (to experientially rehearse the adaptive behaviors), and reinforcement (to stabilize the new behaviors) would be more adequately responsive to the nature of our patient sample. The impact of such a "broad spectrum" approach appears to be a highly promising avenue for further research.

---

[6] Independent of the study's manipulations, and in a manner fully consistent with the correlational findings emerging in several other of our investigations, a correlational analysis revealed a series of significant relationships between patient postmanipulation (preinterview) attraction and both interviewer attraction to the patient ($r = .504$) and patient willingness to disclose ($r = .430$). Furthermore, postinterview patient attraction covaried significantly with patient in interview openness ($r = .488$), and guardedness ($r = -.365$), and interviewer attraction to the patient ($r = .371$).

References

1. Ashby, J. D., Ford, D. H., Guerney, B. G., Jr., & Guerney, L. Effects on clients of a reflective and a leading type of psychotherapy. *Psychological Monographs*, 1957, 7, 1–32.

2. Bromberg, W. Acting and acting out. *American Journal of Psychotherapy*, 1958, 12, 264–268.

3. Carp, E. Psychodrama. Z. *Psychotherapie Medical Psychologie*, 1954, 4, 163–170.

4. Cohen, A. R. & Latané, B. An experiment on choice in commitment to counter-attitudinal behavior. In J. W. Brehm & A. R. Cohen (Eds.), *Explorations in cognitive dissonance*. New York: Wiley, 1962. Pp. 88–91.

5. Culbertson, F. M. Modification of an emotionally held attitude through role playing. *Journal of Abnormal and Social Psychology*, 1957, 54, 230–233.

6. Davis, K. & Jones, E. E. Changes in interpersonal perception as a means of reducing cognitive dissonance. *Journal of Abnormal and Social Psychology*, 1960, 61, 402–410.

7. Edwards, E. D. Observation of the use and efficacy of changing a patient's concept of his role—a psychotherapeutic device. Unpublished master's thesis, Fort Hays State College, 1940.

8. Goodman, J. M. Nondirective psychodramatic play therapy. *American Journal of Orthopsychiatry*, 1962, 32, 532–534.

9. Harrow, G. The effects of psychodrama group therapy on role behavior of schizophrenic patients. *Group Psychotherapy*, 1951, 3, 316–320.

10. Harvey, O. J. & Beverly, G. D. Some personality correlates of concept change through role playing. *Journal of Abnormal and Social Psychology*, 1961, 63, 125–130.

11. Hollander, T. G. The effects of role playing on attraction, disclosure and attitude change in a psychotherapy analogue. Unpublished doctoral dissertation, Syracuse University, 1970.

12. Janis, I. L. & King, B. T. The influence of role playing on opinion change. *Journal of Abnormal and Social Psychology*, 1954, 49, 211–218.

13. Janis, I. & Mann, L. Effectiveness of emotional role playing in modifying smoking habits and attitudes. *Journal of Experimental Research in Personality*, 1965, 1, 84–90.

14. Jones, F. D. & Peters, A. N. An experimental evaluation of group psychotherapy. *Journal of Abnormal and Social Psychology*, 1952, 47, 345–353.

15. Jourard, S. M. *The transparent self*. Princeton, N.J.: Van Nostrand, 1964.

16. Kelly, G. A. *The psychology of personal constructs*. New York: Norton, 1955.

17. King, B. T. & Janis, I. L. Comparison of the effectiveness of improvised vs. non-improvised role playing in producing opinion changes. *Human Relations*, 1956, **9**, 177–186.

18. Krasner, L. Role taking research and psychotherapy. Research reports of Veterans Administration, Palo Alto, Calif., 1959, No. 5.

19. Lazarus, A. A. Behavior rehearsal vs. non-directive therapy vs. advice in effecting behavior change. *Behaviour Research and Therapy*, 1966, **4**, 209–212.

20. Liberman, B. The effect of modeling procedures on attraction and disclosure in a psychotherapy analogue. Unpublished doctoral dissertation, Syracuse University, 1970.

21. Mann, J. H. Experimental evaluations of role playing. *Psychological Bulletin*, 1956, **53**, 227–234.

22. Moreno, J. L. *Group psychotherapy, a symposium.* New York: Beacon House, 1945.

23. O'Connell, W. W. Adlerian psychodrama with schizophrenics. *Journal of Individual Psychology*, 1963, **19**, 69–76.

24. Riessman, F. & Goldfarb, J. Role playing and the poor. In F. Riessman, J. Cohen, & A. Pearl (Eds.), *Mental health of the poor.* New York: Free Press, 1964. Pp. 336–347.

25. Robinson, A. J. Further validation of role therapy. Unpublished master's thesis, Fort Hays State College, 1940.

26. Rosenberg, P. An experimental analysis of psychodrama. Unpublished doctoral dissertation, Harvard University, 1952.

27. Scott, W. A. Attitude change through reward of verbal behavior. *Journal of Abnormal and Social Psychology*, 1957, **55**, 72–75.

28. Shoobs, N. E. Role playing in the individual psychotherapy interview. *Journal of Individual Psychology*, 1964, **20**, 84–89.

29. Shulman, B. H. A psychodramatically oriented action technique in group psychotherapy. *Group Psychotherapy*, 1960, **13**, 34–39.

30. Stampfl, T. G. & Lewis, D. J. Implosive therapy—a behavioral therapy? *Behaviour Research and Therapy*, 1968, **6**, 31–36.

31. Strean, H. S. Treating parents of emotionally disturbed children through role playing. *Psychoanalysis and Psychoanalytic Review*, 1960, **47**, 67–76.

32. Zilboorg, G. & Henry, G. W. *A history of medical psychology.* New York: Norton, 1941.

Chapter XI

Group Cohesiveness

A very substantial body of social-psychological, small group research has focused upon the implications of varying levels of group cohesiveness. In operational terms, cohesiveness has been defined in these investigations as the group's overall level of member-to-member attraction, thus making concern with cohesiveness directly relevant to the focus of the present book. A number of antecedents, concomitants, and consequents of cohesive group structure have been identified. Thus, for example, it has been demonstrated that members of highly cohesive groups, in contrast to members of groups in which the level of attraction is low, will:

(a) remain in the group longer,

(b) be absent less often,

(c) be more open to influence by other members,

(d) be more accepting of member hostility,

(e) place greater value on the group's goals,

(f) be more equal participants in group discussions,

(g) be more active participants in group discussions, and

(h) be less susceptible to disruption as a group when a member terminates his membership.

In short, at least with reference to training, educational, problem-solving, and other nonpsychotherapeutic groups, cohesiveness is a powerful influence on the functioning of group members. Whether group cohesiveness is of similar potency in a psychotherapeutic context is a largely untested question. *A priori* positions on this question are diverse, with both pro (3, 10) and con (16, 22) viewpoints represented. Clarifying evidence is very sparse. The single study of cohesiveness in therapy groups of which this writer is aware was conducted by Truax (19). He examined the effects of group cohesiveness upon depth of patient intrapersonal exploration. Three psychotherapy groups involving a total of 39 psychiatric inpatients were his subjects. Three-minute samples of verbal interaction were randomly selected from recordings of 42 successive hours of group psychotherapy from each of the three groups. Ratings of these segments constituted the cohesiveness data, with intrapersonal exploration data being obtained from Process and Insight Scales completed by independent judges. His data revealed significant, positive correlations between these variables, leading Truax to conclude:

> These results indicate that cohesion, long a central concept in the analysis of small group behavior, is also of importance in the analysis of group psychotherapy: successful group psychotherapy groups are cohesive. . . . These findings not only suggest the fruitfulness of applying knowledge of attitude change obtained from studies of experimental groups, but also point to a variable unique to the group setting and one which is susceptible to external manipulation. (19, p. 10)

Thus encouraged by the singularly positive results of small group cohesiveness research, as well by Truax's findings, we undertook three investigations relevant to attraction in group psychotherapy.

Conformity

Conformity behavior has long been an active focus of social-psychological research. Much of this work has concerned perceptual phenomena and has taken form in one variant or another of the basic experimental paradigm developed by Sherif (18). His design involved exposing small groups of "subjects" (all but one of whom were cohorts previously instructed by the experimenter) to a stationary point of light in a dark room. The amount of apparent movement (the autokinetic effect) reported by the actual subject in each group was demonstrated to be markedly influenced by the degree of movement reported by the cohorts. Asch's (2) well-known elaboration of the Sherif study required subjects to estimate line lengths in comparison with a standard. His subjects were run in groups of eight individuals, one of whom was the subject and seven of whom were preinstructed cohorts. As Sherif had found, a large proportion of subjects (35 percent) were markedly responsive to the cohorts' (objectively erroneous) judgments, even though such judgments departed from the objective reality of the perceptual task. Subsequent studies conducted by Asch demonstrated that a single (cohort) dissenter from the erroneous majority was sufficient to enable subjects to make no mistaken estimates. Further, he found that conformity pressure reached a maximum level after erroneous reports from three or four cohorts, and then leveled out, so that a greater number of cohort reports produced no increase in conformity by the subjects. Perhaps of greater consequence with regard to our own extrapolatory effort in this research domain, Asch was able to demonstrate a more powerful conformity effect the more ambiguous the area being judged, e.g., politics, religion, or morality were more easily influenced than were judgments involving an objective referent (line length, color, shape, etc.).

Crutchfield (5) replicated Asch's initial findings and, further, extended the paradigm to yet other domains involving social, rather than objective, frames of reference. Blake and Brehm (4) provided the methodological improvement of substituting tape-recorded conformity pressure statements apparently coming from other group members in separate cubicles for actual cohorts, thus enabling the investigator to run several subjects simultaneously. Using this procedure, Blake and Brehm successfully replicated Sherif's demonstration of the influence of conformity pressure on the autokinetic effect. A number of subsequent investigations of conformity behavior have sought to identify subject or cohort characteristics resulting in the greatest degree of conformity. Thus it now appears clear that the most successful inducing group of cohorts is or appears to be the same age, sex, and status as the subject. Females consistently tend to conform more than males, and high-authoritarian subjects more than low-authoritarian (1, 7, 9, 14).

The broad intent of our first extrapolatory study of conformity, for which Himmelsbach (13) was the principal investigator, was to ascertain whether conformity pressure operationalized in terms of the classical paradigm discussed above could influence the level of subject attraction to a psychotherapist. Our subjects were 108 female university students randomly selected from all such students participating in Introductory Psychology classes, and randomly assigned to six experimental conditions.

The two 25-minute taped psychotherapy sessions developed for Orenstein's (17) study of modeling and attraction enhancement were also utilized for this investigation. Our utilization of both a High and a Low Attraction tape enabled us to conduct, in effect, two independent tests of the effects of conformity pressure on subject attraction. Conformity pressure took form in seeking to influence the subject to either agree or disagree with cohorts' judgments about the attractiveness of the taped therapist. Thus this investigation was implemented in terms of two 1 x 3 cell arrangements. That is, for both the High and Low Attraction tapes separately, there was conformity pressure exerted to *agree* with the taped patient's attraction to the taped therapist, to disagree with the level of attraction expressed, and a *neutral* condition in which no conformity pressure was exerted—as a means of checking on the attraction-pull of each tape per se.

Concretely, subjects came to the experimental suite in groups of four, and were escorted to separate offices. Each office contained a desk, chair, microphone, headset, and a rating scale consisting of the response format section of the CPRQ, without the actual items. As each subject was able to see before entering the office, wires ran from each microphone-headset combination under the office door to a central tape recorder and amplifier. This physicial arrangement added subsequent credibility to the impression that what subjects were hearing during the experiment proper came from other group members and not, as was actually the case, from a prerecorded tape. Each of the four subjects was told she was subject number four and that she was to respond (both into the microphone and on the scale) only when her number was called. All microphones were actually dead.

Subjects were asked to place the (live) earphones on their heads and the tape playing then began. Two tapes were played to each subject. The first was, depending upon experimental condition, either the High or Low Attraction taped therapy session. The second tape played implemented conformity pressure. Subjects, of course, had been led to believe that the voices on this second tape were the experimenter and other subjects speaking live, and not a tape recording. E stated:

> O.K., now as I read each statement (from the CPRQ) I want you to think about it and form a judgment on the scale from Strongly Agree to Strongly Disagree. I will read each statement only once. I will then ask each of you for your opinion. Remember to also circle the number which corresponds to your judgment.

The subject then heard the 16 items from the CPRQ. After each of the first 12 items, the taped E stated, "Subject number one," and then a taped voice gave her rating—either "Strongly Agree" or "Strongly Disagree." E then called upon subjects two and three in turn, and each in turn gave the same rating as had subject number one. Subject number four was then called upon, after which all four real subjects more or less simultaneously spoke their ratings into the (dead) microphone and each recorded them on her own copy of the rating scale. Thus, in the two conditions in which pressure was to be exerted to have the subject conform to the judgment that the taped therapist was high in attractiveness (Low Attraction tape-Pressure toward High Attraction Condition; High Attraction tape-Pressure toward High Attraction Condition) the subject heard the other "subjects" state "Strongly Agree" to positive CPRQ items and "Strongly Disagree" to negative CPRQ items. In a similar manner, taped cohorts agreed or disagreed in response to the two therapy tapes in the direction of pressure toward low attraction in the two other conformity pressure conditions. No such

conformity pressure was exerted on the last four CPRQ items, as a
minor means of examining the carry over of conformity pressure effects. In the two no conformity pressure conditions, the subjects heard
E read each statement and then gave her own response, with no inter-
vening judgments from other "subjects." After completion of this
procedure, each subject filled out a Willingness to Disclose Scale (15),
a measure seeking to determine whether the effects of conformity pressure went beyond attraction to subject estimates of how open they
would be about personal matters if they were to meet with the taped
therapist. Subjects then left at 90-second intervals, to minimize the
likelihood they would learn that each of them had been subject
number four.

Prior to our major data analyses, and as a check on the attraction-
pull of the two therapy tapes, CPRQ scores for subjects assigned to
the two neutral conditions were compared. As had been predicted,
subjects exposed to what we designed as the High Attraction tape and
to no conformity pressure were significantly more attracted to the
taped therapist than were Low Attraction tape-no pressure subjects
($t = 7.87$, $df = 34$, $p < .001$).[1]

Table 11.1

Attraction and Disclosure Enhancement with Conformity
Pressure Present and Absent

Dependent Variable	F	df	p
Attraction, conformity pressure present:			
High Attraction Tape	79.30	2,53	.001
Low Attraction Tape	34.51	2,53	.001
Attraction, conformity pressure absent:			
High Attraction Tape	9.30	2,53	.01
Low Attraction Tape	3.26	2,53	.05
Willingness to Disclose:			
High Attraction Tape	8.54	2,53	.01
Low Attraction Tape	.79	2,53	NS

Separate one-way analyses of variance were then performed on the
two attraction measures (with conformity pressure, i.e., items 1-12;

[1] Although it was not the experimental focus of this investigation, it is of interest
to note that this simple check on the pull of our experimental tapes also consti-
tutes evidence in support of attraction enhancement by use of modeling procedures.

without conformity pressure, i.e., items 13-16) and the Willingness to Disclose measure for subjects exposed to the High Attraction tape and, separately, for those hearing the Low Attraction tape. Results indicated that the conformity pressure was successful in all instances but one. These findings are presented in Table 11.1.

This array of significant overall results permitted us to conduct an extended series of post hoc cell comparisons, in this instance operationalized in terms of Neuman-Keul (21) mean comparisons tests. These post hoc comparisons yielded support for almost all study predictions. Subjects exposed to both a High Attraction tape and messages from experimenter cohorts to the effect that they judged the therapist as attractive rated this therapist as significantly more attractive than did subjects who heard no messages or negative messages from the cohorts. The attraction difference between no pressure (neutral condition) subjects and pressure toward low attraction subjects was also significant, with no pressure subjects proving more attracted. This same "order of finish"—high attraction conformity pressure subjects, no pressure subjects, low attraction conformity pressure subjects—emerged on the measure of attraction in the absence of conformity pressure and the Willingness to Disclose measure. Again, all between-condition differences were statistically significant.

Of greater importance with reference to the issue of attraction enhancement are this study's results for those three conditions in which the tape played to subjects depicted a patient who expressed repeated dissatisfaction with her therapist. When cohorts consistently rated this therapist as attractive (in contrast to the patient messages on the tape), subjects judged him to be significantly more attractive than when either no conformity pressure was applied or when the cohorts judged him negatively. An analogous significant difference also emerged for attraction in the absence of conformity pressure, but not for subject Willingness to Disclose scores. Furthermore, comparisons of the neutral and pressure toward unattractiveness conditions revealed significantly greater attraction to the therapist but not willingness to disclose among neutral condition subjects.

A final analysis performed of these data sought to clarify the nature of a possible tape by conformity pressure interaction effects. A 3 x 2 analysis of variance on the main attraction score was conducted across all six study conditions. No main effect for type of conformity pressure was either predicted or obtained due to the mutually antagonistic nature of the conformity pressures induced. There was, however, a significant tape effect ($F = 57.70$, $df = 1$, $p < .001$) such that the High Attraction tape pulled significantly more attraction to the therapist across conditions than did the Low Attraction tape. This finding may be viewed as simply an additional check on our therapy tape construction, a check overlapping with, but a bit more elaborate than the pilot test comparison of subject attraction in the two no pressure conditions reported earlier. As noted above, examination of a possible tape by conformity pressure interaction effect was the primary goal of this analysis. Results indicated that this interaction effect was highly significant ($F = 96.76$, $df = 2, 107$, $p < .001$). Of the several significant results emerging from post hoc cell comparisons on these data, the one of greatest relevance to the issue of attraction enhancement in psychotherapy concerns subjects hearing the Low Attraction tape followed by cohort pressure to high attraction versus the High Attraction tape followed by no conformity pressure. The former yielded significantly greater attraction to the therapist than did the latter, thus suggesting even greater robustness than we had anticipated for the attraction-enhancing effects of conformity pressure.

We may thus distill from these several findings the broad conclusion that conformity pressure as operationalized in this investigation has a powerful and consistent influence upon subject attraction and, further, that the effects of such pressure extend at least minimally beyond the immediate period of conformity pressure implementation. Yet, it has quite often been the case in social-psychological laboratory research (including conformity studies) that those positive effects which have been obtained prove to be nonenduring even on moderately short follow-up. Himmelsbach's study demonstrated that the attraction-enhancing effects of group conformity pressure continue to operate immediately after the removal of such pressure when, however, the subject is still in the pressure-exerting experimental setting. Do such pressures continue to have a demonstrable effect on attraction when the subject has left the group context and begun participating in another task? This was the broad question to which our next investigation, conducted by Walsh (20), was oriented. Stated in a manner more relevant to psychotherapy, Walsh sought to determine if the attraction-enhancing effects of group conformity pressure carried over to a therapy-like interview and the subject's evaluation of a live interviewer—when the latter was the same interviewer he had heard and rated earlier on the conformity tape. With a few exceptions, Walsh's procedures paralleled those used by Himmelsbach. In contrast to the latter investigation, in which the taped patient verbalized high or low attraction statements to the taped therapist, all such statements were eliminated from the present study's tape. This removal of any "objective" basis for subsequent subject attraction judgments provided us, we felt, with the opportunity for discerning more clearly the effects of conformity pressure per se. Pilot work with this tape clearly demonstrated its neutral tape pull with regard to attraction to the therapist. We also added a fourth experimental condition to this investigation. Specifically, 60 female college undergraduates were randomly assigned to High Attraction, Low Attraction, No Pressure, and Interview Only experimental conditions. The interview only subjects were included to provide, in effect, base rate information regarding the attractiveness of the interviewer. Subjects in the three tape conditions participated in experimental procedures identical to those used by Himmelsbach. These subjects, and the interview only subjects, then participated in a broadly exploratory, intake-like interview which was conducted by the same interviewer subjects in the first three conditions had heard on the conformity tape. Following this interview, all subjects completed a CPRQ. The interviews were tape-recorded and content-analyzed for openness and guardedness using our usual content analysis procedures.[2]

Analyses of variance conducted across the study's data clearly confirmed and extended Himmelsbach's findings. The CPRQ-derived ratings completed during tape listening *and* conformity pressure yielded a significant between-groups difference ($F = 34.35$, $df = 2, 42$, $p < .01$). A post hoc analysis on these data (Neuman-Keuls tests) revealed all possible differences to be significant. That is, subjects exposed to high attraction conformity pressure were significantly more attracted to the taped therapist than were subjects receiving no pressure, and these latter subjects were significantly more attracted than were subjects who heard low attraction ratings from taped group cohorts. When conformity pressure was removed, during the rating of the last four items of this scale, a significant finding was again obtained ($F = 3.82$, $df = 2, 42$, $p < .05$). High attraction conformity pressure subjects were significantly more attracted than subjects who had earlier heard low attraction conformity ratings. There were no significant differences involving no pressure subjects on this set of items. As noted earlier, this investigation sought not only to essentially replicate the findings of our initial conformity study but, perhaps more important, to discern whether such effects of conformity pressure on attraction continue to operate when S leaves the context of direct conformity pressure and enters a therapy-like interview. Positive findings in this latter regard would contribute importantly to our confidence in suggesting the usefulness of such conformity manipulations for attraction-enhancement

[2] Interjudge reliability = .83 (Pearson *r*).

purposes in a psychotherapeutic setting. Our experimental results in these regards provide just such materials. Both postinterview CPRQ scores ($F = 3.51$, $df = 3, 56$, $p < .05$) and openness scores[3] derived from a content analysis of the interview ($F = 4.22$, $df = 3, 56$, $p < .05$) yielded significant group differences. Subsequent Neuman-Keuls tests revealed that with regard to both of these scores, openness in the interview and postinterview attraction, high attraction pressure and interview only subjects were significantly higher than low attraction pressure subjects. In neither of these comparisons did significant differences emerge involving no pressure subjects. In addition, in no between-group comparisons were there significant differences in terms of guardedness scores.

With reference to the circumstance of a low level of patient attraction to the psychotherapist in the context of group psychotherapy, and also as a means for preparing resistant patients in advance for individual or group psychotherapy, we take these findings to suggest the possibility that cohort-exerted conformity pressure in the direction of high perceived attraction offers a viable means for attraction enhancement. These findings also suggest that there may well be other protherapeutic ends toward which the use of cohorts may be put, particularly in the context of group psychotherapy. This possibility is examined more closely in the remainder of the present chapter.

The Planted Patient

The discussion which follows presents a less formal research project than those examined elsewhere in this book. Its nature and intent relates more to generating than to testing hypotheses. Consistent with this more expansive intent, our procedures aimed not only at attraction enhancement, but also toward augmenting other potentially protherapeutic group processes. Our extrapolatory base for this investigation consisted of the several, social-psychological studies of small groups in which the investigator employed a cohort, accomplice, stooge, shill, or plant as an aid in implementing the independent variable manipulation. In much of this group dynamics literature, the plant's role was structured to be attraction-relevant. For example, the plant may serve as an opinion deviate, one whose stated views depart markedly from the group's norm on a given issue. Emerson (6), Festinger et al. (8), and Horowitz et al. (14) have demonstrated that intermember attrac-

---

[3] Since the interviews varied in length, rather than using subjects' raw scores for openness, we used an arcsin transformation of these scores—thus taking into account variable interview length.

tion will increase in response to the threat posed by the deviate plant
and, further, will increase even more if they are successful in "winning
him over." Other investigators, such as Gula (12), have made use of
accomplices for modeling purposes and have similarly been able to
effect an increase in intermember attraction. It was in response to findings such as these that we integrated special procedures into two psychotherapy groups we were constituting (10). One group consisted of
six university students and met at the University's Counseling Center.
The second group, also of six members, was drawn from a psychiatric
outpatient population and met at a county psychiatric clinic. Each
group was led by two therapists who were advanced graduate students in clinical psychology. In addition to the two therapists and six
bona fide patients, a graduate student was planted as a patient in
each group.

The therapy supervisor, the therapists, and the "plants" held regular
planning and role-playing sessions. These discussions sought to define
and redefine, in concrete terms, the manner in which the plants might
serve optimal therapeutic roles. Toward this end, we had to consider
not only ease of enactment and avoiding discovery but, most important, the functional roles needed but unfilled within each group.
Stated otherwise, each plant's "mandate" was built around our predictions regarding the evolving needs of each group. Since much of what
we sought to accomplish required that the plant serve at times as a
model for the other patients to emulate, it was necessary to maximize
his credibility as a model. This we attempted by building into each
plant's "cover story" the fact that he had been in group therapy before
and was already familiar with its procedures, tensions, potential benefits, and so forth. Our instructions to the plants in this regard were to
act "five sessions ahead" of the typical real group member. We sought
here a "potentiating effect through modeling." For example, in the first
session of each group, when member-disclosure anxiety was at a maximum and cohesiveness apparently minimal, the plants (with largely
feigned reticence) "opened up" by tentatively revealing their own
supposed psychopathology. Via what clearly appeared to us to be a
modeling process, several members of each group discussed their own
psychopathology during these sessions more rapidly and more deeply
than we have observed in other, plantless groups. In later sessions, the
plants also appeared to serve in disclosure- and attraction-enhancing
ways by enacting the role of opinion deviate, in a manner similar to
that used in the investigations cited above.

A wide variety of other potentially protherapeutic plant roles were
developed, rehearsed, and enacted as the two groups continued. Thus,

when needed, the plants reassured, attacked, befriended, argued, yielded, encouraged, or elaborated in detail their own purported psychopathology. They related in-group to out-group behavior; inspected, as Bach (3) has termed it, the group's interpersonal traffic; fought the therapists; agreed with the therapists; led the therapists; followed their lead; and set the emotional level of the group's going around, psychodramas, and marathon sessions. The plants at times aided in quieting monopolizers, permitted themselves to be "intimidated" by patients in need of assertiveness experience, augmented feelings of universalization, assisted in clique-busting and clique-formation, and encouraged other patients to discuss material during the group session which had originally been revealed to the plants during postsessions without the therapists. The plants showed "improvement" for modeling purposes, thus apparently raising the overall group level of expectancy for change and, perhaps most important from our theoretical perspective, markedly shortened the time necessary for the groups to develop an essentially group-centered mode of functioning.

Mistakes were also made by us, although none appeared enduringly harmful to the groups' progress. The plants at times subtly slid into the role of therapist, an error which interestingly was corrected by one patient or another interpreting the plant's apparent resistance. Reciprocally, the therapists on occasion tended to ignore the plant and endangered his role by failing to give him his "fair share" of treatment time. Again, other patients tended to correct this error. At times the plants failed to behave in a manner consistent with their stated psychopathology, and again were typically called on it by a sensitive patient. For example, the plant in our student group supposedly found it difficult to get close to people and, in other ways, purported to suffer from marked interpersonal insensitivity. The night we had to deal with the several exquisitely sensitive interpersonal observations he made has come to be known by us as the night the plant became a weed. Finally, a language problem emerged at times. It was rather startling to hear a supposedly unsophisticated group-therapy patient (the plant), in the midst of a heated argument about how much group agreement there was on a highly salient issue, use the term "consensual validation." In all, however, it was our clinical impression that the plants served an immensely useful and wide variety of protherapeutic purposes in these groups.

Although no control group or base rate information was obtained for purposes of evaluating these planted-patient procedures, we did wish to get beyond solely impressionistic evidence, at least as far as estimating attraction enhancement was concerned. To do so, we had all patients complete a sociometric questionnaire[4] following each odd-numbered session, and an attraction-to-group questionnaire after each even-numbered session.[5] The sociometric instrument focused primarily upon the therapeutic impact and likability of one's co-patients. In both groups it was clear that the plants were not the most popular or best-liked group members. However, as had been our intent, the plants were consistently seen as the the most protherapeutic patient in their respective groups.

We determined the average attraction-to-group score for each group and for each occasion of measurement. These means are reported in Figure 1. The trend for both groups is clear and upward. In the absence of control group information we can only conclude that it seems likely that in neither group did the plants have a negative influence on attraction and, most probably, functioned to increase inter-member attraction.

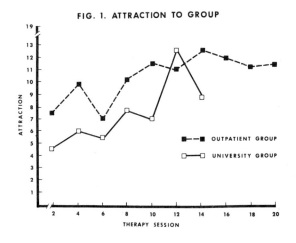

FIG. 1. ATTRACTION TO GROUP

References

1. Allen, V. L. Effect of knowledge of deception on conformity. *Journal of Social Psychology*, 1966, **69**, 101–106.

2. Asch, S. E. Effects of group pressure upon the modification and distortion and judgments. In H. Guetzkow (Ed.), *Groups, leadership and men*. Pittsburgh: Carnegie Press, 1951.

3. Bach, G. R. *Intensive group psychotherapy*. New York: Ronald Press, 1954.

[4] See Appendix I, pp. 222–223.
[5] *Ibid.*, p. 198.

4. Blake, R. R. & Brehm, J. W. The use of tape recorders to simulate a group atmosphere. *Journal of Abnormal and Social Psychology*, 1954, **49**, 311–313.

5. Crutchfield, R. S. Conformity and character. *American Psychologist*, 1955, **10**, 191–195.

6. Emerson, R. M. Deviation and rejection: An experimental replication. *American Sociological Review*, 1954, **19**, 688–693.

7. Feldman, M. J. & Goldfarb, M. R. Validity of group judgment and factors effecting independent and conformity behavior. *Journal of Social Psychology*, 1962, **58**, 289–294.

8. Festinger, L., Gerard, H., Hymovetch, B., Kelley, H., & Raven, B. The influence process in the presence of extreme deviates. *Human Relations*, 1952, **5**, 327–346.

9. Gerard, H. B. Conformity and commitment to the group. *Journal of Abnormal and Social Psychology*, 1964, **68**, 209–211.

10. Goldstein, A. P., Gassner, S., Greenberg, R., Gustin, A., Land, J., Liberman, B., & Streiner, D. The use of planted patients in group psychotherapy. *American Journal of Psychotherapy*, 1967, **21**, 767–773.

11. Goldstein, A. P., Heller, K., & Sechrest, L. B. *Psychotherapy and the psychology of behavior change.* New York: Wiley, 1966.

12. Gula, M. Boy's House—The use of a group for observation and treatment. *Mental Hygiene*, 1944, **28**, 430–437.

13. Himmelsbach, J. The influence of conformity pressure on psychotherapeutic attraction. Unpublished master's thesis, Syracuse University, 1970.

14. Horowitz, M. W., Lyons, J., & Perlmutter, H. V. Induction of forces in discussion groups. *Human Relations*, 1951, **4**, 57–75.

15. Jourard, S. M. *The transparent self.* Princeton, N.J.: Van Nostrand, 1964.

16. Locke, N. M. *Group psychoanalysis.* New York: New York University Press, 1961.

17. Orenstein, R. The influence of self-esteem on modeling behavior in a psychotherapy analogue. Unpublished master's thesis, Syracuse University, 1970.

18. Sherif, M. *The psychology of social norms.* New York: Harper, 1936.

19. Truax, C. B. The process of group psychotherapy. *Psychological Monographs*, 1961, **75**, Whole No. 511.

20. Walsh, W. The effects of conformity pressure on attraction to an interviewer. Unpublished master's thesis, Syracuse University, 1970.

21. Winer, B. J. *Statistical principles in experimental design.* New York: McGraw-Hill, 1962.

22. Wolf, A. & Schwartz, E. K. *Psychoanalysis in groups.* New York: Grune & Stratton, 1962.

Chapter XII

Summary

Our primary focus throughout this research program has been upon utilizing attraction-enhancement precedures developed in the social-psychological laboratory to analogously enhance the attractiveness of the therapist-patient relationship in psychotherapy. In each of our subseries of studies in which it was possible, our extrapolatory effort extended to two different types of settings and populations. The first was typically a university setting, involving an analogue or in-therapy design and randomly selected or moderately disturbed college students as subject-patients. Following such limited extrapolation, we tested our several hypotheses in psychiatric hospitals or outpatient clinics, prisons, and related settings—involving patients considerably more disturbed than those seeking help at a counseling center. Our major findings relevant to attraction enhancement are broadly summarized in Table 12.1.

One of the more important conclusions that may be drawn from Table 12.1 concerns the limits or parameters of our extrapolatory research. Concretely, note that almost all of the procedures successfully utilized to enhance interpersonal attraction in the social-psychological laboratory were similarly successful in the context of an analogue design or, *in vivo*, in our Counseling Center, while almost all such efforts failed in their intended purpose in the hospital and clinic settings. Extrapolation from laboratory to counseling center involves deriving procedures from subjects who are alert, bright, highly motivated, articulate, and the several other positive qualities represented by the term "YAVIS," and extrapolating these procedures to what are in most ways the *same* types of individuals, currently experiencing psychological difficulties. Thus we note from Table 12.1 that YAVIS-nonpatient to YAVIS-patient extrapolation is indeed a successful enterprise. Attraction-enhancing procedures and, perhaps more broadly, a general psychology of social influence, does appear to extend from laboratory to clinic when essentially similar types of individuals are involved. We may thus generally conclude that our research program provides a major initial step toward a technology of psychotherapeutic attraction enhancement.

Yet, and this is a most crucial stipulation, as is true of so many

Table 12.1

Summary of Attraction-Enhancement Research Results

Attraction-Enhancing Procedure	Subjects and Experimental Setting		
	YAVIS,[a] Laboratory	YAVIS, University (Analogue or Counseling Center)	NON-YAVIS Hospital, Clinic
1. Direct Structuring	Yes	Yes (desensitization) No (interview)	No
2. Trait Structuring	Yes	Yes	Yes (analogue) No (interview)
3. Therapist Structuring	Yes	Yes	not tested
4. Status	Yes	Yes	No
5. Effort-Consolidation	Yes	Yes	No
6. Modeling	Yes	Yes	No
7. Matching a) Interpersonal orientation b) Attitude similarity	Yes Yes	not tested No	Yes No
8. Role Playing	Yes	not tested	No
9. Conformity Pressure	Yes	Yes	not tested

[a] Studies conducted by other investigators, in the social-psychological laboratory.

aspects of contemporary psychotherapy, we have here a contribution to primarily a YAVIS-relevant technology. As the last column of Table 12.1 so fully indicates, to seek to extrapolate to what we have earlier described as NON-YAVIS patients appears to be almost a completely different enterprise. We would speculate that it is not only degree of psychopathology that is critical in this context but, perhaps even more important, the many characteristics of the NON-YAVIS patient that make a psychology of social influence *derived from college student subjects* largely irrelevant to such patients. What is vital here, for extrapolatory research to become a viable endeavor for NON-YAVIS patients, appears to be a psychology of social influence developed from investigations using NON-YAVIS persons as subjects. Such an enterprise would focus not so much on degree or type of psychopathology, but on differences between YAVIS and NON-YAVIS individuals of likely relevance to cognitive, emotional, and personality change.[1] Thus we would ask, in developing a psychology of social influence for NON-YAVIS people, what is the likely relevance of their temporal perspective, achievement motivation, need for approval, psychological-mindedness, authoritarianism, ability to delay gratification, persuasibility, verbal fluency, and so forth? Characteristics such as the foregoing are both relevant to behavior in an experimental setting and representative of those qualities frequently described as differentiating between middle-class and lower-class life styles.

It is of interest in this context that two of our extended extrapolations that were partially successful did involve hospitalized patients who in many ways were more YAVIS- than NON-YAVIS-like. Davidoff's (1) attempt to enhance attraction via direct structuring failed when her VA hospital sample was considered as a whole. A post hoc analysis, however, revealed success for these procedures on a subsample of patients rated by staff psychologists as having a good prognosis and high functioning intelligence. It will also be recalled that Liberman's (5) investigation demonstrated successful use of modeling procedures to increase the level of patient disclosure in an interview context. His experimental setting was a hospital for alcoholics and most of his patient sample reflected a much more middle-class life style than was the case in any of our other extended extrapolation investigations.

Thus we have proposed here that extrapolatory research involving a rather modest leap from YAVIS subjects to YAVIS patients appears to be an appropriate and fruitful research strategy. Before taking the more substantial jump to NON-YAVIS patient populations, a new springboard is needed—research on social influence using as subjects individuals whose dispositional characteristics are more similar to the target patient populations.

---

[1] Schultz, drawing upon both his own (7) and Smart's (8) extended surveys of psychological journals, has commented in this regard: ". . . approximately 80% of our research is performed on the 3% of the population currently enrolled in college. Regardless of how much our college enrollments may increase, college students most likely will never be truly representative of the total adult population, in terms of level of intelligence alone. Further, this pronounced emphasis on college students means that most of our research is conducted with a very young group. . . . There is also the problem of social class representation . . . the college student population contains more upper- and middle-class people and fewer lower-class people than the general population" (7, p. 218).

These recommendations, and the thrust of our research program in general, are in no way inconsistent with the notion that both evolutionary and revolutionary changes in contemporary psychotherapy must be forthcoming if we are to meaningfully assist the NON-YAVIS patient. Our research program exemplifies one evolutionary approach, in that it seeks to develop new procedures to indoctrinate such patients into traditional forms of psychotherapy. Simultaneous with this orientation, new and different approaches to psychological intervention must be sought. Several aspects of the growing community mental health movement exemplify this more radical, revolutionary approach to behavior change. We would hope, however, that eventually both orientations, evolutionary and revolutionary, may profit greatly by recourse to the types of nonclinical investigations of behavior change from which our own research program has grown.

There are two other characteristics of future extrapolatory research we wish to briefly suggest. When Davidoff moved from analysis of her entire sample to a more restricted group of patients, she not only was examining a more YAVIS-like group of patients, but also a more *homogeneous* group of patients. Time and again in our extended extrapolation studies we found exceedingly large within-group variance. The use of more homogeneous patient samples as well as other experimental and statistical procedures for reducing such error variance appear to be a vital methodological step.

A further methodological consideration involves the power of our independent variable manipulations throughout the present research program. Beyond the observation that such manipulations rarely had their intended effect with NON-YAVIS subjects, it should also be noted that we have little evidence regarding the durability of these effects when they indeed did work. Our several approaches to attraction enhancement with YAVIS subjects and patients did generally increase their attraction to the therapist, but our dependent variable measurement was typically limited to the initial interviews or the experimental session proper. Since analogous manipulations rather rarely endure in the social-psychological laboratory, our hunch would be that in the absence of further experimenter or therapist interventions, the effects of attraction-enhancing manipulations in psychotherapy may similarly wash out over time. Thus, for the NON-YAVIS patient for whom there was no effect and for the YAVIS patient for whom the effect may not have been enduring, we would propose the need for a *series* of related or repetitive experimental manipulations. Such an approach might be implemented (in a manner analogous to what occurs in psychotherapeutic practice) by the straightforward administration of a variety of related stimuli, e.g., a series of modeling tapes, a series of role-play scripts. Or, this methodological orientation might assume a form more similar to an operant paradigm in which measures on the dependent variable are obtained after each individual manipulation in the series, with reinforcement provided in response to subject behaviors that are in the "desired" direction, i.e., behavioral shaping.

We wish also to comment on substantive areas, other than attraction enhancement, of potential use for the extrapolatory study of psychotherapy. A few years ago the present writer, in collaboration with Kenneth Heller and Lee Sechrest, presented an extended statement (3) of the orientation to psychotherapy and psychotherapy research which the present book has sought to begin implementing. In our earlier formulation, in addition to laboratory extrapolations relevant to psychotherapeutic attraction, we drew upon research on attitude change, on characteristics of persuasive messages, and on personality dispositions toward persuasibility as ways of framing hypotheses relevant to psychotherapeutic communication with restive patients. We turned to research on time estimation and time perspective to propose predictions of relevance to time-limited psychotherapy. We drew upon studies of sensory deprivation and social isolation to formulate hypotheses about optimal patient anxiety level in psychotherapy. Our concern about the minimal psychotherapeutic use to which between-session hours are put led us to extrapolate from laboratory studies of emotional sensitivity training. The usefulness of group dynamics research for the enhancement of group psychotherapy was also of major concern to us. Thus we considered research on group leadership at some length, distilling predictions from such research relevant to the leadership of psychotherapy groups. Investigations of communication networks in problem-solving groups were drawn upon to frame hypotheses about optimal patterns of group psychotherapeutic communication, and barriers thereto. Group dynamics studies on member expectations, intergroup competition, clique-formation, and goal setting were all considered for their relevance to the development of cohesiveness in psychotherapy groups. In a similar manner, laboratory studies were useful in developing hypotheses about such other characteristics of psychotherapy groups as therapist-like behavior by patients, open versus closed groups, the use of postsessions, and phase movement.

Though our extrapolations were many, and several relevant to attraction have been presented in the present book, it must be noted that social psychology's potential contribution to psychotherapy extends well beyond our particular extrapolations and investigations.

Others concerned with the advance of psychotherapy have recently proposed further extrapolatory formulations (2, 4, 6, 9). The scope and substance of laboratory and field research conducted by social psychologists are both considerable and growing. We urge others concerned with psychotherapeutic effectiveness to pursue further tests of this research strategy.

References

1. Davidoff, L. Schizophrenic patients in psychotherapy: The effects of degree of information and compatibility expectations on behavior in the interview setting: An operant conditioning analogue. Unpublished doctoral dissertation, Syracuse University, 1969.

2. Durkin, H. E. Toward a common basis for group dynamics: Group and therapeutic processes in group psychotherapy. *International Journal of Group Psychotherapy*, 1957, 7, 115–130.

3. Goldstein, A. P., Heller, K., & Sechrest, L. B. *Psychotherapy and the psychology of behavior change*. New York: Wiley, 1966.

4. Lakin, M. & Carson, R. C. A therapeutic vehicle in search of a theory of therapy. *Journal of Applied Behavioral Science*, 1966, 2, 27–40.

5. Liberman, B. The effect of modeling procedures on attraction and disclosure in a psychotherapy analog. Unpublished doctoral dissertation, Syracuse University, 1970.

6. Parloff, M. B. Group dynamics and group psychotherapy: The state of the union. Presented at American Group Psychotherapy Association, Washington, D.C., January, 1963.

7. Schultz, D. P. The human subject in psychological research. *Psychological Bulletin*, 1969, 72, 214–228.

8. Smart, R. Subject selection bias in psychological research. *Canadian Psychologist*, 1966, 7, 115–121.

9. Strong, S. R. Counseling: An interpersonal influence process. *Journal of Counseling Psychology*, 1968, 15, 215–224.

Appendices

Appendix I

Questionnaires

(Present Self Questionnaire)

Name _____

Date _____

Listed below are common problems that people sometimes have. Directly under each problem are statements showing how much like or unlike a person each problem can be. Please read each of the problems carefully and decide how much it is like or unlike you *now*. Then place an X in the parentheses ( ) over the statement which best fits how well the problem describes you *now*. Since each statement is not in the same place after each problem, please read them very carefully. There are no right or wrong answers to these problems; we are only interested in *your* feelings about them.

Examples:

If you worry about unimportant things ALMOST ALWAYS, you would place an X over the statement "almost always like me" as shown below:

1. Worry about unimportant things:

(X)	( )	( )	( )	( )
almost always like me	often like me	sometimes like me	seldom like me	never like me

If you worry about unimportant things OFTEN, you would place an X over the statement "often like me" as shown below:

1. Worry about unimportant things:

( )	( )	( )	(X)	( )
never like me	seldom like me	sometimes like me	often like me	almost always like me

If you worry about unimportant things SOMETIMES, you would place an X over the statement "sometimes like me" as shown below:

1. Worry about unimportant things:

( )	( )	(X)	( )	( )
never like me	seldom like me	sometimes like me	often like me	almost always like me

If you worry about unimportant things SELDOM, you would place an X over the statement "seldom like me" as shown below:

1. Worry about unimportant things:

( )	( )	( )	(X)	( )
almost always like me	often like me	sometimes like me	seldom like me	never like me

If you NEVER worry about unimportant things, you would place an X over the statement "never like me" as shown below:

1. Worry about unimportant things:

(X)	( )	( )	( )	( )
never like me	seldom like me	sometimes like me	often like me	almost always like me

---

Do not spend much time on any one problem. When you are finished, check to see that you have answered every question.

1. Worry about unimportant things:

( )	( )	( )	( )	( )
almost always like me	often like me	sometimes like me	seldom like me	never like me

2. Difficulty in sleeping:

( )	( )	( )	( )	( )
almost always like me	often like me	sometimes like me	seldom like me	never like me

3. Feeling afraid in many situations:

( )	( )	( )	( )	( )
never like me	seldom like me	sometimes like me	often like me	almost always like me

4. Nausea or upset stomach:

( )	( )	( )	( )	( )
never like me	seldom like me	sometimes like me	often like me	almost always like me

5. Queer unpleasant feeling in my body:

( )	( )	( )	( )	( )
never like me	seldom like me	sometimes like me	often like me	almost always like me

6. Finding it hard to keep my mind on things:

( )	( )	( )	( )	( )
never like me	seldom like me	sometimes like me	often like me	almost always like me

7. Shortness of breath:

( )	( )	( )	( )	( )
almost always like me	often like me	sometimes like me	seldom like me	never like me

8. Feeling useless to myself and others:

( )	( )	( )	( )	( )
never like me	seldom like me	sometimes like me	often like me	almost always like me

9. Getting tired easily:

( )	( )	( )	( )	( )
almost always like me	often like me	sometimes like me	seldom like me	never like me

10. Feeling lonely:

( )	( )	( )	( )	( )
never like me	seldom like me	sometimes like me	often like me	almost always like me

11. Feeling that I'm getting a raw deal from life:

( )	( )	( )	( )	( )
never like me	seldom like me	sometimes like me	often like me	almost always like me

12. Pains in the lower part of my back:

( )	( )	( )	( )	( )
never like me	seldom like me	sometimes like me	often like me	almost always like me

13. Getting mad easily:

( )	( )	( )	( )	( )
never like me	seldom like me	sometimes like me	often like me	almost always like me

14. Feeling that I'm no good at all:

( )	( )	( )	( )	( )
never like me	seldom like me	sometimes like me	often like me	almost always like me

15. Feeling that no one seems to understand me:

( )	( )	( )	( )	( )
almost always like me	often like me	sometimes like me	seldom like me	never like me

16. Getting upset easily:

( )	( )	( )	( )	( )
never like me	seldom like me	sometimes like me	often like me	almost always like me

17. Feeling I can't do anything well:

( )	( )	( )	( )	( )
never like me	seldom like me	sometimes like me	often like me	almost always like me

18. Worrying about my weight:

( )	( )	( )	( )	( )
almost always like me	often like me	sometimes like me	seldom like me	never like me

19. Trouble with my bowel movements:

( )	( )	( )	( )	( )
almost always like me	often like me	sometimes like me	seldom like me	never like me

20. Finding that my feelings are easily hurt:

( )	( )	( )	( )	( )
almost always like me	often like me	sometimes like me	seldom like me	never like me

21. Poor appetite:

( )	( )	( )	( )	( )
almost always like me	often like me	sometimes like me	seldom like me	never like me

22. Getting discouraged easily:

( )	( )	( )	( )	( )
never like me	seldom like me	sometimes like me	often like me	almost always like me

23. Trouble with my eyes or ears:

( )	( )	( )	( )	( )
almost always like me	often like me	sometimes like me	seldom like me	never like me

24. Cough, sore throat, or trouble swallowing:

( )	( )	( )	( )	( )
never like me	seldom like me	sometimes like me	often like me	almost always like me

25. Feeling nervous:

( )	( )	( )	( )	( )
never like me	seldom like me	sometimes like me	often like me	almost always like me

26. Shaking or trembling:

( )	( )	( )	( )	( )
almost always like me	often like me	sometimes like me	seldom like me	never like me

27. Headaches:

( )	( )	( )	( )	( )
almost always like me	often like me	sometimes like me	seldom like me	never like me

28. Finding I can't make up my mind about things:

( )	( )	( )	( )	( )
never like me	seldom like me	sometimes like me	often like me	almost always like me

29. Getting embarrassed easily:

( )	( )	( )	( )	( )
almost always like me	often like me	sometimes like me	seldom like me	never like me

30. Skin eruptions or rashes:

( )	( )	( )	( )	( )
never like me	seldom like me	sometimes like me	often like me	almost always like me

31. Feeling sad, getting the blues:

( )	( )	( )	( )	( )
never like me	seldom like me	sometimes like me	often like me	almost always like me

32. Feeling inferior:

( )	( )	( )	( )	( )
never like me	seldom like me	sometimes like me	often like me	almost always like me

33. Feeling ill at ease with other people:

( )	( )	( )	( )	( )
almost always like me	often like me	sometimes like me	seldom like me	never like me

34. Pains in the arms or legs:

( )	( )	( )	( )	( )
never like me	seldom like me	sometimes like me	often like me	almost always like me

35. Faintness or dizziness:

( )	( )	( )	( )	( )
almost always like me	often like me	sometimes like me	seldom like me	never like me

36. Feeling I take things too seriously:

( )	( )	( )	( )	( )
never like me	seldom like me	sometimes like me	often like me	almost always like me

37. Feeling guilty without a good reason for it:

( )	( )	( )	( )	( )
never like me	seldom like me	sometimes like me	often like me	almost always like me

38. Feeling I have too many responsibilities:

( )	( )	( )	( )	( )
almost always like me	often like me	sometimes like me	seldom like me	never like me

39. Feeling that other people aren't fair to me:

( )	( )	( )	( )	( )
never like me	seldom like me	sometimes like me	often like me	almost always like me

40. Feeling that my luck is very bad:

( )	( )	( )	( )	( )
never like me	seldom like me	sometimes like me	often like me	almost always like me

41. Feeling that I'm too sensitive:

( )	( )	( )	( )	( )
almost always like me	often like me	sometimes like me	seldom like me	never like me

42. Worrying a lot about the future:

( )	( )	( )	( )	( )
almost always like me	often like me	sometimes like me	seldom like me	never like me

43. Pains in my chest:

( )	( )	( )	( )	( )
never like me	seldom like me	sometimes like me	often like me	almost always like me

44. Feeling that I don't get along with my family:

( )	( )	( )	( )	( )
almost always like me	often like me	sometimes like me	seldom like me	never like me

45. Hot or cold spells:

( )	( )	( )	( )	( )
never like me	seldom like me	sometimes like me	often like me	almost always like me

46. Feeling afraid without knowing why:

( )	( )	( )	( )	( )
never like me	seldom like me	sometimes like me	often like me	almost always like me

47. Worrying a lot about the past:

( )	( )	( )	( )	( )
never like me	seldom like me	sometimes like me	often like me	almost always like me

48. Feel my heart is pounding or racing:

( )	( )	( )	( )	( )
almost always like me	often like me	sometimes like me	seldom like me	never like me

49. Sore muscles:

( )	( )	( )	( )	( )
never like me	seldom like me	sometimes like me	often like me	almost always like me

50. Sweating a lot, even on cold days:

( )	( )	( )	( )	( )
never like me	seldom like me	sometimes like me	often like me	almost always like me

(Expected Self Questionnaire)

Name _____

Date _____

Listed below are common problems that people sometimes have. Directly under each problem are statements showing how much a person can expect each problem to be like or unlike them. Please read each of the problems carefully and decide how much you *expect* it to be like or unlike you *after your treatment here*. Then place an X in the parentheses ( ) over the statement which best fits how you *realistically expect* the problem to describe you *after your treatment here*. Do *not* answer these problems on the basis of what you hope, wish, or would like to be; only consider your realistic expectations. Since each statement is not in the same place after each problem, please read them very carefully. There are no right or wrong answers to these problems; we are only interested in *your* feelings about them.

Examples:

If you realistically expect to worry about unimportant things ALMOST ALWAYS after your treatment here, you would place an X over the statement "expect almost always like me" as shown below:

1. Worry about unimportant things:

(X)	( )	( )	( )	( )
expect almost always like me	expect often like me	expect sometimes like me	expect seldom like me	expect never like me

If you realistically expect to worry about unimportant things OFTEN, you would place an X over the statement "expect often like me" as shown below:

1. Worry about unimportant things:

( )	( )	( )	(X)	( )
expect never like me	expect seldom like me	expect sometimes like me	expect often like me	expect almost always like me

If you realistically expect to worry about unimportant things SOME-TIMES, you would place an X over the statement "expect sometimes like me" as shown below:

1. Worry about unimportant things:

( )	( )	(X)	( )	( )
expect never like me	expect seldom like me	expect sometimes like me	expect often like me	expect almost always like me

If you realistically expect to worry about unimportant things SELDOM, you would place an X over the statement "expect seldom like me" as shown below:

1. Worry about unimportant things:

( )	( )	( )	(X)	( )
expect almost always like me	expect often like me	expect sometimes like me	expect seldom like me	expect never like me

If you realistically expect to worry about unimportant things NEVER after your treatment here, you would place an X over the statement "expect never like me" shown below:

1. Worry about unimportant things:

(X)	( )	( )	( )	( )
expect never like me	expect seldom like me	expect sometimes like me	expect often like me	expect almost always like me

---

Do not spend much time on any one problem. When you are finished, check to see that you have answered every question.

1. Worry about unimportant things:

( )	( )	( )	(	( )
expect almost always like me	expect often like me	expect sometimes like me	expect seldom like me	expect never like me

2. Difficulty in sleeping:

( )	( )	( )	( )	( )
expect almost always like me	expect often like me	expect sometimes like me	expect seldom like me	expect never like me

3. Feeling afraid in many situations:

( )	( )	( )	( )	( )
expect never like me	expect seldom like me	expect sometimes like me	expect often like me	expect almost always like me

4. Nausea or upset stomach:

( )	( )	( )	( )	( )
expect never like me	expect seldom like me	expect sometimes like me	expect often like me	expect almost always like me

5. Queer unpleasant feeling in my body:

( )	( )	))	( )	( )
expect almost always like me	expect often like me	expect sometimes like me	expect seldom like me	expect never like me

6. Finding it hard to keep mind on things:

( )	( )	( )	( )	( )
expect never like me	expect seldom like me	expect sometimes like me	expect often like me	expect almost always like me

7. Shortness of breath:

( )	( )	( )	( )	( )
expect almost always like me	expect often like me	expect sometimes like me	expect seldom like me	expect never like me

8. Feeling useless to myself and others:

( )	( )	( )	( )	( )
expect never like me	expect seldom like me	expect sometimes like me	expect often like me	expect almost always like me

9. Getting tired easily:

( )	( )	( )	( )	( )
expect almost always like me	expect often like me	expect sometimes like me	expect seldom like me	expect never like me

10. Feeling lonely:

( )	( )	( )	( )	( )
expect almost always like me	expect often like me	expect sometimes like me	expect seldom like me	expect never like me

11. Feeling that I'm getting a raw deal from life:

( )	( )	( )	( )	( )
expect never like me	expect seldom like me	expect sometimes like me	expect often like me	expect almost always like me

12. Pains in the lower part of my back:

( )	( )	( )	( )	( )
expect never like me	expect seldom like me	expect sometimes like me	expect often like me	expect almost always like me

13. Getting mad easily:

( )	( )	( )	( )	( )
expect never like me	expect seldom like me	expect sometimes like me	expect often like me	expect almost always like me

14. Feeling that I'm no good at all:

( )	( )	( )	( )	( )
expect never like me	expect seldom like me	expect sometimes like me	expect often like me	expect almost always like me

15. Feeling that no one seems to understand me:

( )	( )	( )	( )	( )
expect almost always like me	expect often like me	expect sometimes like me	expect seldom like me	expect never like me

16. Getting upset easily:

( )	( )	( )	( )	( )
expect never like me	expect seldom like me	expect sometimes like me	expect often like me	expect almost always like me

17. Feeling I can't do anything well:

( )	( )	( )	( )	( )
expect never like me	expect seldom like me	expect sometimes like me	expect often like me	expect almost always like me

18. Worrying about my weight:

( )	( )	( )	( )	( )
expect almost always like me	expect often like me	expect sometimes like me	expect seldom like me	expect never like me

19. Trouble with my bowel movements:

( )	( )	( )	( )	( )
expect almost always like me	expect often like me	expect sometimes like me	expect seldom like me	expect never like me

20. Finding that my feelings are easily hurt:

( )	( )	( )	( )	( )
expect almost always like me	expect often like me	expect sometimes like me	expect seldom like me	expect never like me

21. Poor appetite:

( )	( )	( )	( )	( )
expect almost always like me	expect often like me	expect sometimes like me	expect seldom like me	expect never like me

22. Getting discouraged easily:

( )	( )	( )	( )	( )
expect never like me	expect seldom like me	expect sometimes like me	expect often like me	expect almost always like me

23. Trouble with my eyes or ears:

( )	( )	( )	( )	( )
expect almost always like me	expect often like me	expect sometimes like me	expect seldom like me	expect never like me

24. Cough, sore throat, or trouble swallowing:

( )	( )	( )	( )	( )
expect never like me	expect seldom like me	expect sometimes like me	expect often like me	expect almost always like me

25. Feeling nervous:

( )	( )	( )	( )	( )
expect never like me	expect seldom like me	expect sometimes like me	expect often like me	expect almost always like me

26. Shaking or trembling:

( )	( )	( )	( )	( )
expect almost always like me	expect often like me	expect sometimes like me	expect seldom like me	expect never like me

27. Headaches:

( )	( )	( )	( )	( )
expect almost always like me	expect often like me	expect sometimes like me	expect seldom like me	expect never like me

28. Finding I can't make up my mind about things:

( )	( )	( )	( )	( )
expect never like me	expect seldom like me	expect sometimes like me	expect often like me	expect almost always like me

29. Getting embarrassed easily:

( )	( )	( )	( )	( )
expect almost always like me	expect often like me	expect sometimes like me	expect seldom like me	expect never like me

30. Skin eruptions or rashes:

( )	( )	( )	( )	( )
expect never like me	expect seldom like me	expect sometimes like me	expect often like me	expect almost always like me

31. Feeling sad, getting the blues:

( )	( )	( )	( )	( )
expect never like me	expect seldom like me	expect sometimes like me	expect often like me	expect almost always like me

32. Feeling inferior:

( )	( )	( )	( )	( )
expect never like me	expect seldom like me	expect sometimes like me	expect often like me	expect almost always like me

33. Feeling ill at ease with other people:

( )	( )	( )	( )	( )
expect almost always like me	expect often like me	expect sometimes like me	expect seldom like me	expect never like me

34. Pains in the arms or legs:

( )	( )	( )	( )	( )
expect never like me	expect seldom like me	expect sometimes like me	expect often like me	expect almost always like me

35. Faintness or dizziness:

( )	( )	( )	( )	( )
expect almost always like me	expect often like me	expect sometimes like me	expect seldom like me	expect never like me

36. Feeling I take things too seriously:

( )	( )	( )	( )	( )
expect never like me	expect seldom like me	expect sometimes like me	expect often like me	expect almost always like me

37. Feeling guilty without a good reason for it:

( )	( )	( )	( )	( )
expect never like me	expect seldom like me	expect sometimes like me	expect often like me	expect almost always like me

38. Feeling I have too many responsibilities:

( )   ( )   ( )   ( )   ( )

| expect almost always like me | expect often like me | expect sometimes like me | expect seldom like me | expect never like me |

39. Feeling that other people aren't fair to me:

( )   ( )   ( )   ( )   ( )

| expect never like me | expect seldom like me | expect sometimes like me | expect often like me | expect almost always like me |

40. Feeling that my luck is very bad:

( )   ( )   ( )   ( )   ( )

| expect never like me | expect seldom like me | expect sometimes like me | expect often like me | expect almost always like me |

41. Feeling that I'm too sensitive:

( )   ( )   ( )   ( )   ( )

| expect almost always like me | expect often like me | expect sometimes like me | expect seldom like me | expect never like me |

42. Worrying a lot about the future:

( )   ( )   ( )   ( )   ( )

| expect almost always like me | expect often like me | expect sometimes like me | expect seldom like me | expect never like me |

43. Pains in my chest:

( )   ( )   ( )   ( )   ( )

| expect never like me | expect seldom like me | expect sometimes like me | expect often like me | expect almost always like me |

44. Feeling that I don't get along with my family:

( )   ( )   ( )   ( )   ( )

| expect almost always like me | expect often like me | expect sometimes like me | expect seldom like me | expect never like me |

45. Hot or cold spells:

( )   ( )   ( )   ( )   ( )
_____
expect   expect   expect   expect   expect
never   seldom   sometimes   often   almost
like me   like me   like me   like me   always
                                                          like me

46. Feeling afraid without knowing why:

( )   ( )   ( )   (( )
_____
expect   expect   expect   expect   expect
never   seldom   sometimes   often   almost
like me   like me   like me   like me   always
                                                          like me

47. Worrying a lot about the past:

( )   ( )   ( )   ( )   ( )
_____
expect   expect   expect   expect   expect
never   seldom   sometimes   often   almost
like me   like me   like me   like me   always
                                                          like me

48. Feel my heart is pounding or racing:

( )   ( )   ( )   ( )   ( )
_____
expect   expect   expect   expect   expect
almost   often   sometimes   seldom   never
always   like me   like me   like me   like me
like me

49. Sore muscles:

( )   ( )   ( )   ( )   ( )
_____
expect   expect   expect   expect   expect
never   seldom   sometimes   often   almost
like me   like me   like me   like me   always
                                                          like me

50. Sweating a lot, even on cold days:

( )   ( )   ( )   ( )   ( )
_____
expect   expect   expect   expect   expect
never   seldom   sometimes   often   almost
like me   like me   like me   like me   always
                                                          like me

(Friend's Problem Inventory)

Name _____

Date _____

Listed below are common problems that people sometimes have. For each problem ask yourself the question: If a close friend said that he (she) had this problem and asked me to whom he (she) should go to help solve it, in what order would I recommend the sources of help? For *each* problem, put the number 1 next to the source of help you would recommend first, the number 2 next to the source of help you would recommend second, etc.

Example:

If your friend said that he (she) was "worrying about unimportant things" and, to help solve this problem, you would recommend that he (she) seek help first from his Clergyman, place the number 1 next to the word Clergyman. If the second source of help you would recommend is this Clinic, place the number 2 next to the word Clinic. If your third recommendation would be not to send your friend to anyone, that he should work on the problem by himself, place the number 3 next to the words No one. If your fourth choice was his parents, place the number 4 next to the word Parents. If your fifth recommendation was a friend, place the number 5 next to the word Friend. Your completed answer for this problem, therefore, would be as shown below:

a. Worry about unimportant things:

Friend 5   No one 3   Clinic 2   Clergyman 1   Parents 4

Do not spend much time on any one problem. When you are finished, check to see that you have answered every problem.

1. Worry about unimportant things:
   Parents___ Clinic___ Clergyman___ No one___ Friend___
2. Difficulty in sleeping:
   Clergyman___ Friend___ Clinic___ No one___ Parents___
3. Feeling afraid in many situations:
   Friend___ No one___ Clinic___ Parents___ Clergyman___

4. Nausea or upset stomach:
   Parents___ Clinic___ Clergyman___ No one___ Friend___
5. Queer unpleasant feeling in my body:
   Clergyman___ Clinic___ Parents___ No one___ Friend___
6. Finding it hard to keep my mind on things:
   No one___ Clergyman___ Clinic___ Friend___ Parents___
7. Shortness of breath:
   Clergyman___ Parents___ Clinic___ Friend___ No one___
8. Feeling useless to myself and others:
   Parents___ Clinic___ Clergyman___ No one___ Friend___
9. Getting tired easily:
   Friend___ Parents___ No one___ Clinic___ Clergyman___
10. Feeling lonely:
    Clergyman___ Parents___ Friend___ No one___ Clinic___
11. Feeling that I'm getting a raw deal from life:
    Clinic___ Clergyman___ Parents___ No one___ Friend___
12. Pains in the lower part of my back:
    No one___ Clergyman___ Friend___ Clinic___ Parents___
13. Getting mad easily:
    No one___ Clergyman___ Friend___ Clinic___ Parents___
14. Feeling that I'm no good at all:
    Parents___ Friend___ Clergyman___ Clinic___ No one___
15. Feeling that no one seems to understand me:
    Friend___ Clinic___ Parents___ Clergyman___ No one___
16. Getting upset easily:
    Clinic___ Clergyman___ Friend___ Parents___ No one___
17. Feeling I can't do anything well:
    Clinic___ Friend___ No one___ Clergyman___ Parents___
18. Worrying about my weight:
    Friend___ Parents___ Clergyman___ Clinic___ No one___
19. Trouble with my bowel movements:
    Parents___ Clergyman___ Friend___ Clinic___ No one___
20. Finding that my feelings are easily hurt:
    No one___ Parents___ Clinic___ Clergyman___ Friend___
21. Poor appetite:
    No one___ Clinic___ Parents___ Friend___ Clergyman___
22. Getting discouraged easily:
    Friend ___Clergyman___ No one___ Parents___ Clinic___
23. Trouble with my eyes or ears:
    Clinic___ No one___ Friend___ Clergyman___ Parents___
24. Cough, sore throat, or trouble swallowing:
    Clergyman___ Clinic___ Parents___ No one___ Friend___
25. Feeling nervous:
    Friend___ Clergyman___ Clinic___ Parents___ No one___
26. Shaking or trembling:
    Friend___ Clinic___ Parents___ Clergyman___ No one___
27. Headaches:
    No one___ Friend___ Parents___ Clinic___ Clergyman___
28. Finding I can't make up my mind about things:
    No one___ Parents___ Clinic___ Clergyman___ Friend___

29. Getting embarrassed easily:
    Clinic___ Clergyman___ No one___ Parents___ Friend___
30. Skin eruptions or rashes:
    No one___ Friend___ Clinic___ Parents___ Clergyman___
31. Feeling sad, getting the blues:
    Clinic___ Clergyman___ Parents___ No one___ Friend___
32. Feeling inferior:
    Clergyman___ Parents___ Friend___ No one___ Clinic___
33. Feeling ill at ease with other people:
    No one___ Clergyman___ Friend___ Parents___ Clinic___
34. Pains in the arms or legs:
    Clinic___ No one___ Friend___ Clergyman___ Parents___
35. Faintness or dizziness:
    No one___ Friend___ Clergyman___ Parents___ Clinic___
36. Feeling I take things too seriously:
    Parents ___Friend___ Clergyman___ No one___ Clinic___
37. Feeling guilty without a good reason for it:
    Clinic___ Parents___ No one___ Clergyman___ Friend___
38. Feeling I have too many responsibilities:
    No one___ Friend___ Parents ___Clinic___ Clergyman___
39. Feeling that other people aren't fair to me:
    Parents___ No one___ Clinic___ Friend___ Clergyman___
40. Feeling that my luck is very bad:
    Friend___ Parents___ No one___ Clinic___ Clergyman___
41. Feeling that I'm too sensitive:
    Friend___ No one___ Clinic ___Parents___ Clergyman___
42. Worrying a lot about the future:
    Friend___ No one___ Clinic___ Parents___ Clergyman___
43. Pains in my chest:
    Clinic___ Friend___ Parents___ Clergyman___ No one___
44. Feeling that I don't get along with my family:
    Clergyman___ Parents___ Friend___ No one___ Clinic___
45. Hot or cold spells:
    Clinic___ Friend___ Clergyman___ No one___ Parents___
46. Feeling afraid without knowing why:
    Clergyman___ No one___ Parents___ Clinic___ Friend___
47. Worrying a lot about the past:
    Friend___ Clinic___ Clergyman___ Parents___ No one___
48. Feeling my heart is pounding or racing:
    Friend___ No one___ Clergyman___ Clinic___ Parents___
49. Sore muscles:
    Clinic___ Parents___ Friend___ No one___ Clergyman___
50. Sweating a lot, even on cold days:
    Clinic___ Parents___ Friend___ No one___ Clergyman___

(Patient-Therapist Matching Scale)

Below is a list of statements made by other patients, like yourself, when they were asked to describe the kind of interviewer with whom they would most like to meet. Please read each statement carefully and decide how much you wish *your* interviewer to behave the way each statement describes. Circle one answer for each statement.

If you wish your interviewer to be . . .

. . . *not at all* that way,	circle *1.*
. . . *a little bit* that way,	circle *2.*
. . . *quite a bit* that way,	circle *3.*
. . . *very much* that way,	circle *4.*

HOW MUCH DO YOU WISH YOUR INTERVIEWER TO . . .

1.	act warm and friendly toward you?	1	2	3	4
2.	expect you to accept his ideas and opinions?	1	2	3	4
3.	try to help you help yourself?	1	2	3	4
4.	tell you what to do about difficult decisions?	1	2	3	4
5.	say what he thinks frankly and directly?	1	2	3	4
6.	try to get you to see things his way?	1	2	3	4
7.	show a real liking for you?	1	2	3	4
8.	let you know when he doesn't agree with you?	1	2	3	4
9.	act cool and detached?	1	2	3	4
10.	encourage you to depend on him for help?	1	2	3	4
11.	treat you as an equal?	1	2	3	4
12.	act as though he knew all the answers?	1	2	3	4
13.	encourage you to rely on others more?	1	2	3	4
14.	encourage you to rely on others less?	1	2	3	4
15.	relate to you as though you were a friend?	1	2	3	4
16.	be logical and stick to the facts?	1	2	3	4
17.	be critical and not easily impressed?	1	2	3	4
18.	ask you many questions?	1	2	3	4
19.	mostly sit quietly and wait for you to talk?	1	2	3	4
20.	seek underlying reasons for your problem?	1	2	3	4
21.	agree with your opinions all the time?	1	2	3	4
22.	ask you to take certain tests?	1	2	3	4
23.	refuse calls or other interruptions during your interviews?	1	2	3	4
24.	see you for as many interviews as *you* wish?	1	2	3	4

(Therapist's Personal Reaction Questionnaire)

During therapy, therapists have many different feelings and reactions. These reactions are sometimes negative, sometimes positive, and sometimes mixed. Leaders in various schools of therapy seem to agree that having varied feelings and reactions toward clients is not undesirable as long as the therapist recognizes and understands them. We are interested in learning what these feelings are and how they change. Your answers to this questionnaire will have nothing to do with your therapy. They will *not* be made available to your supervisor or anyone else except the researchers.

There are five possible answers to each of the items in the questionnaire:

1. Not characteristic of my present feelings.
2. Slightly characteristic of my present feelings.
3. Moderately characteristic of my present feelings.
4. Quite characteristic of my present feelings.
5. Highly characteristic of my present feelings.

Put a circle around the answer most representative of your *present* feelings. Be sure to put a circle around one answer for each item. Do not spend too much time on any one item. The numbers may appear in different orders after each item, but they always signify the same answer. Thank you for your cooperation.

1.	I like this client more than most.	1	2	3	4	5
2.	I was relieved when the interview was over.	5	4	3	2	1
3.	I couldn't get this client to open up.	5	4	3	2	1
4.	I have a more warm, friendly reaction to this client than others I have seen.	5	4	3	2	1
5.	I was seldom in doubt about what the client was trying to say.	1	2	3	4	5
6.	The client seemed to appreciate my efforts.	1	2	3	4	5
7.	Sometimes I got pretty tense during the interview.	5	4	3	2	1
8.	In general, I could not ask for a better client.	1	2	3	4	5
9.	I got pretty bored during the interview.	1	2	3	4	5
10.	I usually found significant things to respond to in what the client said.	5	4	3	2	1
11.	Interviews like this are bright spots in my schedule.	1	2	3	4	5
12.	I felt pretty ineffective with this client.	5	4	3	2	1
13.	I think I did a pretty competent job with this client.	5	4	3	2	1
14.	I disagree with this client about some basic matters.	5	4	3	2	1
15.	I think this client is trying harder to solve his (her) problems than most others I've seen.	1	2	3	4	5
16.	It was hard to know how to respond to this client in a helpful way.	5	4	3	2	1
17.	It's easier for me to see exactly how this client would feel in the situations he describes than it is with other clients.	1	2	3	4	5

18. I prefer working with this client more than others I've worked with.   1 2 3 4 5
19. I don't think this client will stand out in my pleasant memories of cases.   1 2 3 4 5
20. I didn't particularly enjoy my hour with this client.   5 4 3 2 1
21. I am more confident this client will work out his problems than I've been with others.   1 2 3 4 5
22. In comparison with other clients, I found it hard to get involved with this client's problems.   1 2 3 4 5
23. The therapy hour with this client was a more rewarding experience for me than with many others I've had.   5 4 3 2 1
24. I feel in need of help with this client.   1 2 3 4 5
25. I think we had a pretty relaxed, understanding kind of relationship.   1 2 3 4 5
26. I was more absorbed in what this client was saying than with others I've had.   5 4 3 2 1
27. Sometimes I felt pretty frustrated during the interview.   5 4 3 2 1
28. I found it easier to understand and communicate with this client than with others I've had.   1 2 3 4 5
29. It was really an effort to "stay with" this client.   5 4 3 2 1
30. I had a good feeling after the interview with this client.   5 4 3 2 1
31. I sometimes felt "pushed" by this client.   5 4 3 2 1
32. I would have like to have been able to feel more warmth toward this client than I did.   1 2 3 4 5
33. I got more satisfaction out of working with this client than with most I've seen.   5 4 3 2 1
34. I couldn't get close to this client.   1 2 3 4 5
35. I was sometimes at a loss as to how to respond to this client.   1 2 3 4 5
36. Sometimes I resented the client's attitude.   1 2 3 4 5
37. I got anxious about what to do or say with this client less frequently than with others I've had.   5 4 3 2 1
38. I felt more comfortable in the session with this client than in others I've had.   1 2 3 4 5
39. I doubt if any therapist could do much for this client.   5 4 3 2 1
40. I'm glad this particular client was assigned to me.   1 2 3 4 5

Client's Name —————————————————————

Date of Session ———————————————————

Your Name ——————————————————
(to be removed after coding)

(Client's Personal Reaction Questionnaire)

During therapy, people have many different feelings and reactions. We know that these reactions are sometimes negative, sometimes positive, and often mixed. Your responses to the following questionnaire will help us understand people's reactions to therapy. This will have nothing to do with *your* therapy. It will be *completely confidential*. Neither your therapist nor his superiors will be informed of your responses.

There are five possible answers to each of the items in the questionnaire:

1. Not characteristic of my present feelings.
2. Slightly characteristic of my present feelings.
3. Moderately characteristic of my present feelings.
4. Quite characteristic of my present feelings.
5. Highly characteristic of my present feelings.

Put a circle around the answer most representative of your *present* feelings. Be sure to put a circle around *one* answer for *each* item. Do not spend too much time on any one item. Thank you for your cooperation.

1. I'm pleased with my therapist's interest
   and attention.   1 2 3 4 5
2. I wish I felt as sure of myself in all
   social situations as I did with my therapist.   1 2 3 4 5
3. I doubt if many people get much help out of
   these interviews.   5 4 3 2 1
4. I have a very warm feeling toward my
   therapist.   5 4 3 2 1
5. It was hard for me to talk about myself
   with the therapist.   1 2 3 4 5
6. I wish I had some friends who were as understanding as my therapist.   5 4 3 2 1
7. I told the therapist a lot, but he (she)
   didn't give me much help.   5 4 3 2 1
8. I wish I could feel other people respected
   and liked me as much as my therapist seemed to.   1 2 3 4 5
9. I felt comfortable talking with my therapist.   1 2 3 4 5
10. Many of the things we talked about didn't seem
    to be related to my problems.   5 4 3 2 1
11. I wish I were more like my therapist.   1 2 3 4 5
12. I feel that my therapist regards me as a
    likable person.   5 4 3 2 1
13. Many of the things my therapist said just
    seemed to hit the nail on the head.   5 4 3 2 1
14. I sometimes hesitated to tell my therapist
    what I was really thinking.   5 4 3 2 1
15. I felt that the therapist really liked to
    spend the therapy session with me.   1 2 3 4 5
16. It was easier for me to talk with the
    therapist than with most other people.   5 4 3 2 1

17. If I had had someone else as a therapist I would have probably felt freer to discuss my problems.   1 2 3 4 5
18. I think I could criticize or get angry at my therapist and he (she) wouldn't resent it.   1 2 3 4 5
19. My therapist must be one of the best ones here.   1 2 3 4 5
20. I wish I had asked for this kind of help sooner.   5 4 3 2 1
21. I wish I could have spent more time with the therapist.   5 4 3 2 1
22. I frequently found it difficult to think of things to say when I was with my therapist.   1 2 3 4 5
23. I have the feeling that the therapist is one person I can really trust.   5 4 3 2 1
24. I got irritated at some of my therapist's comments.   1 2 3 4 5
25. I can't see where my therapist can do much to help me solve my problems.   1 2 3 4 5
26. I would like to behave toward other people like my therapist behaved toward me.   5 4 3 2 1
27. I don't know exactly why, but I felt nervous during the therapy hour.   1 2 3 4 5
28. It was sometimes hard for me to pay attention to what the therapist was saying.   5 4 3 2 1
29. I'm glad this particular therapist was assigned to me.   5 4 3 2 1
30. The therapist's looking at me all the time made me uncomfortable.   1 2 3 4 5
31. I'm sure that my therapist would take anything I could say or do without getting upset.   5 4 3 2 1
32. I was afraid to express my real feelings in the therapy session.   1 2 3 4 5
33. My therapist is a warm and friendly person.   1 2 3 4 5
34. I felt the need to keep the conversation moving during the therapy hour.   5 4 3 2 1
35. The interview seemed like a waste of time to me.   1 2 3 4 5
36. I sometimes felt like I was being put on the spot during the therapy hour.   1 2 3 4 5
37. I sometimes felt like leaving before the interview was over.   5 4 3 2 1
38. The things my therapist said and did gave me confidence in him.   1 2 3 4 5
39. I really felt the interview was worthwhile.   1 2 3 4 5

Name _____ Date _____
(to be removed after coding)

(Staff Rating Questionnaire)

As you probably know, _____ recently participated in some research which some graduate students at Syracuse University are conducting. It is desirable to have certain information on each patient which cannot be obtained from the hospital record. Your cooperation would be greatly appreciated.

Please rate this patient *on the basis of his overall behavior* within the last week or two. If you feel you have insufficient knowledge to make a rating, please check the box "No Knowledge."

1. Estimate the patient's current level of intellectual functioning.
___a. Below Average
___b. Average (Consider average approximately 90-100 IQ)
___c. Above Average
___d. No Knowledge

2. Estimate the patient's current span of attention for an intellectual task.
___a. Very Short (1-10 minutes)
___b. Short (10-30 minutes)
___c. Medium (30-60 minutes)
___d. Long (over 60 minutes)
___e. No Knowledge

3. Estimate the patient's current severity of pathology. (Adjustment is defined here as minimal vocational and/or social adaptation as a member of a community.)
___a. Very severe (Poor prognosis for adjustment outside the hospital)
___b. Moderate (50-50 chance for adjustment outside the hospital)
___c. Good (Good prognosis for adjustment outside the hospital)
___d. No Knowledge

4. Estimate the patient's current amount of seeking approval and companionship from other patients.
___a. Low
___b. Moderate
___c. High
___d. No Knowledge

5. Estimate the patient's current amount of seeking approval and companionship from staff members at the hospital.
___a. Low
___b. Moderate
___c. High
___d. No Knowledge

(Attraction to Group Questionnaire)

Name _____ Date _____

Group Psychotherapy Questionnaire A

Below are listed a number of feelings and attitudes a person may have towards his therapy group. Read each statement carefully and decide how strongly it describes your present feelings or attitudes about your therapy group. Then circle the number of your answer in the answer column.

IF YOU PRESENTLY FEEL . . .

. . . *not at all* that way, circle *1.*
. . . *a little* that way, circle *2.*
. . . *quite a bit* that way, circle *3.*
. . . *extremely* that way, circle *4.*

I WOULD LIKE TO . . .

1. remain a member of this group.	1 2 3 4
2. try a different kind of treatment, instead of the group meetings.	1 2 3 4
3. have longer group meetings.	1 2 3 4
4. see certain members quit the group.	1 2 3 4
5. meet with the group outside the therapy hour.	1 2 3 4
6. change some of the procedures now followed in the group.	1 2 3 4
7. see the group meet less often than it now does.	1 2 3 4
8. become close friends with most of the other group members.	1 2 3 4
9. recommend this kind of meeting to others.	1 2 3 4
10. persuade any member thinking of quitting the group to change his mind and stay on.	1 2 3 4
11. have different kinds of topics discussed in the group, instead of what we usually talk about.	1 2 3 4

(General Attraction to Treatment Scale)

Name _____ Date _____

Please describe your feelings toward the following items. **Choose the number** on the rating scale below that which most accurately conveys your feelings and place it in the blank space next to each item.

Rating Scale

1. very positive
2. positive
3. slightly positive
4. neutral
5. slightly negative
6. negative
7. very negative

a. instructor___
b. relaxation procedure___
c. visualization while relaxing___
d. discussion___
e. rest of group___

(Student-Instructor Matching Scale)

Name _____

Your instructor will not be shown this form; it is for assignment purposes only.

Below is a list of statements made by other students like yourself when they were asked to describe the kind of instructor with whom they would most like to take a class. It has been found worthwhile to try and assign each student to an instructor who most closely matches the student's "ideal" of an instructor for this type of course. In order to attempt this for you, please read each statement carefully and decide how much you wish *your* instructor to behave the way each statement describes. Circle one answer for each statement.

$$1 = No, \text{ not at all}$$
$$2 = \text{A little bit}$$
$$3 = \text{Quite a bit}$$
$$4 = Yes, \text{ very much}$$

HOW MUCH DO YOU WISH YOUR INSTRUCTOR TO . . . .

1.	act warm and friendly toward you?	1	2	3	4
2.	expect you to accept his ideas and opinions?	1	2	3	4
3.	try to help you help yourself?	1	2	3	4
4.	tell you what to do about difficult decisions?	1	2	3	4
5.	say what he thinks frankly and directly?	1	2	3	4
6.	try to get you to see things his way?	1	2	3	4
7.	show a real liking for you?	1	2	3	4
8.	let you know when he doesn't agree with you?	1	2	3	4
9.	act cool and detached?	1	2	3	4
10.	encourage you to depend on him for help?	1	2	3	4
11.	treat you as an equal?	1	2	3	4
12.	act as though he knew all the answers?	1	2	3	4
13.	encourage you to rely on others more?	1	2	3	4
14.	encourage you to rely on others less?	1	2	3	4
15.	relate to you as though you were a friend?	1	2	3	4
16.	be logical and stick to the facts?	1	2	3	4
17.	be critical and not easily impressed?	1	2	3	4
18.	ask you many questions?	1	2	3	4
19.	mostly sit quietly and wait for you to talk?	1	2	3	4
20.	seek underlying reasons?	1	2	3	4
21.	agree with your opinions all the time?	1	2	3	4
22.	ask you to take certain tests?	1	2	3	4
23.	refuse to allow interruptions during your class?	1	2	3	4
24.	see you for as many classes as *you* wish?	1	2	3	4

(Tape Rating Scale)

Name _____

Date _____

Indicate your degree of agreement or disagreement with each of the following statements by putting a circle around one answer for each item. There are seven possible answers for each item:

1. Strongly disagree
2. Moderately disagree
3. Slightly disagree
4. Neither agree nor disagree
5. Slightly agree
6. Moderately agree
7. Strongly agree

Do not spend too much time on any one item. Thank you for your cooperation.

1. The therapist seemed to understand the way the client really felt.   1   2   3   4   5   6   7
2. I enjoyed listening to the tape.   1   2   3   4   5   6   7
3. I felt like the client was being put on the spot during the therapy hour.   1   2   3   4   5   6   7
4. The client didn't seem to do his share during the session.   1   2   3   4   5   6   7
5. The therapist seemed like a warm person.   1   2   3   4   5   6   7
6. How people do on the qualifying tests seems unrelated to their tape-judging ability.   1   2   3   4   5   6   7
7. The therapist seemed unable to handle some of the client's statements.   1   2   3   4   5   6   7
8. I'm glad I signed up for this experiment.   1   2   3   4   5   6   7
9. The therapist gave the client reason to want to return.   1   2   3   4   5   6   7
10. Probably only a small number of those who try psychotherapy benefit from it.   1   2   3   4   5   6   7
11. The therapist seemed to patronize the client.   1   2   3   4   5   6   7
12. People can learn a lot from participating in psychological experiments.   1   2   3   4   5   6   7

13. Taking the qualifying tests required much effort on my part.　1　2　3　4　5　6　7

14. The therapist is probably quite experienced.　1　2　3　4　5　6　7

15. I felt uncomfortable while listening to the therapy tape.　1　2　3　4　5　6　7

16. The therapist seemed to confuse the client.　1　2　3　4　5　6　7

17. I would like a person like this client for a friend.　1　2　3　4　5　6　7

18. The therapist seemed eager to help the client.　1　2　3　4　5　6　7

19. Psychological tests are an invasion of one's personal privacy.　1　2　3　4　5　6　7

20. The therapist talked too much.　1　2　3　4　5　6　7

21. Psychological tests can pick out things that are not readily apparent to everyone.　1　2　3　4　5　6　7

22. The therapist made it easy for the client to talk of difficult things.　1　2　3　4　5　6　7

23. I don't see how this kind of experiment can help psychology much.　1　2　3　4　5　6　7

24. The therapist somehow seemed to miss the client's meaning.　1　2　3　4　5　6　7

25. Society needs many more psychotherapists.　1　2　3　4　5　6　7

26. I would recommend this therapist to a friend.　1　2　3　4　5　6　7

27. Psychological research really only proves the obvious.　1　2　3　4　5　6　7

28. If the client had had someone else as his therapist, he would have probably felt freer to discuss his problems.　1　2　3　4　5　6　7

29. I would not mind listening to tapes of other therapy sessions.　1　2　3　4　5　6　7

30. This therapist seemed very competent.　1　2　3　4　5　6　7

31. I didn't feel that this client was being very truthful.　1　2　3　4　5　6　7

32. In many ways the session seemed like a waste of time for the client.　1　2　3　4　5　6　7

33. I like to take psychological tests.　1　2　3　4　5　6　7

34. The therapist seemed to be vague.　1　2　3　4　5　6　7

35. I would consider participating in another experiment like this one even if I didn't get credit.　1　2　3　4　5　6　7

36. The client will probably benefit from his sessions with this therapist.　1　2　3　4　5　6　7

37. Participation in experiments should be dropped from the Psychology 5 requirements.　1　2　3　4　5　6　7

38. The therapist seemed genuinely interested in the client's problems.　1　2　3　4　5　6　7

39. I would urge a friend who was having trouble getting along with others to enter psychotherapy.   1 2 3 4 5 6 7
40. The tape-listening session seemed to drag.   1 2 3 4 5 6 7
41. I like this client.   1 2 3 4 5 6 7
42. At times the therapist seemed unsure as to what he should do next.   1 2 3 4 5 6 7
43. I would not recommend this experiment to a friend.   1 2 3 4 5 6 7
44. Psychotherapy seems to be an inefficient technique.   1 2 3 4 5 6 7
45. Psychological research is interesting.   1 2 3 4 5 6 7
46. What was the client's name?

47. Did the client state his age?   Yes   No
48. Did the client admit to feeling depressed during the session?   Yes   No
49. Did the client discuss his relationships with women?   Yes   No
50. How many minutes did the tape session last?

(Persuasibility Questionnaire)

Name _____

Age (in years) _____

This is a survey to find out what opinions people have about psychotherapy patients.

There are no definite "right" or "wrong" answers to these questions. They are matters of personal opinion based on your impressions of the patient as you heard him. The best answer is your own opinion.

These questions were also submitted to the therapist you heard, after the session. For each question we have put down the therapist's opinion so that you can see how your opinion compares with his.

Please turn the page, read the instructions, and begin.

Instructions:

Read each of the following statements.

The therapist's opinion is given following each of the statements.

Give your own opinion about the statement on the line below, by drawing a circle around the words which best tell how you feel about the statement.

Please give your opinion for *all* of the statements.

1. The patient is a more serious person than most other people. (Therapist's opinion—DISAGREE SLIGHTLY)

Agree strongly	Agree fairly much	Agree slightly	Neither agree nor disagree	Disagree slightly	Disagree fairly much	Disagree strongly

2. The patient probably often leaves work unfinished. (Therapist's opinion —AGREE STRONGLY)

Agree strongly	Agree fairly much	Agree slightly	Neither agree nor disagree	Disagree slightly	Disagree fairly much	Disagree strongly

3. The patient has a good sense of humor. (Therapist's opinion—NEITHER AGREE NOR DISAGREE)

Agree strongly	Agree fairly much	Agree slightly	Neither agree nor disagree	Disagree slightly	Disagree fairly much	Disagree strongly

4. The patient would rather work with things than ideas. (Therapist's opinion—AGREE STRONGLY)

Agree strongly	Agree fairly much	Agree slightly	Neither agree nor disagree	Disagree slightly	Disagree fairly much	Disagree strongly

5. The patient probably has headaches often. (Therapist's opinion—AGREE STRONGLY)

Agree strongly	Agree fairly much	Agree slightly	Neither agree nor disagree	Disagree slightly	Disagree fairly much	Disagree strongly

6. The patient would go out of his way to help other people. (Therapist's opinion—AGREE STRONGLY)

Agree strongly	Agree fairly much	Agree slightly	Neither agree nor disagree	Disagree slightly	Disagree fairly much	Disagree strongly

7. The patient daydreams frequently. (Therapist's opinion—DISAGREE STRONGLY)

Agree strongly	Agree fairly much	Agree slightly	Neither agree nor disagree	Disagree slightly	Disagree fairly much	Disagree strongly

8. The patient is probably more creative than the average person. (Therapist's opinion—DISAGREE SLIGHTLY)

Agree strongly	Agree fairly much	Agree slightly	Neither agree nor disagree	Disagree slightly	Disagree fairly much	Disagree strongly

9. The patient is likely to overestimate a person's abilities. (Therapist's opinion—DISAGREE STRONGLY)

Agree strongly	Agree fairly much	Agree slightly	Neither agree nor disagree	Disagree slightly	Disagree fairly much	Disagree strongly

10. It is probably unusual for the patient to express strong approval or disapproval of the actions of others. (Therapist's opinion—NEITHER AGREE NOR DISAGREE)

Agree strongly	Agree fairly much	Agree slightly	Neither agree nor disagree	Disagree slightly	Disagree fairly much	Disagree strongly

11. The patient probably likes to belong to clubs. (Therapist's opinion—
AGREE STRONGLY)

Agree strongly	Agree fairly much	Agree slightly	Neither agree nor disagree	Disagree slightly	Disagree fairly much	Disagree strongly

12. The patient feels like giving up quickly when things go wrong. (Therapist's opinion—DISAGREE SLIGHTLY)

Agree strongly	Agree fairly much	Agree slightly	Neither agree nor disagree	Disagree slightly	Disagree fairly much	Disagree strongly

13. The patient finds it hard to take no for an answer. (Therapist's opinion—AGREE STRONGLY)

Agree strongly	Agree fairly much	Agree slightly	Neither agree nor disagree	Disagree slightly	Disagree fairly much	Disagree strongly

14. The patient is more nervous than most other people. (Therapist's opinion—AGREE SLIGHTLY)

Agree strongly	Agree fairly much	Agree slightly	Neither agree nor disagree	Disagree slightly	Disagree fairly much	Disagree strongly

15. The patient is careful not to hurt people's feelings. (Therapist's opinion—NEITHER AGREE NOR DISAGREE)

Agree strongly	Agree fairly much	Agree slightly	Neither agree nor disagree	Disagree slightly	Disagree fairly much	Disagree strongly

16. The patient is not easily impressed. (Therapist's opinion—DISAGREE STRONGLY)

Agree strongly	Agree fairly much	Agree slightly	Neither agree nor disagree	Disagree slightly	Disagree fairly much	Disagree strongly

17. The patient is likely to keep his resentments to himself. (Therapist's opinion—AGREE SLIGHTLY)

Agree strongly	Agree fairly much	Agree slightly	Neither agree nor disagree	Disagree slightly	Disagree fairly much	Disagree strongly

18. The patient probably tends to get over-excited. (Therapist's opinion—
DISAGREE SLIGHTLY)

Agree strongly	Agree fairly much	Agree slightly	Neither agree nor disagree	Disagree slightly	Disagree fairly much	Disagree strongly

19. The patient does things at a rather slow pace. (Therapist's opinion—
DISAGREE STRONGLY)

Agree strongly	Agree fairly much	Agree slightly	Neither agree nor disagree	Disagree slightly	Disagree fairly much	Disagree strongly

20. The patient seldom worries about his physical health. (Therapist's opinion—DISAGREE STRONGLY)

Agree strongly	Agree fairly much	Agree slightly	Neither agree nor disagree	Disagree slightly	Disagree fairly much	Disagree strongly

21. The patient probably has many friends. (Therapist's opinion—AGREE SLIGHTLY)

Agree strongly	Agree fairly much	Agree slightly	Neither agree nor disagree	Disagree slightly	Disagree fairly much	Disagree strongly

22. The patient probably often becomes jealous of others. (Therapist's opinion—NEITHER AGREE NOR DISAGREE)

Agree strongly	Agree fairly much	Agree slightly	Neither agree nor disagree	Disagree slightly	Disagree fairly much	Disagree strongly

23. The patient probably often has difficulty falling asleep or staying asleep. (Therapist's opinion—AGREE STRONGLY)

Agree strongly	Agree fairly much	Agree slightly	Neither agree nor disagree	Disagree slightly	Disagree fairly much	Disagree strongly

24. The patient misinterprets the behavior of others. (Therapist's opinion—AGREE SLIGHTLY)

Agree strongly	Agree fairly much	Agree slightly	Neither agree nor disagree	Disagree slightly	Disagree fairly much	Disagree strongly

25. The patient is probably much more outspoken outside of therapy. (Therapist's opinion—DISAGREE SLIGHTLY)

Agree strongly	Agree fairly much	Agree slightly	Neither agree nor disagree	Disagree slightly	Disagree fairly much	Disagree strongly

26. The patient probably finds it hard to speak in public. (Therapist's opinion—DISAGREE STRONGLY)

Agree strongly	Agree fairly much	Agree slightly	Neither agree nor disagree	Disagree slightly	Disagree fairly much	Disagree strongly

27. The patient is likely to give advice to other people in trouble. (Therapist's opinion—DISAGREE STRONGLY)

Agree strongly	Agree fairly much	Agree slightly	Neither agree nor disagree	Disagree slightly	Disagree fairly much	Disagree strongly

28. The patient seeks excitement. (Therapist's opinion—DISAGREE STRONGLY)

Agree strongly	Agree fairly much	Agree slightly	Neither agree nor disagree	Disagree slightly	Disagree fairly much	Disagree strongly

29. The patient enjoys philosophical discussions. (Therapist's opinion—NEITHER AGREE NOR DISAGREE)

Agree strongly	Agree fairly much	Agree slightly	Neither agree nor disagree	Disagree slightly	Disagree fairly much	Disagree strongly

30. The patient probably gets into more accidents than others do. (Therapist's opinion—DISAGREE STRONGLY)

Agree strongly	Agree fairly much	Agree slightly	Neither agree nor disagree	Disagree slightly	Disagree fairly much	Disagree strongly

31. The patient's friends probably think it is hard to get to know him well. (Therapist's opinion—AGREE SLIGHTLY)

Agree strongly	Agree fairly much	Agree slightly	Neither agree nor disagree	Disagree slightly	Disagree fairly much	Disagree strongly

32. The patient is probably absentminded. (Therapist's opinion—AGREE STRONGLY)

Agree strongly	Agree fairly much	Agree slightly	Neither agree nor disagree	Disagree slightly	Disagree fairly much	Disagree strongly

33. The patient probably often says things on the spur of the moment that he later regrets. (Therapist's opinion—DISAGREE SLIGHTLY)

Agree strongly	Agree fairly much	Agree slightly	Neither agree nor disagree	Disagree slightly	Disagree fairly much	Disagree strongly

34. The patient probably enjoys being with children more than most other people do. (Therapist's opinion—AGREE STRONGLY)

Agree strongly	Agree fairly much	Agree slightly	Neither agree nor disagree	Disagree slightly	Disagree fairly much	Disagree strongly

35. The patient would rather be alone than with others. (Therapist's opinion—AGREE SLIGHTLY)

Agree strongly	Agree fairly much	Agree slightly	Neither agree nor disagree	Disagree slightly	Disagree fairly much	Disagree strongly

36. The patient probably often has an upset stomach. (Therapist's opinion —DISAGREE STRONGLY)

Agree strongly	Agree fairly much	Agree slightly	Neither agree nor disagree	Disagree slightly	Disagree fairly much	Disagree strongly

37. The patient probably has more trouble concentrating than others have. (Therapist's opinion—AGREE STRONGLY)

Agree strongly	Agree fairly much	Agree slightly	Neither agree nor disagree	Disagree slightly	Disagree fairly much	Disagree strongly

38. The patient will easily put trust in others. (Therapist's opinion— NEITHER AGREE NOR DISAGREE)

Agree strongly	Agree fairly much	Agree slightly	Neither agree nor disagree	Disagree slightly	Disagree fairly much	Disagree strongly

39. The patient probably likes to read a lot. (Therapist's opinion—AGREE STRONGLY)

Agree strongly	Agree fairly much	Agree slightly	Neither agree nor disagree	Disagree slightly	Disagree fairly much	Disagree strongly

40. The patient probably does not like animals too much. (Therapist's opinion—DISAGREE SLIGHTLY)

Agree strongly	Agree fairly much	Agree slightly	Neither agree nor disagree	Disagree slightly	Disagree fairly much	Disagree strongly

(Willingness to Meet)

The Psychology Department has had many inquiries over the past year from students regarding their problems. To help with some of these problems the Department is thinking of asking a number of therapists, including the one you just heard, to the university to speak to students. Indicate below whether or not you would be willing to meet with the therapist you just heard.

I would be willing to attend a meeting to discuss student problems.

_____

(signature)

I would not be willing to attend a meeting to discuss student problems.

_____

(signature)

(Prognosis-Evaluation Questionnaire)

The following questions deal with your impressions about the film you just saw. Please answer them all as spontaneously as you can.

1. What would you recommend to this patient? (Check one)

   __Hospitalization   __Supportive treatment
   __Foster home placement   __Medication only
   __Long-term intensive   __No treatment
       treatment

2. Check one of the following labels to indicate the patient's dominant personality type.

   __Anxiety   __Cyclothymic
   __Hysteria   __Schizoid
   __Obsessive   __Paranoid
   __Psychopathic   __Neurotic

3. How much ego strength does this patient seem to have?

   __A great deal   __Relatively little
   __A fair amount   __Very little

4. How much anxiety does this patient seem to have?

   __A great deal   __Relatively little
   __A fair amount   __Very little

5. How much insight does this patient seem to have into his problem?

   __A great deal   __Relatively little
   __A fair amount   __Very little

6. To what extent does the patient appear to be capable of self-observation and self-appraisal as opposed to the tendency to rationalization?

   __Very capable   __Slightly capable
   __Fairly capable   __Not at all capable

7. How would you rate this patient's overall emotional maturity?

   __Very mature   __Fairly immature
   __Fairly mature   __Very immature

8. How would you characterize the patient's social adjustment?

__Very adequate   __Fairly inadequate
__Fairly adequate   __Very inadequate

9. Considering the entire range of mental disorder, how would you characterize the degree of disturbance in this patient?

__Very mildly disturbed   __Moderately disturbed
__Mildly disturbed   __Seriously disturbed
                    __Extremely disturbed

10. Assuming the patient's life situation remained about the same, how would you expect him to get along if *no* therapy were undertaken?

__He would probably get much better.
__He would probably get a little better.
__He would probably remain about the same.
__He would probably get a little worse.
__He would probably get much worse.

11. Assuming your recommendations for treatment were followed, how would you rate the prognosis for this patient?

__Very favorable   __Somewhat unfavorable
__Somewhat favorable   __Very unfavorable
                    __Neither favorable nor unfavorable

(Test Rating Scale)

Name _____

Date _____

Indicate your degree of agreement or disagreement with each of the following statements by putting a circle around one answer for each item. There are seven possible answers for each item:

1. Strongly disagree
2. Moderately disagree
3. Slightly disagree
4. Neither agree or disagree
5. Slightly agree
6. Moderately agree
7. Strongly agree

Do not spend too much time on any one item. Thank you for your cooperation.

1. I would have preferred it if the tester wrote down my answers.   1   2   3   4   5   6   7
2. I don't see how this kind of experiment can help psychology much.   1   2   3   4   5   6   7
3. I enjoyed taking the test.   1   2   3   4   5   6   7
4. I would have preferred it if there were no limit for each answer.   1   2   3   4   5   6   7
5. I felt personally involved during the testing session.   1   2   3   4   5   6   7
6. Taking the test was effortful.   1   2   3   4   5   6   7
7. The tester seemed quite experienced.   1   2   3   4   5   6   7
8. Psychological tests are an unfair invasion of privacy.   1   2   3   4   5   6   7
9. The test got harder as it went along.   1   2   3   4   5   6   7
10. I would have preferred to write my answers.   1   2   3   4   5   6   7
11. The testing session seemed to drag.   1   2   3   4   5   6   7
12. The tester seemed like a warm person.   1   2   3   4   5   6   7
13. Psychological tests are not very useful.   1   2   3   4   5   6   7

14. I would consider participating in
    another experiment like this one even
    if I didn't get credit.   1 2 3 4 5 6 7

15. I would have liked to have had more time
    to make up answers.   1 2 3 4 5 6 7

16. The tester didn't talk enough.   1 2 3 4 5 6 7

17. This test can help people learn a lot
    about themselves.   1 2 3 4 5 6 7

18. I found it hard to give answers.   1 2 3 4 5 6 7

19. I like to take psychological tests.   1 2 3 4 5 6 7

20. Psychological research really only
    proves the obvious.   1 2 3 4 5 6 7

21. If I had had someone else as my tester,
    I would have felt freer to talk.   1 2 3 4 5 6 7

22. People can learn a lot from partic-
    ipating in psychological experiments.   1 2 3 4 5 6 7

23. I felt uncomfortable while taking the test. 1 2 3 4 5 6 7

24. I was made uncomfortable by the tape
    recorder.   1 2 3 4 5 6 7

25. Psychological tests have many valuable
    applications.   1 2 3 4 5 6 7

(General and Alcoholism Attitudes Scale)

Indicate your degree of agreement or disagreement with each of the following statements by putting a circle around the one answer for *each* item that is most representative of your present feelings. There are no right or wrong answers. All questions are matters of opinion. Do not spend too much time on any one item.

1. It is better if people sometimes act on impulse rather than engage in careful consideration.

| Agree strongly | Agree fairly much | Agree slightly | Disagree slightly | Disagree fairly much | Disagree strongly |

2. People with a purpose in life have no need for alcohol.

| Agree strongly | Agree fairly much | Agree slightly | Disagree slightly | Disagree fairly much | Disagree strongly |

3. Racial integration in public schools is a mistake.

| Agree strongly | Agree fairly much | Agree slightly | Disagree slightly | Disagree fairly much | Disagree strongly |

4. Alcoholics are usually born that way.

| Agree strongly | Agree fairly much | Agree slightly | Disagree slightly | Disagree fairly much | Disagree strongly |

5. Birth control techniques should be used by more people.

| Agree strongly | Agree fairly much | Agree slightly | Disagree slightly | Disagree fairly much | Disagree strongly |

6. I like people who drink a little better than those who do not drink at all.

| Agree strongly | Agree fairly much | Agree slightly | Disagree slightly | Disagree fairly much | Disagree strongly |

7. It is very enjoyable to listen to classical music.

| Agree strongly | Agree fairly much | Agree slightly | Disagree slightly | Disagree fairly much | Disagree strongly |

8. A person with a drinking problem cannot be expected to make good decisions about everyday problems.

| Agree strongly | Agree fairly much | Agree slightly | Disagree slightly | Disagree fairly much | Disagree strongly |

9. Premarital sex relations are generally harmful to the people involved.

| Agree strongly | Agree fairly much | Agree slightly | Disagree slightly | Disagree fairly much | Disagree strongly |

10. One of the main causes of alcoholism is a lack of moral strength.

| Agree strongly | Agree fairly much | Agree slightly | Disagree slightly | Disagree fairly much | Disagree strongly |

11. Money is one of the most important goals of life.

| Agree strongly | Agree fairly much | Agree slightly | Disagree slightly | Disagree fairly much | Disagree strongly |

12. Alcoholics have only themselves to blame for their drinking; in most cases they just haven't tried hard enough to stop.

| Agree strongly | Agree fairly much | Agree slightly | Disagree slightly | Disagree fairly much | Disagree strongly |

13. Novels are boring to read.

| Agree strongly | Agree fairly much | Agree slightly | Disagree slightly | Disagree fairly much | Disagree strongly |

14. Alcoholics cannot tell right from wrong when they are drunk.

| Agree strongly | Agree fairly much | Agree slightly | Disagree slightly | Disagree fairly much | Disagree strongly |

15. The father should discipline the children more than the mother.

| Agree strongly | Agree fairly much | Agree slightly | Disagree slightly | Disagree fairly much | Disagree strongly |

16. Everyone has characteristics similar to those of alcoholics.

| Agree strongly | Agree fairly much | Agree slightly | Disagree slightly | Disagree fairly much | Disagree strongly |

17. For many people divorce would be a good thing.

| Agree strongly | Agree fairly much | Agree slightly | Disagree slightly | Disagree fairly much | Disagree strongly |

18. An alcoholic cannot be trusted.

| Agree strongly | Agree fairly much | Agree slightly | Disagree slightly | Disagree fairly much | Disagree strongly |

19. There is nothing wrong with a mother taking a job.

| Agree strongly | Agree fairly much | Agree slightly | Disagree slightly | Disagree fairly much | Disagree strongly |

20. Alcoholism is a sickness just like any other.

| Agree strongly | Agree fairly much | Agree slightly | Disagree slightly | Disagree fairly much | Disagree strongly |

(Attitudes Toward Psychotherapy and Psychotherapists Scale)

Directions

Both psychiatrists and psychologists are doctors who try to help people with mental or nervous problems by talking to them.

The 25 questions on the following pages are being asked to learn *your opinion* about psychiatrists and psychologists.

Nothing you tell us will be told to the VA staff. Everything is strictly confidential.

Each question has seven possible answers:

1. Strongly agree
2. Moderately agree
3. Slightly agree
4. Neither agree nor disagree
5. Slightly disagree
6. Moderately disagree
7. Strongly disagree

Circle only *one* number for each question on the following pages which best tells how *you* feel.

Name _____

Date _____

Years in School _____ Age _____

Ward _____

1. Psychiatrists and psychologists are not very
   much help in solving people's problems.   1 2 3 4 5 6 7

2. Most people would go to a psychiatrist
   or psychologist if they felt they had
   mental or nervous problems.   1 2 3 4 5 6 7

3. Many of the people who go to psychiatrists
   or psychologists are made worse by the
   treatment they get.   1 2 3 4 5 6 7

4. Talking about your problems to a
   psychiatrist or psychologist is mostly
   a waste of time.   1 2 3 4 5 6 7

5. Every school child should be given a
   psychiatric examination.   1 2 3 4 5 6 7

6. Psychiatrists and psychologists are warm
   and friendly people.   1 2 3 4 5 6 7

7. If you live a good, clean life, you shouldn't need to talk to a psychiatrist or psychologist.

    1 2 3 4 5 6 7

8. Most people would feel comfortable talking to a psychiatrist or psychologist about their problems.

    1 2 3 4 5 6 7

9. Most people would be afraid to tell their real feelings during a therapy session where they talked with a psychiatrist or psychologist.

    1 2 3 4 5 6 7

10. Psychiatrists and psychologists really know more about mental and nervous conditions than other doctors do.

    1 2 3 4 5 6 7

11. Unhappy people should go to a psychiatrist or psychologist for help.

    1 2 3 4 5 6 7

12. People with mental or nervous problems should be able to pull themselves together without the help of a psychiatrist or a psychologist.

    1 2 3 4 5 6 7

13. A psychiatrist or psychologist usually says things that give patients confidence in him.

    1 2 3 4 5 6 7

14. Most people would find it hard to talk about themselves to a psychiatrist or psychologist.

    1 2 3 4 5 6 7

15. Most people cannot understand how talking with a psychiatrist or psychologist could do much to solve their problems.

    1 2 3 4 5 6 7

16. It would be easier for a person to talk with a psychiatrist or psychologist than with most other people.

    1 2 3 4 5 6 7

17. Talking with a psychiatrist or psychologist is the best way to deal with mental, nervous, and emotional problems.

    1 2 3 4 5 6 7

18. Psychiatrists and psychologists, compared to other kinds of doctors, are more successful in helping their patients.

    1 2 3 4 5 6 7

19. Psychiatrists and psychologists would not be needed if people had willpower of their own.

    1 2 3 4 5 6 7

20. When a psychiatrist or psychologist tries to treat a person with little schooling, neither one really understands the other.

    1 2 3 4 5 6 7

21. Talking with a psychiatrist or
    psychologist gives people many ideas
    about their problems which help them
    to understand themselves better.   1 2 3 4 5 6 7

22. Most people would hesitate to tell a
    psychiatrist or psychologist what they
    were really thinking.   1 2 3 4 5 6 7

23. Talking with your minister if you have
    a problem is better than talking to a
    psychiatrist or psychologist.   1 2 3 4 5 6 7

24. It would be difficult to think of things
    to say during a therapy session where
    you talked about your problems to a
    psychiatrist or psychologist.   1 2 3 4 5 6 7

25. Psychiatrists and psychologists,
    compared with other kinds of doctors,
    are more interested in the well-being
    of their patients.   1 2 3 4 5 6 7

(Sociometric Questionnaire)

Group Psychotherapy Questionnaire S

Below you will find some questions concerning your feelings toward the other members of your therapy group. For each question you are asked to write in the name of one or more members of your group, or none of them as your answer. You are free to choose as many members as you wish for each question, can choose the same member as often as you wish, or you may choose no one. You may choose yourself if you feel such choice is appropriate, but do *not* include your psychotherapists among those from whom you choose. Consider only those members present at *tonight's* meeting and the last two meetings. Your answers will be kept in the strictest confidence; they will *not* be shown to any other group member.

1. Who do you feel advances or helps most the group's therapeutic work?
_____

2. Who do you feel blocks or diverts the group's therapeutic work?
_____

3. Which member(s) of this group would you like very much to have as a close friend? _____

4. Which member(s) of this group would you very much not like to have as a close friend? _____

5. Who is most like yourself?_____
_____

6. Who is least like yourself?_____
_____

7. Who is easiest to talk to? _____
_____

8. Who is most difficult to talk to? _____
_____

9. Who do you feel brings up the most useful material with respect to your own problems? _____

10. Who in the group makes you feel uncomfortable? _____

11. Who do you feel is the "best" group member in terms of making a real effort to solve his or her problems? _____

12. With whom would you be the most afraid to disagree?

13. With whom would you be the least afraid to disagree?

14. If a secret ballot were taken to eliminate one group member, whom would you vote to eliminate? _____

15. Which member of the group would you most prefer to be like, as far as his or her behavior *in the group* is concerned?

16. Whose departure from the group would disturb you the most?

Appendix II

Content Analysis Criteria

Client Verbal Behavior Categories[1]
General Rules

1. A client response is a client statement or 15 seconds of silence between two therapist statements. If a client's statement is longer than 15 seconds it is divided into 15-second units. The last part of a client statement between a previous 15-second portion and the time the therapist speaks is categorized even though it may be less than 15 seconds long, unless it is a pause.

2. The category N is used for the client only when there is nothing in the client's response to call for a classification anywhere else.

3. If a statement cannot definitely be placed in a category other than N, because it is not complete at 15 seconds when the recording machine is stopped, put it in that N category. But its meaning is allowed to have bearing on the categorization of the next 15-second portion of the client's response. If, on the other hand, enough of the client's statement is heard to put it definitely in a category, do so even though the sentence may not be complete.

4. The same *sentence* cannot be categorized in two places (unless it is an Interruption, Blocking, or Change of Topic), but more than one category may be used for the same 15-second interval.

5. If in conflict between two or more categorizations of the same client sentence, place it where the least inference is required.

6. We are interested in the variables being measured here only as they are manifest in the counseling situation itself. Client statements which indicate only that the client is or has been, for example, guarded outside of the therapy hour does not fall under the Guardedness category here.

Openness

Openness is defined as: the extent to which the client freely discusses his problems, deviations from the "normal," his culturally frowned-upon traits, behavior, and motivations; and, in general, his willingness to expose himself to potential criticism and change, particularly his willingness to discuss thoroughly those areas which seem most threatening. He does this without at the same time qualifying, hedging, and engaging in defensive verbal maneuvers.

In a way this category is the opposite of the "Guardedness" category. When the client's statement does not exhibit any guardedness in a dis-

[1] The descriptions which follow are from Ashby, J. D., Ford, D. H., Guerney, B. G., Jr., & Guerney, L. Effects on clients of a reflective and leading type of psychotherapy. *Psychological Monographs*, 1957, 7, 1-32.

cussion area in which a clinician would often expect a person to be guarded, the client's statement is categorized under "Openness." This category is meant to reflect the ability or willingness of a client to "open himself up" to the counselor, to expose himself to possible criticism, to expose himself to the prospect of modifying his self-concept, without at the same time feeling the need to defend himself as he is to his own or to the counselor's eyes. A confidence in the therapist's understanding, noncriticalness, and trustworthiness is presumed to underlie such openness, i.e., the statements that are considered "open" are not such as one would tell to one's critics or even newfound friends.

1. Unqualified[2] admission to a problem,[3] deficiency, inadequacy, undesirable characteristic, trait, behavior pattern or act, feelings, or attitudes.

2. Unqualified statements pointing to personal deviation from the norm in a culturally or personally undesirable direction.

3. Unqualified statements that admit to possession of culturally or personally undesirable characteristics, traits, behavior, feelings, or attitudes.

Note: Simple acceptance of a therapist's statement placing the client in an undesirable light is not scored "Open." It is only when the client proceeds in such a way as to place his statement under any of the criteria listed above that his statement is categorized "Open."

A simple statement of a problem qualifies as an "Open" response if it is unqualified.

A description of a particular conflict is not necessarily "Open." But an unqualified admission of having important unresolved contradictions or irrationalities within oneself is categorized "Open."

The following statements are some examples to clarify the categorization of "Openness":

[2] An admission to a problem is "qualified" when it is coupled with expression of uncertainty (e.g., "maybe," "perhaps," "probably," etc.; the term "I think," however, is not considered to indicate uncertainty). Qualifications may also exist in any minimization of the problem in terms of the extent or severity of the problem. Such minimization is, of course, a different thing than clarification and specification, and the coder must make a decision as to whether the client is being cautious and guarded, or merely giving some definitive information to his counselor. When the case is ambiguous to the coder he should not categorize it as "Openness" (or "Guardedness") but as "None." A qualification must occur in the same 15-second interval as a statement in order for it to disqualify the statement as "open." If an admission is accompanied (i.e., in the same 15-second interval) by anything that calls for a "Guardedness" categorization it is not categorized as "Openness." These categories are mutually exclusive in the same client response.

[3] The word "problem" is defined in the section on "Guardedness."

1. Client (speaking about husband or father): "As far as really deep feelings—I have none for him." . . . O.

This is an unqualified admission to culturally unacceptable attitude or feeling.

2. "My conversational ability is pretty weak. I can't carry on a long continuous conversation." . . . O.

This is an unqualified admission of an inadequacy.

3. Therapist: "That seems kind of contradictory." Client: "When I think about it, that's true; as far as things have gone in the past I have no reason to feel inferior." . . . O.

The client accepts and *elaborates* upon therapist statement pointing to important contradiction or irrationality in client.

4. "Most of the time I'm worried about people—what they're thinking of me." . . . O.

This is an unqualified admission of a psychological problem.

5. Therapist: "And you feel like he's thinking only of himself." Client: "Not exactly. I don't blame him particularly. I guess I do in a way. I don't want to, but I do. I want him to accept me and my needs." . . . O.

This is an admission to a feeling toward which a personal distaste is made clear.

Guardedness

Guardedness is defined as the extent to which the client exhibits wariness and hedging in regard to presenting and working on his problem, admitting to faults, and exposing himself to potential criticism and change. This includes self-stimulated denial, or minimization, of his problems or his deviations from the "normal," and denial of culturally undesirable feelings, traits, and motivations. It also includes the need to justify himself or his actions to the therapist and expectations or anticipations of criticism from the therapist.

A key question for the judge to ask himself in listening to a client's statement with reference to this category is whether the client is in any way engaged in "protecting" himself from potential criticism or potential change in his self-concept. Some of the cues to listen for are presented below.

1. Statements denying, qualifying, minimizing, or belittling the extent of a problem or the existence of one.[4] The denial is not in response

---

[4] "Problem" is broadly defined here as anything which is culturally frowned-upon, *or* which bothers the client personally. To qualify under the latter the client must make his personal distaste clear. Physical symptoms or manifesta-

to a question or statement of the therapist or any other particular person.

2. Statements pointing to nondeviation from the "norm," "average," "everyone," "other," etc.—either as a person in general or in some particular aspect of thought, feeling, or behavior (e.g., "I guess we all have a tendency to talk in circles."). If such a statement is purely descriptive and factual or is in the nature of a complaint, rather than being something which is *comforting to the client*, it does not receive a Guardedness categorization.

3. Statements denying possession of an undesirable characteristic, trait, feeling, attitude, or denying an undesirable act or motivation. This category is not used when the characteristic has been attributed to the client by the therapist or some specific other person.

4. Statements in which the client attempts to justify an act, thought, feeling, statement, etc. to the therapist. "Justify" here means to hold forth one's behavior as just, right, warranted, to declare oneself guiltless, absolve or acquit oneself, to attempt to show satisfactory excuse or reason for something that is culturally or personally undesirable. The reason that is offered by the client is usually one that is primarily "outside" of the self, i.e., the undesirable thing is a result of the behavior of others or circumstances. This category does not apply if the client has been asked to justify himself by the therapist or some specific other persons.

5. A statement indicating that the client might be anticipating a critical or differing thought or statement from the therapist. (For example, "That's the way I think about it; you may think differently, I don't know."). Such phrases as "sound to you" or "look to you" from the client to the therapist should alert the coder to the possibility that such a statement is an anticipation of difference or criticalness between the client and the counselor.

Some such statements could serve to beat the therapist to the punch. "All this must sound foolish to you." Here the expectation by the client of a critical attitude on the therapist's part is overt. In some cases the anticipation of a critical attitude is only implied by the client's overt acceptance of the blame or fault-finding he expects from the therapist. He will thus make a statement taking fault or responsibility upon himself while he is in reality rejecting the blame or criticism. Sometimes this takes the form of a much-qualified acceptance of a statement by

---

tions of problems (e.g., headaches, crying, sweating, shaking) stated only as a physical problem are not considered to fall under the definition of "problem." But psychological symptoms (e.g., nervousness, feeling depressed, etc.) are considered to be "problems."

the therapist or some other person which places the client in a bad light. Admitting to blame does not, of course, automatically indicate that the statement should be categorized as Guardedness. Such a statement may belong in the *N* or *OP* category, depending on the way it is said and:

1. The extent of qualification. As a rule, in doubtful cases, do not categorize as *G* an unqualified statement accepting blame (e.g., "I'm being foolish."). Do not categorize as *G* a statement containing a single qualification (e.g., "Maybe I'm being foolish."). Do categorize as *G* such a statement which contains a plural number of qualifications (e.g., "I guess maybe I'm being foolish.").

2. The nature of the elaboration on the statement that is found within the same client response. As a rule, in doubtful cases: (a) the latter part of the client's response is considered more important—if the acceptance of fault follows the blaming of outside circumstances or other people, it should probably not be categorized as *G*. On the other hand, if the blaming of outside factors follows self-blame, this should probably be categorized as *G*; (b) the more detailed and specific part of the client's response is considered more important and the vague, more general, part considered to be less important. Thus, if a client states he is at fault in some general way but criticizes another person or a circumstance in a more specific way, the statement is likely to be a Guardedness statement.

Note: A simple rejection of a therapist's statement whatever it may have been, is not categorized as *G*. It is only when the client proceeds in such a way as to place his statement under any of the criteria listed above that his statement is categorized as Guardedness.

The following statements are some examples to clarify the categorization of Guardedness:

1. "I wonder if I have any problems. Maybe it's just that I think I have problems. Maybe that's all there is to the whole thing." . . . G.
This is minimization of the problem.

2. "I guess everybody feels that way about something." . . . G.
This is self-stimulated pointing to nondeviation from the norm.

3. "I was proud of the medal, and I showed it to everyone, as every successful athlete would." . . . G.
The client is pointing to nondeviation from the norm in regard to the culturally frowned-upon trait of pride.

4. "I don't like to visit my family because when I have too much work to do it bothers me." . . . G.
This is justification.

5. Therapist: "You feel inferior to them." Client: "Maybe that's

true. I don't know. Anyway, they kept talking about things with which I wasn't familiar, which I thought was very inconsiderate of them." . . .

If the manner in which the statement is said is consistent with such a categorization, this doubly qualified acceptance is put in the G category as an overt acceptance of a therapist's statement placing the client in an undesirable light which is really emotionally rejected by the client.

6. Therapist: "You feel inferior to them." Client: "No, it wasn't that. It was just that they kept talking about things with which I wasn't familiar, which I thought was very inconsiderate of them." . . . N.

A rejection of a therapist's statement placing the client in an undesirable light is not categorized G unless it also falls in one of the criteria listed for G.

Covert Resistance

Covert resistance is defined as the extent to which the client manifests indirect or impersonalized criticism of the therapist or therapy, also blocking, delaying tactics, failure to recall or report things, changing the subject, interrupting the therapist. It is resistance or hostility toward therapy, therapist, progress in therapy, or toward things which are thought of as being conducive to such progress. But the resistance is not directly expressed verbally; instead, other more subtle escapes or hostilities are restorted to by the client.

1. **Long Pauses (LP):** A 15-second "response" in which the client does not talk.

2. **Short Answer (SA):** An unelaborated simple thought statement not longer than four or five words that is followed by a pause. This category is not used when the client's response is in reply to a question by the therapist which can be given a simple affirmative, negative, or factual answer.

3. **Changing Topic (TC):** Client initiated changes in the topic being discussed. The new topic is clearly unrelated to the previous statements of the counselor or client. Client statements which serve to cut off a topic (e.g., "That's all I have to say about it.") are also included here.

4. **Blocking (Bl):** Incomplete sentences that are not the product of an interruption by the therapist. Retracing and rephrasing or fumbling of sentences. Pauses in mid-sentence (at least 5 seconds in length). Any statement of, or indication of, failure or inability to think or talk

about something in particular or anything in general; inability to recall a word, situation, or example; inability or failure to give reasons or motivations; inability to give any label to one's own feelings, attitudes, or perceptions.

5. Interruption (Int): Client interruptions or overriding of therapist's verbalizations. (Agreement inserted into a therapist's verbalizations with no intent to cut him off are not included here.)

6. Verbalization or intellectualization (v): Talking about minutiae or irrelevant details. *Abstract* discussions of politics, religion, etc. Such statements bear no discernible relationship to the client's problems as he has been expressing them in the interview. To qualify for a categorization here such a statement must take up a whole 15-second interval. However, if the client spends time groping for an irrelevant detail his response is categorized here whether or not the whole 15 seconds is spent on irrelevancies.

7. Resistance toward therapy or therapist (Th): Indirect or disguised reference to the inadequacy of therapy or therapist. This includes indirect or subtle minimizations of the benefits being derived from therapy. These statements are not made with any reference to the client's own feelings or thoughts about therapy or therapist, or the client is not taking any definite stand or position in his statement.

Statements indicating unwillingness to abide by therapeutic limits or demands when this unwillingness is only indirectly expressed. Any reason—other than open admission of not wanting to do so—for not appearing on time. Indecision about attending the next interview without stating any desire not to.

8. Inability to understand (U): Client statements indicating feigned or real inability to understand the therapist when the therapist's statement is judged to be clear in meaning. Requests for clarification of such therapist statements are included here, but not requests for further elaboration (which are included in Dependence).

Note: A rejection of a therapist's statement or interpretation is not considered resistance, unless it also happens to meet one of the above criteria.

The following statements are some examples to clarify the categorization of Covert Resistance:

1. "I can't define how I felt in that situation." . . . CR. "Bl" (blocking).

2. Therapist: "I wonder where they get that idea?" Client: "I don't know." . . . N.

Client's inability to provide labels, motivations, etc., for *other* people is not considered resistance.

3. "If I could be hypnotized that would help." . . . CR.

This is an indirect reference to inadequacy of therapy.

4. "And I was going to tell him off, so I went down there about two o'clock (pause), or was it three o'clock (pause), I think it was two o'clock, and I said to him." . . . CR.

This "Verbalization," groping for irrelevant detail.

5. "Since I talked about this thing with you I felt much better in class than I had before, but I think that was because I was sitting somewhere else this time." . . . CR ("Th").

This is indirect minimization of the benefits being derived from therapy.

6. Therapist: "You felt uncomfortable in that situation." Client: "What did you say?" . . . CR.

This is real or feigned inability to understand a clear therapist statement.

7. "I don't know if I'll be able to make it next time; I have an exam coming up." . . . CR ("Th").

Client gives reason, other than not wanting to, for possibility of not coming to therapy session.

Open Resistance

Briefly defined, "open resistance" is the extent to which the client *verbalizes criticism*—in an open way—of the therapist or the therapeutic technique. *Also,* personal and verbalized opposition to staying within the limits set by the particular kind of therapy which the client is receiving. This is *verbalized unwillingness* as opposed to "inability" or failure per se.

This is resistance or hostility toward the same things as are mentioned in "covert resistance," but here these things are admitted by the client.

1. Criticism or negative attitudes about the therapist or therapy verbally expressed. Statements are frequently expressed in the form of doubts, sarcastic remarks, and only thinly veiled criticism of the therapy or therapist. These statements admittedly convey the thoughts or feelings of the client himself and the client is taking a stand about his opinions or doubts.

2. Open admission of unwillingness (not "inability") to talk, or discuss any particular area, or to follow the conditions and limits of the kind of therapy the client is receiving.

The following statements are some examples to clarify the categorization of Open Resistance:

1. "I can't see how this is going to help very much." . . . Op. Res.

2. "All that's been happening so far is I've been answering questions, when am I going to get some answers?" . . . Op. Res.

3. "Isn't there some way we could speed this business up?" . . . Op. Res.

4. "That's something I'd rather not talk about right now" . . . Op. Res.

5. "I'd like to take a break from this for a while. I'll call you again when I want another appointment if that's O.K. with you." . . . Op. Res.

Empathy Scale[5]

General Definition

Accurate empathy involves more than just the ability of the therapist to sense the client or patient's "private world" as if it were his own. It also involves more than just his ability to know what the patient means. Accurate empathy involves both the therapist's *sensitivity to current feelings* and his *verbal ability to communicate this understanding* in a language attuned to the client's current feelings.

It is not necessary—indeed, it would seem undesirable—for the therapist to *share* the client's feelings in any sense that would require him to feel the same emotions. It is instead an appreciation and a sensitive awareness of those feelings. At deeper levels of empathy, it also involves enough understanding of patterns of human feelings and experience to sense feelings that the client only partially reveals. With such experience and knowledge, the therapist can communicate what the client knows as well as meanings in the client's experience of which he is scarcely aware.

At a *high* level of accurate empathy the message "I am *with* you" is unmistakably clear—the therapist's remarks fit perfectly with the client's mood and content. His responses not only indicate his sensitive understanding of the obvious feelings, but also serve to clarify and expand the client's awareness of his own feelings or experiences. Such empathy is communicated by both the language used and all the voice qualities which unerringly reflect the therapist's seriousness and depth of feeling. The therapist's intent concentration upon the client keeps him continuously aware of the client's shifting emotional content so that he can shift his own responses to correct for language or content errors when he temporarily loses touch and is not "with" the client.

At a *low* level of accurate empathy the therapist may go off on a

[5] The Empathy and Warmth Scales are from Truax, C. B. & Carkhuff, R. R. *Toward effective counseling and psychotherapy.* Chicago: Aldine, 1967.

tangent of his own or may misinterpret what the client is feeling. At a very low level he may be so preoccupied and interested in his own intellectual interpretations that he is scarcely aware of the client's "being." The therapist at this low level of accurate empathy may even be uninterested in the client, or may be concentrating on the intellectual content of what the client says rather than what he "is" at the moment, and so may ignore or misunderstand the client's current feelings and experiences. At this low level of empathy the therapist is doing something other than "listening," "understanding," or "being sensitive"; he may be evaluating the client, giving advice, sermonizing, or simply reflecting upon his own feelings or experiences. Indeed, he may be accurately describing psychodynamics to the patient—but in the wrong language for the client, or at the wrong time, when these dynamics are far removed from the client's current feelings, so that the interaction takes on the flavor of "teacher-pupil."

Stage 1

Therapist seems completely unaware of even the most conspicuous of the client's feelings; his responses are not appropriate to the mood and content of the client's statements. There is no determinable quality of empathy, and hence no accuracy whatsoever. The therapist may be bored, and disinterested, or actively offering advice, but he is not communicating an awareness of the client's current feelings.

Stage 2

Therapist shows an almost negligible degree of accuracy in his responses, and that only toward the client's most obvious feelings. Any emotions which are not clearly defined he tends to ignore altogether. He may be correctly sensitive to obvious feelings and yet misunderstand much of what the client is really trying to say. By his response he may block off or may misdirect the patient. Stage 2 is distinguishable from Stage 3 in that the therapist ignores feelings rather than displaying an inability to understand them.

Stage 3

Therapist often responds accurately to client's more exposed feelings. He also displays concern for the deeper, more hidden feelings which he seems to sense must be present, though he does not understand their nature or sense their meaning to the patient.

Stage 4

Therapist usually responds accurately to the client's more obvious feelings and occasionally recognizes that some are less apparent. In the process of this tentative probing, however, he may misinterpret some present feelings and anticipate some which are not current. Sensitivity and awareness do exist in the therapist, but he is not entirely "with" the patient in the *current* situation or experience. The desire and effort to understand are both present, but his accuracy is low. This stage is distinguishable from Stage 3 in that the therapist does occasionally recognize less apparent feelings. He also may seem to have a theory about the patient and may even know how or why a patient feels a particular way, but he is definitely not "with" the patient. In short, the therapist may be diagnostically accurate, but not empathically accurate in his sensitivity to the patient's current feelings.

Stage 5

Therapist accurately responds to all of the client's more readily discernible feelings. He also shows awareness of many less evident feelings and experiences, but he tends to be somewhat inaccurate in his understanding of these. However, when he does not understand completely, this lack of complete understanding is communicated without an anticipatory or jarring note. His misunderstandings are not disruptive by their tentative nature. Sometimes in Stage 5 the therapist simply communicates his awareness of the problem of understanding another person's inner world. This stage is the midpoint of the continuum of accurate empathy.

Stage 6

Therapist recognizes most of the client's present feelings, including those which are not readily apparent. Although he understands their content, he sometimes tends to misjudge the intensity of these veiled feelings, so that his reponses are not always accurately suited to the exact mood of the client. The therapist does deal directly with feelings the patient is currently experiencing although he may misjudge the intensity of those less apparent. Although sensing the feelings, he is often unable to communicate meaning to them. In contrast to Stage 7, the therapist's statements contain an almost static quality in the sense that he handles those feelings that the patient offers but does not bring new elements to life. He is "with" the client, but does not encourage exploration. His manner of communicating his understanding is such that he makes of it a finished thing.

Stage 7

Therapist responds accurately to most of the client's present feelings and shows awareness of the precise intensity of most of the underlying emotions. However, his responses move only slightly beyond the client's own awareness, so that feelings may be present which neither the client nor therapist realizes. The therapist initiates moves toward more emotionally laden material and may communicate simply that he and the patient are moving towards more emotionally significant material. Stage 7 is distinguishable from Stage 6 in that often the therapist's response is a kind of precise pointing of the finger toward emotionally significant material.

Stage 8

Therapist accurately interprets all the client's present, acknowledged feelings. He also uncovers the most deeply shrouded of the client's feelings, voicing meanings in the client's experience of which the client is scarcely aware. Since the therapist must necessarily utilize a method of trial-and-error in the new uncharted areas, there are minor flaws in the accuracy of his understanding, but these inaccuracies are held tentatively. With sensitivity and accuracy he moves into feelings and experiences that the client has only hinted at. The therapist offers specific explanations or additions to the patient's understanding so that underlying emotions are both pointed out and specifically talked about. The content that comes to life may be new but it is not alien.

Although the therapist in Stage 8 makes mistakes, these mistakes are not jarring because they are covered by the tentative character of the response. Also, this therapist is sensitive to his mistakes and quickly changes his response in midstream, indicating that he has recognized what is being talked about and what the patient is seeking in his own explorations. The therapist reflects a togetherness with the patient in tentative trial-and-error exploration. His voice tone reflects the seriousness and depth of his empathic grasp.

Stage 9

The therapist in this stage unerringly responds to the client's full range of feelings in their exact intensity. Without hesitation he recognizes each emotional nuance and communicates an understanding of every deepest feeling. He is completely attuned to the client's shifting emotional content; he senses each of the client's feelings and reflects them in his words and *voice*. With sensitive accuracy, he expands the client's hints into a full-scale (though tentative) elaboration of feeling or experience. He shows precision both in understanding and in communication of this understanding, and expresses and experiences them without hesitancy.

Warmth Scale

General Definition

The dimension of *nonpossessive warmth* or unconditional positive regard ranges from a high level, where the therapist warmly accepts the patient's experience as part of that person without imposing conditions, to a low level, where the therapist evaluates a patient or his feelings, expresses dislike or disapproval, or expresses warmth in a selective or evaluative way.

Thus a warm positive feeling toward the client may still rate quite low in this scale if it is given conditionally. Nonpossessive warmth for the client means accepting him as a person with human potentialities. It involves a nonpossessive caring for him as a separate person and, thus, a willingness to share equally his joys and aspirations or his depressions and failures. It involves valuing the patient as a person, separate from any evaluation of his behavior or thoughts. Thus a therapist can evaluate the patient's behavior or his thoughts but still rate high on warmth if it is quite clear that his valuing of the individual as a person is uncontaminated and unconditional. At its highest level this unconditional warmth involves a nonpossessive caring for the patient as a separate person who is allowed to have his own feelings and experiences; a prizing of the patient for himself regardless of his behavior.

It is not necessary—indeed, it would seem undesirable—for the therapist to be nonselective in reinforcing, or to sanction or approve thoughts and behaviors that are disapproved by society. Nonpossessive warmth is present when the therapist appreciates such feelings or behaviors and their meaning to the client, but shows a nonpossessive caring for the person and not for his behavior. The therapist's response to the patient's thoughts or behaviors is a search for their meaning or value within the patient rather than disapproval or approval.

Stage 1

The therapist is actively offering advice or giving clear negative regard. He may be telling the patient what would be "best for him," or in other ways actively approving or disapproving of his behavior. The therapist's actions make himself the locus of evaluation; he sees himself as *responsible for* the patient.

Stage 2

The therapist responds mechanically to the client, indicating little positive regard and hence little nonpossessive warmth. He may ignore the patient or his feelings or display a lack of concern or interest. The therapist ignores the client at times when a nonpossessively warm response would be expected; he shows a complete passivity that communicates almost unconditional lack of regard.

Stage 3

The therapist indicates a positive caring for the patient or client, but it is a *semipossessive* caring in the sense that he communicates to the client that his behavior matters to him. That is, the therapist communicates such things as, 'It is not all right if you act immorally," "I want you to get along at work," or "It's important to me that you get along with the ward staff." The therapist sees himself as *responsible for* the client.

Stage 4

The therapist clearly communicates a very deep interest and concern for the welfare of the patient, showing a nonevaluative and unconditional warmth in almost all areas of his functioning. Although there remains some conditionality in the more personal and private areas, the patient is given freedom to be himself and to be liked as himself. There is little evaluation of thoughts and behaviors. In deeply personal areas, however, the therapist may be conditional and communicate the idea that the client may act in any way he wishes— *except* that it is important to the therapist that he be more mature, or not regress in therapy, or accept and like the therapist. In all other areas, however, nonpossessive warmth is communicated. The therapist sees himself as *responsible to* the client.

Stage 5

The therapist communicates warmth without restriction. There is a deep respect for the patient's worth as a person and his rights as a free individual. At this level the patient is free to be himself even if this means that he is regressing, being defensive, or even disliking or rejecting the therapist himself. At this stage the therapist cares deeply for the patient as a person, but it does not matter to him how the patient chooses to behave. He genuinely cares for and deeply prizes the patient for his human potentials, apart from evaluations of his behavior or his thoughts. He is willing to share equally the patient's joys and aspirations or depressions and failures. The only channeling by the therapist may be the demand that the patient communicate personally relevant material.

Criteria for Rating Self-Referring Statements[6]

A statement was defined as a clause with subject and verb, recognizable as either:

1. a simple sentence,
2. a complex sentence,
3. a coordinate clause of a compound sentence,[7]
4. a clause containing a subject and verb but never completed.

Raters counted self-referring statements according to the following rules:

1. Any statement which contains one or more references to "I," "me," "we," "us," regardless of whether it occurs in a main or subordinate clause, should be treated as one self-referring statement.

2. "My," "mine," "our," "ours," should be counted as self-referring only when they refer to the subject's own mental or physical person, life, group, achievement, or performance. Do not count "my," "mine," "our," "ours" if they primarily refer to objects outside the person—relatives, friends, professionals, etc. *Example:* Count "my family," "my hobby"; do not count "my father," "my car."

3. Count self-referring questions.

4. Count self-referring statements twice if they are repeated for emphasis.

[6] From Davidoff, L. L. Schizophrenic patients in psychotherapy: The effects of degree of information and compatibility expectations on behavior in the interview setting: An operant conditioning analogue. Uupublished doctoral dissertation, Syracuse University, 1969.

[7] All compound sentences were analyzed into their component coordinate clauses and treated as two or more simple sentences. Sometimes several clauses joined by "and," "or," or "but" had the necessary number of verbs for each clause but were missing a stated subject. If they clearly expressed two or more separate thoughts, they were treated as separate coordinate clauses, instead of as a compound verb in a simple or complex sentence.

5. Count self-referring quotations, even if the self-reference has been transformed to "you" or "he" for grammatical reasons.
6. Do not count self-referring statements in poetry recited.
7. Certain expressions have become conversational clichés that automatically express certain ideas. The expressions that follow, and their like, should be counted only when they are followed by or preceded by self-referring words or when they refer to actual thoughts, opinions, or feeling of the individual subject, as opposed to statements of fact. The expressions that follow should also be counted as self-referring if they contain a direct object.

Expressions

I think	I don't know
I'll tell you	I believe it was
Why, I don't know	As far as I know
As I say	I mean
I would say	I suppose
Know what I mean?	I guess
As I understood it	Last I heard
Like I say	I hear
I do believe	As I said before
I don't know of	I remember
I know	I mentioned

8. Do not count as self-referring, questions to the interviewer about the task, the experiment, the interviewer, the hospital facilities, etc. And if expressions similar to the following refer to the present situation, do not count them as self-referring:

Expressions

I can't think of the word
What else can I tell you?
Should I keep on?
What else do I do?
Let me think
That's about all I could say
Believe me
My foot's asleep
How am I doing?
I'd like a cigarette
I'm lost
I have to leave

Author Index

Subject Index